The participation of my ministry in the research and writing of this book has been a great opportunity to mobilise the key stakeholders in the agriculture sector around the importance of evaluation and the incomparable benefits of developing public policy based on evidence.
—*Bonaventure Kouakanou, Deputy Minister of Agriculture, Benin*

I highly recommend this book. It is a cogent analysis of why all policy-makers ought to use evidence and citizen engagement, routinely, to improve decision-making.
—*Judi Wakhungu, EGH, Kenya Ambassador to France, Portugal, Serbia & Holy Sea; previously Cabinet Secretary, Ministry of Environment and Natural Resources*

Profiling the work of policy-makers to use evidence in their decision-making is so important, and the world has much to learn from our experiences in Africa. This book makes a valuable contribution for all of us working to support better decisions based on better evidence.
—*Ruth Stewart, Africa Centre for Evidence, University of Johannesburg, South Africa; Chair, Africa Evidence Network*

In an era of Africa awakening, there is no time to waste on traditions, fads, success stories, and intuitions. The time has come for African policy-makers and development professionals to move to evidence-based decision making and actions. This book showcases the rich use of evidence from selected African countries that can serve as a guide for those interested to learn what others have done in an African context.
—*David Sarfo Ameyaw, CEO/President, The International Centre for Evaluation and Development, Kenya*

Using Evidence in Policy and Practice

This book asks how governments in Africa can use evidence to improve their policies and programmes, and ultimately, to achieve positive change for their citizens. Looking at different evidence sources across a range of contexts, the book brings policy makers and researchers together to uncover what does and doesn't work and why.

Case studies are drawn from five countries and the ECOWAS (west African) region, and a range of sectors from education, wildlife, sanitation, through to government procurement processes. The book is supported by a range of policy briefs and videos intended to be both practical and critically rigorous. It uses evidence sources such as evaluations, research synthesis and citizen engagement to show how these cases succeeded in informing policy and practice. The voices of policy makers are key to the book, ensuring that the examples deployed are useful to practitioners and researchers alike.

This innovative book will be perfect for policy makers, practitioners in government and civil society, and researchers and academics with an interest in how evidence can be used to support policy making in Africa.

Ian Goldman, Advisor on Evaluation and Evidence Systems, CLEAR Anglophone Africa; Adjunct Professor, University of Cape Town, South Africa.

Mine Pabari, Visiting Research Fellow, CLEAR Anglophone Africa, Kenya.

Rethinking Development

Rethinking Development offers accessible and thought-provoking overviews of contemporary topics in international development and aid. Providing original empirical and analytical insights, the books in this series push thinking in new directions by challenging current conceptualisations and developing new ones.

This is a dynamic and inspiring series for all those engaged with today's debates surrounding development issues, whether they be students, scholars, policy makers and practitioners internationally. These interdisciplinary books provide an invaluable resource for discussion in advanced undergraduate and postgraduate courses in development studies as well as in anthropology, economics, politics, geography, media studies and sociology.

Energy and Development
Frauke Urban

Power, Empowerment and Social Change
Edited by Rosemary McGee and Jethro Pettit

Innovation for Development in Africa
Jussi S. Jauhiainen and Lauri Hooli

Women, Literature and Development in Africa
Anthonia C. Kalu

Rural Development in Practice
Evolving Challenges and Opportunities
Willem van Eekelen

Using Evidence in Policy and Practice
Lessons from Africa
Edited by Ian Goldman and Mine Pabari

www.routledge.com/Rethinking-Development/book-series/RD

Using Evidence in Policy and Practice

Lessons from Africa

Edited by
Ian Goldman and Mine Pabari

First published 2021
by Routledge
2 Park Square, Milton Park, Abingdon, Oxon OX14 4RN

and by Routledge
52 Vanderbilt Avenue, New York, NY 10017

Routledge is an imprint of the Taylor & Francis Group, an informa business

© 2021 selection and editorial matter, The University of the Witwatersrand, Johannesburg; individual chapters, the contributors

The right of Ian Goldman and Mine Pabari to be identified as the authors of the editorial matter, and the authors for their individual chapters, has been asserted by them. The copyright for the selection and arrangement of the Work as a whole will remain the property of The University of the Witwatersrand, in accordance with sections 77 and 78 of the Copyright, Designs and Patents Act 1988.

The Open Access version of this book, available at www.taylorfrancis.com, has been made available under a Creative Commons Attribution 4.0 license.

Trademark notice: Product or corporate names may be trademarks or registered trademarks, and are used only for identification and explanation without intent to infringe.

British Library Cataloguing-in-Publication Data
A catalogue record for this book is available from the British Library

Library of Congress Cataloging-in-Publication Data
Names: Goldman, Ian, editor. | Pabari, Mine, editor.
Title: Using evidence in policy and practice : lessons from Africa / edited by Ian Goldman and Mine Pabari.
Description: Abingdon, Oxon ; New York, NY : Routledge, 2020. | Includes bibliographical references and index.
Identifiers: LCCN 2020004937 (print) | LCCN 2020004938 (ebook) | ISBN 9780367440121 (hardback) | ISBN 9780367440077 (paperback) | ISBN 9781003007043 (ebook)
Subjects: LCSH: Education and state—Africa. | Sustainable development—Government policy—Africa. | Conservation of natural resources—Government policy—Africa. | Africa—Social policy. | Africa—Economic policy.
Classification: LCC JQ1875.A55 P78 2020 (print) | LCC JQ1875.A55 (ebook) | DDC 320.6096—dc23
LC record available at https://lccn.loc.gov/2020004937
LC ebook record available at https://lccn.loc.gov/2020004938

ISBN: 978-0-367-44012-1 (hbk)
ISBN: 978-0-367-44007-7 (pbk)
ISBN: 978-1-003-00704-3 (ebk)

Typeset in Bembo
by Apex CoVantage, LLC

Contents

List of figures	ix
List of tables	x
List of boxes	xi
List of contributors	xii
Foreword by Prime Minister of the Republic of Uganda	xvi
Foreword by Professor Paul Cairney, Stirling University	xvii
Acknowledgements	xix
List of abbreviations	xxi

1 **Introduction to the book** 1
IAN GOLDMAN AND MINE PABARI

2 **An introduction to evidence-informed policy and practice in Africa** 13
IAN GOLDMAN AND MINE PABARI

3 **Using evidence in Africa: a framework to assess what works, how and why** 34
LAURENZ LANGER AND VANESA WEYRAUCH

4 **Mere compliance or learning – M&E culture in the public service of Benin, Uganda and South Africa** 54
IAN GOLDMAN, WOLE OLALEYE, STANLEY SIXOLILE NTAKUMBA, MOKGOROPO MAKGABA AND CARA WALLER

5 **Using evaluations to inform policy and practice in a government department: the case of the Department of Basic Education in South Africa** 75
NEDSON POPHIWA, CAROL NUGA DELIWE, JABULANI MATHE AND STEPHEN TAYLOR

6 Use of evidence in a complex social programme: case of an evaluation of the state's response to violence against women and children in South Africa 92
MATODZI M. AMISI, THABANI BUTHELEZI AND SIZA MAGANGOE

7 The influence of local ownership and politics of the use of evaluations in policy making: the case of the public procurement evaluation in Uganda 115
ISMAEL KAWOOYA, TIMOTHY LUBANGA, ABDUL MUWANIKA, EDWIN MUHUMUZA AND RHONA MIJUMBI-DEVE

8 Rapidly responding to policy queries with evidence: learning from Rapid Response Services in Uganda 133
ISMAEL KAWOOYA, ISAAC DDUMBA, EDWARD KAYONGO AND RHONA MIJUMBI-DEVE

9 The potential and the challenges of evaluations to positively influence reforms: working with producers in the Benin agricultural sector 152
BONAVENTURE KOUAKANOU, DOSSA AGUEMON, MARIUS S. AINA, ABDOULAYE GOUNOU AND EMMANUEL M. DAVID-GNAHOUI

10 Parliament and public participation in Kenya: the case of the Wildlife Conservation and Management Act 2013 169
MINE PABARI, YEMESERACH TESSEMA, AMINA ABDALLA, JUDI WAKHUNGU, AHMED HASSAN ODHOWA AND ALI KAKA

11 The contribution of civil society generated evidence to the improvement of sanitation services in Ghana 188
LAILA SMITH, DEDE BEDU-ADDO, MOHAMMED AWAL AND ANTHONY MENSAH

12 Using evidence for tobacco control in West Africa 206
PAPA YONA BOUBACAR MANE, ABDOULAYE DIAGNE AND SALIFOU TIEMTORE

13 Lessons for using evidence in policy and practice 224
IAN GOLDMAN AND MINE PABARI

Index 242

Figures

1.1	Simplified version of the analytical framework	9
2.1	Policy/programme cycle used in training in Africa	17
2.2	Supply, demand and knowledge brokering for evidence	25
2.3	Different evidence: policy dynamics	26
2.4	Levels of knowledge brokering	28
3.1	Science of Using Science conceptual framework	41
3.2	Combined analytical framework	45
6.1	Timeline showing the evolution of VAWC-related national policy	95
7.1	Procurement timeline reform	121
9.1	The journey of the agricultural sector policy	154
10.1	The WCMA 2013 journey	176
12.1	Milestones in the ECOWAS new tobacco fiscal directive process	209
13.1	The analytical framework showing the Context, Mechanism, Outcome relationships	225

Tables

3.1	Evidence use mechanisms	40
3.2	Dimensions of context according to the Context Matters framework	43
3.3	Immediate outcomes	47
4.1	The situation with regard to evaluation/M&E units in each country	57
4.2	Perceived responses when the ministry/department's performance is *below* expectation	60
4.3	Values and culture barriers to effective use of evaluation in decision making, learning and accountability in your department	61
4.4	How evaluation recommendations are used	65
4.5	Stage at which countries use evaluation evidence	65
4.6	Summary of strengths and weaknesses	67
4.7	Summary of features of the context in Uganda, Benin and South Africa	70
5.1	List of DBE's research and evaluations to date	80
5.2	Use interventions and how these influenced use	85
6.1	Interventions to promote use and their effect	103
6.2	Summary of enabling factors and barriers from the context	104
7.1	Use interventions and their effect	124
9.1	Recommendations from the 2009 evaluation and what has been implemented	158
9.2	Interventions that influenced use	162
Annex 9.1	(Chapter 9): Summary of the main landmarks in Benin's agriculture sector 1990–2009	166
10.1	Use interventions and change mechanisms	179
11.1	Evidence use interventions around the IAA/DLT and the changes these influenced	196
12.1	Use interventions and their influence	217
13.1	Contextual influencers of evidence use emerging in the case studies	226
13.2	The range of evidence use interventions, as part of, or external to, national evaluation systems	229
13.3	The change mechanisms	231

Boxes

2.1	Distinguishing between monitoring and evaluation	20
12.1	Tax categories	212

Contributors

Editors

Ian Goldman, Advisor on Evaluation and Evidence Systems, CLEAR Anglophone Africa; Adjunct Professor, University of Cape Town, ian.goldman@wits.ac.za

Ian was the Head of Evaluation and Research in South Africa's Department of Planning, Monitoring and Evaluation (DPME), where he led the establishment of South Africa's national evaluation system and spearheaded work on evidence-based policy. He is a commissioner of 3ie and a founder of Twende Mbele, a partnership of African governments promoting monitoring and evaluation. He joined CLEAR Anglophone Africa at the University of Witwatersrand in July 2018. In addition, he is an adjunct professor at the Nelson Mandela School of Public Governance at the University of Cape Town and a visiting professor at the University of Reading in the UK.

Mine Pabari, Visiting Research Fellow, CLEAR Anglophone Africa, mine.pabari@athariadvisory.co.ke

Mine has over 20 years' experience in the natural resource management and sustainable development as an evaluator as well as programme manager and implementer. From 2001 to 2004, she was responsible for monitoring and evaluation processes across a large-scale regional initiative covering 12 countries in eastern Africa. Thereafter, from 2005 to 2009, she provided technical advisory services to environmental and agricultural programmes in eastern and southern Africa. This included carrying out evaluations, facilitating self-appraisals and internal evaluations as well as training and supporting the development and implementation of monitoring systems. From 2009 to 2017, she was a senior manager heading up the International Union for the Conservation of Nature (IUCN) regional programme in eastern and southern Africa. She is currently a visiting research fellow with CLEAR Anglophone Africa and the managing partner of Athari Advisory.

Foreword

Hon Dr Ruhakana Rugunda, Prime Minister, Republic of Uganda

Paul Cairney, Professor of Politics and Public Policy, University of Stirling, UK, p.a.cairney@stir.ac.uk

Contributing authors

Hon Amina Abdalla, CBS, Policy Advisor, Governance and Natural Resources Consultant. Previously, nominated MP and Chair Committee on Environment and Natural Resources, Kenya National Assembly, Honaminaabdalla@gmail.com

Dossa Aguemon, Director of Planning and Prospective, Ministry of Agriculture, Livestock and Fisheries (MAEP), Benin, Aguemondossa@yahoo.fr

Marius S. Aina, Deputy Director of Planning and Prospective, Ministry of Agriculture, Livestock and Fisheries (MAEP), Benin, Asmarius@yahoo.fr

Matodzi M. Amisi, Researcher, CLEAR-AA, University of Witwatersrand, South Africa, michellematodzi@gmail.com

Mohammed Awal, Team Leader, Social Accountability & SDGs, Ghana Centre for Democratic Development (CDD-Ghana), m.awal@cddgh.org

Dede Bedu-Addo, Coordinator, Ghana Monitoring & Evaluation Forum (GMEF), abedums@gmail.com

Thabani Buthelezi, Chief Director M&E, Department of Social Development, South Africa, ThabaniB@dsd.gov.za

Emmanuel M. David-Gnahoui, University of Abomey-Calavi, Benin, edavid1@gmail.com

Isaac Ddumba, Assistant District Health Officer, Mukono District Local Government, Uganda iddumba08@outlook.com

Abdoulaye Diagne, Executive Director, Consortium pour la Recherche Economique et Sociale, Université Cheikh Anta Diop de Dakar, Sénégal, adiagne@cres-sn.org

Abdoulaye Gounou, Chief of the Bureau of Evaluation of Public Policies and Government Actions, Presidency, Benin, agounou0@gmail.com

Ali Kaka, Wildlife Sector Policy Advisor to the Cabinet Secretary, Ministry of Tourism and Wildlife, Kenya, ali.kaka@adeptconservation.net

Ismael Kawooya, Research Scientist, The Centre for Rapid Evidence Synthesis (ACRES), Regional East African Health Policy Initiative (REACH PI), Makerere University College of Health Sciences, Uganda, ikawooya@acres.or.ug

Edward Kayongo, Research Scientist, The Centre for Rapid Evidence Synthesis (ACRES), Regional East African Health Policy Initiative (REACH PI), Makerere University College of Health Sciences, Uganda, ekayongo@acres.or.ug

Hon Bonaventure Kouakanou, Deputy Minister of Agriculture, Livestock and Fisheries (MAEP), Benin, bonaventure_kouakanou@yahoo.fr

Laurenz Langer, Senior Researcher, African Centre for Evidence, University of Johannesburg, South Africa, llanger@uj.ac.za

Timothy Lubanga, Commissioner Monitoring & Evaluation, Office of the Prime Minister, Uganda, tlubanga@gmail.com

Siza Magangoe, Chief Director, Families and Social Crime Prevention, Department of Social Development, South Africa, SizaM@dsd.gov.za

Mokgoropo Makgaba, Data Analysis Specialist, Department of Planning, Monitoring and Evaluation (DPME), South Africa, mokgoropo@dpme.gov.za

Papa Yona Boubacar Mane, Coordinateur scientifique, Consortium pour la Recherche Economique et Sociale, Université Gaston Berger–Saint-Louis, Senegal, yonamane@gmail.com

Jabulani Mathe, Formerly Senior Evaluation Specialist, Department of Planning Monitoring and Evaluation, now Senior Advisor, Monitoring and Evaluation, National Planning Commission, Office of the President, Namibia, jmathe@integration.org

Anthony Mensah, Director, EHSD, Ministry of Sanitation and Water Resources, Ghana, mensahanthony@hotmail.com

Rhona Mijumbi-Deve, Senior Research Scientist, The Centre for Rapid Evidence Synthesis (ACRES), Regional East African Health Policy Initiative (REACH PI), Makerere University College of Health Sciences, rmijumbi@acres.or.ug

Edwin Muhumuza, Director Corporate Affairs, Public Procurement and Disposal of Assets (PPDA) Authority, Uganda

Abdul Muwanika, Principal Economist, Office of the Prime Minister, Uganda, abdulmuwanika@hotmail.com

Stanley Sixolile Ntakumba, Acting Director-General, Department of Planning, Monitoring and Evaluation (DPME), South Africa, stanley@dpme.gov.za

Carol Nuga Deliwe, Chief Director, Strategic Planning, Research & Coordination, Department of Basic Education, South Africa; Research Associate, University of Pretoria, carolnuga@gmail.com

Ahmed Hassan Odhowa, Principal Research Officer, Parliament of Kenya, odhowa.ah@gmail.com

Wole Olaleye, PhD Candidate, University of Witwatersrand, South Africa; Visiting Research Associate, CLEAR-AA, wole4467@gmail.com

Nedson Pophiwa, Senior Researcher, National Consumer Commission; Research Fellow, CLEAR AA, pophiwan@gmail.com

Laila Smith, Senior Consultant, Universalia Management Group, lsmith@universalia.com

Stephen Taylor, Director, Research Coordination, Monitoring and Evaluation, Department of Basic Education, South Africa; Research Associate, University of Stellenbosch, taylor.s@dbe.gov.za

Yemeserach Tessema, Researcher, Athari Advisory, Kenya, emi.tessema@athariadvisory.co.ke

Salifou Tiemtore, Director of Customs Union & Taxation, Department of Trade, Customs & Free Movement, ECOWAS, saliftiemtore@yahoo.fr

H.E. Prof. Judi Wakhungu, EGH, Kenya Ambassador to France, Portugal, Serbia & Holy See. Previously Cabinet Secretary, Ministry of Environment and Natural Resources, Kenya, judiwakhungu@gmail.com

Cara Waller, Programme Manager, Twende Mbele programme, based at CLEAR-AA, University of Witwatersrand, cara.waller@wits.ac.za

Vanesa Weyrauch, Co-founder, Politics & Ideas, Argentina, v_weyrauch@yahoo.com

Foreword by Prime Minister of the Republic of Uganda

Africa needs to develop, and to do so we need the best evidence to inform our choices for policies and programmes and how we implement them. In Uganda we have been implementing our evaluation system since 2011, and we now have one of Africa's widely recognised evaluation systems. In fact, we have discovered we already have over 500 policy and programme evaluations that have been undertaken in Uganda! We also have a well-established research system and a growing Science and Innovation Fund, and Makerere University is one of the top universities in Africa with a promising Knowledge Translation (KT) innovation, the Rapid Response Service (RRS). In addition, we have well-established processes for citizen engagement, including our community information fora, Barazas.

We have to use these resources to help inform our policy choices. But how do we do so most effectively? How do we maximise the likelihood that evidence does not just sit on a shelf but is used? This is a timely book to help us in that journey, and it is so refreshing to see these interesting African examples of using evidence for us to learn from, including two examples from Uganda. It also reflects the value that we have obtained from our partnership with Benin, South Africa and more recently Ghana and Kenya through the Twende Mbele programme, and the value of transcending colonial boundaries to learn from our peers across Africa.

We look to our public managers and our scholars to read this book, learn from the experience, and see how it can be applied in our context, so that we don't only generate the evidence, but we are consciously planning how to maximise the likelihood of use. And I see that one of the conclusions is that we need to take the role of our monitoring and evaluation units more seriously, and their role in brokering the demand from policy makers for evidence and ensuring that evidence is generated in a systematic way to inform ministers and senior managers. For countries that have less well-established evaluation and research systems, this provides an idea of what they can be aiming for.

I commend the authors, I welcome the learnings, and I look forward to seeing more high-quality evidence at Cabinet, and in pan-African fora, contributing to improving development outcomes on the African continent.

Dr Ruhakana Rugunda
Prime Minister of the Republic of Uganda

Foreword by Professor Paul Cairney, Stirling University

A lot of the literature on 'evidence-based policymaking' (EBPM) is written from a narrow perspective, such as by researchers commenting on the pathologies of politics and failings of politicians, and in a small number of 'Western' or 'Global North' countries. A very limited perspective often masquerades as general knowledge of the world.

This book represents an important antidote to that problem. First, it focuses on the topic of EBPM partly by examining the experiences of people who use and demand evidence. Second, it seeks to give 'voice to African experience' in the context of a growing movement to decolonise the ways in which people create and use knowledge.

In performing both aims, it reminds us that knowledge production and use is a highly social and political process that varies according to context, rather than a technical process that can be reduced to a small number of 'universal' rules for high-quality research. As such, the relationships and interactions between people can be more important than 'the evidence' to the uptake of certain forms of knowledge.

This book also recognises that we should not expect to find so-called rational policymaking during the completion of a simple, orderly, linear 'policy cycle' in which we know how evidence will be used at each stage. Rather, people combine elements such as cognition, emotion, belief, and tradition to help them understand and cooperate within their world. Further, the policy process is best understood as a 'complex system' or 'environment' in which there are many policymakers and influencers interacting across many levels or types of governance, in which each venue for policymaking has its own rules, dominant ideas, networks and ways to respond to socioeconomic conditions and events. What 'works' in one context may not in another.

As such, we need more in-depth and rich descriptions of case studies of evidence use. They help us to capture the sense that, although we have ways to make comparisons and learn from each other, we recognise that no two case studies are the same and there is no 'blueprint' for evidence uptake.

In that context, this book has two profoundly important lessons for key audiences. First, it provides lessons that are relevant to the development of capacity and culture in evidence generation and use in Africa. A large part of giving voice to African experience is to use case studies from some African countries to enable many more to reflect on their own – current and future – procedures. As the editors describe, this book is part of a trust- and capacity-building exercise to extend policy learning from the short to the long term. Second, it provides lessons to a much wider, global, audience that tends to reply disproportionately on experiences from the Global North. The overall result is a book that is greater than the sum of its highly informative parts.

Paul Cairney
Professor of Politics and Public Policy
University of Stirling, UK
p.a.cairney@stir.ac.uk

Acknowledgements

This book was only able to be produced by the involvement of many people. The 39 contributors are already recognised in the individual chapters and the list of contributors. Many thanks for the dedication to the project and managing to get the research and writing completed quickly, for the additional hours put in, and the backwards and forwards needed to finalise the chapters. We note also the people who developed the framework which was central to the book, Laurenz Langer and David Gough amongst others.

We are very grateful to the Prime Minister of Uganda Hon Dr Ruhakana Rugunda for his championing of evaluation and evidence use in Uganda, his support for the Twende Mbele initiative, and his contributing a foreword for the book. Similarly, Professor Paul Cairney for his insightful writing which has helped inspire us, and also for contributing a foreword.

The advisory group met physically twice and provided very useful guidance and support on the book, as well as many peer reviewed individual chapters. We would like to thank Laila Smith (CLEAR-AA and Universalia) who chaired the Advisory Group; Norma Altschuler of the William and Flora Hewlett Foundation, David Ameyaw (ICED, Kenya); Abdoulaye Gounou (BEPPAG, Benin); Alan Hirsch (University of Cape Town); Beryl Leach, formerly of 3ie; Tim Lubanga (OPM, Uganda); Constance Mabela and David Makhado (DPME, South Africa); Adeline Sibanda (IOCE, EvalPartners, formerly AFREA); Peter Taylor of IDRC, Canada (and now IDS); Eliyah Zulu of AFIDEP. Many thanks for your contributions.

Peer reviewing of chapters was done first by chapter authors of each other's work. Then at draft final stage Advisory Group members and others peer reviewed chapters, providing so much value in their constructive criticism. Apart from the advisory group members we had 16 peer reviewers including Robert Cameron (University of Cape Town), Phil Davies (Oxford Evidentia), Hans de Bruijn (University of Delft), Bridget Dillon (formerly of DFID), Saliem Fakir (World Wildlife Fund), Dugan Fraser (CLEAR-AA), Marie Gaarder (3ie), Gonzalo Hernandez Licona (formerly CONEVAL), Manny Jimenez (formerly 3ie), Patricia Kameri-Mbote (University of Nairobi), Brian Levy (University of Cape Town), Mala Mann (University of Cardiff), Ada Ocampo (UNICEF),

Cosmas Ochieng (AfDB), Lynn Osomo (Makerere University) and George Wamukoya.

Judy Scott-Goldman and Lynn Southey did the detailed editing and added a lot of insight and clarity in the writing. Barbara Herweg managed the finances of the project. Laila Smith and later Dugan Fraser of CLEAR-AA enthusiastically took on the project and have supported it throughout. Thanks to the William and Flora Hewlett Foundation for funding the book and the wider evidence use project and to Norma Altschuler for providing detailed suggestions and inputs, contributing far beyond just funding.

We hope that all of you have learnt from the experience and that it contributes to improving development outcomes in Africa.

Ian Goldman and Mine Pabari

Abbreviations

ABePROFA	*Agence Béninoise de Promotion des Filières Agricoles* (Benin Agency for the Promotion of Agricultural Value Chains)
ACE	African Centre for Evidence
AEN	African Evidence Network
AfDB	African Development Bank
AfrEA	African Evaluation Association
ANA	Annual National Assessments
ANAW	Africa Network for Animal Welfare
ANCB	*Association Nationale des Communes du Bénin* (Benin National Local Government Association)
APNODE	African Parliamentarians Network on Development Evaluation
ASTA	African Tobacco Situation Analysis
BCURE	Building Capacity to Use Research Evidence
BEPP	*Bureau d'Évaluation des Politiques Publiques* (Office for Evaluation of Public Policies)
BEPPAAG	*Bureau d'Evaluation des Politiques Publiques et de l'Analyse de l'Action Gouvernementale* (Office for Evaluation of Public Policies and Government Actions)
CAK	Conservation Association of Kenya
CANAM	Conservancies Association of Namibia
CBO	Community-based organisation
CCIB	*Chambre de Commerce et d'Industrie du Bénin* (Chamber of Commerce and Industry of Benin)
CDD-Ghana	Ghana Centre for Democratic Development
CITES	Convention on International Trade in Endangered Species
CLEAR	Centres for Learning and Evaluation for Results
CLEAR-AA	Centre for Learning on Evaluation and Results for Anglophone Africa
CNOS	*Conseil National d'Orientation et de Suivi* (National Guidance and Monitoring Council)
COMESA	Common Market for Eastern and Southern Africa
CONIWAS	Coalition of NGOs in Water and Sanitation

CPAR	Country Procurement Assessment Report
CRES	*Consortium pour la Recherche Economique et Sociale* (Consortium for Economic and Social Research)
CREST	Centre for Research on Evaluation, Science and Technology
CS	Cabinet secretary
CSO	Civil society organisation
CWSA	Community Water and Sanitation Agency
DA	District Assembly
DAC	Development Assistance Committee of the OECD
DACF	District Assemblies Common Fund
DBE	Department of Basic Education
DCENR	Departmental Committee on Environment and Natural Resources
DESO	District Environmental Sanitation Officer
DESSAP	District Environmental Sanitation Strategy and Action Plan
DFID	Department for International Development (UK)
DGE	*Direction Générale de l'Évaluation* (Directorate General for Evaluation)
DHET	Department of Higher Education and Training
DHO	District health officer
DHT	District health team
DoH	Department of Health
DP	Development partner
DPAT	District Performance Assessment Tool
DPCU	District Planning and Coordinating Unit
DPDR	*Déclaration de Politique de Développement Rural* (Declaration of Rural Development Policy)
DPME	Department of Performance, Monitoring and Evaluation, South Africa (in 2014 renamed the Department of Planning, Monitoring and Evaluation)
DRC	Democratic Republic of the Congo
DSD	Department of Social Development
DUR	Department of Urban Roads
EAWLS	East African Wildlife Society
EBPM	Evidence-based policy making
ECD	Early childhood development
ECOWAS	Economic Community of West African States
EHSD	Environmental Health and Sanitation Directorate
EIDM	Evidence-informed decision making
EIPP	Evidence-informed policy and practice
EPA	Environmental Protection Agency
ESC	Evaluation Steering Committee (South Africa)
ESC	Evaluation Sub-committee (Uganda)
ETWG	Evaluation Technical Working Group
EU	European Union

FCTC	Framework Convention on Tobacco Control	
FLBP	Funza Lushaka Bursary Programme	
GAIN	Global Alliance for Improved Nutrition	
GBV	Gender-based violence	
GDP	Gross domestic product	
GEF	Government Evaluation Facility	
GIZ	*Deutsche Gesellschaft fur Internationale Zusammenarbeit* (German Society for International Cooperation)	
GMEF	Ghana Monitoring and Evaluation Forum	
GoG	Government of Ghana	
GPRS	Ghana Poverty Reduction Strategy	
GPRSII	Growth and Poverty Reduction Strategy	
GWCL	Ghana Water Company Limited	
HC	Health centre	
HSD	Health sub-district	
ICT	Information and Communication Technology	
IDLO	International Development of Law Organisation	
IDRC	International Development Research Centre	
IE	Impact Evaluation	
IGG	Inspector General of Government	
IMC	Inter-Ministerial Committee	
IP	Implementation partner	
IRC	International Research Centre	
ISS	Institute for Security Studies	
ITE	Initial Teacher Education	
IUCN ESARO	International Union for Conservation of Nature, Eastern and Southern Africa Regional Office	
JBSF	Joint Budget Support Framework	
KEPSA	Kenya Private Sector Alliance	
KUAPO	Kenyans United Against Poaching	
KWCA	Kenya Wildlife Conservancies Association	
KWCF	Kenya Wildlife Conservation Forum	
KWS	Kenya Wildlife Service	
LDPDR	*Lettre de Déclaration de Politique de Développement Rural* (Letter of Declaration of Rural Development Policy)	
LWF	Laikipia Wildlife Forum	
M&E	Monitoring and Evaluation	
MAEP	*Ministère de l'Agriculture, de l'Élevage et de la Pêche* (Ministry of Agriculture, Livestock and Fisheries)	
MDA	Ministries, Departments and Agencies	
MDG	Millennium Development Goal	
MDGLAAT	*Ministère de la Décentralisation, de la Gouvernance Locale, de l'Administration et de l'Aménagement du Territoire* (Ministry of Decentralisation, Local Governance, Administration and Land-use Planning)	

MDR	*Ministère du Développement Rural* (Ministry of Rural Development)
MESTI	Ministry of Environment, Science, Technology and Innovation
MEWNR	Ministry of Wildlife, Environment, Water and Natural Resources
MLGRD	Ministry of Local Government and Rural Development
MMDAs	Metropolitan, Municipal and District Assemblies
MoEM	Ministry of Energy and Mineral Development
MoFPED	Ministry of Finance, Planning and Economic Development
MOH	Ministry of Health
MoME	Ministry of Monitoring and Evaluation
MoWT	Ministry of Works and Transport
MPD	*Ministère du Plan et du Développement* (Ministry of Planning and Development)
MPDEPP-CAG	*Ministère du Plan, du Développement, de l'Évaluation des Politiques Publiques et du Contrôle de l'Action Gouvernementale* (Ministry of Planning, Development, Evaluation of Public Policies and Monitoring of Government Implementation)
MSWR	Ministry of Sanitation and Water Resources
MWRWH	Ministry of Water Resources, Works and Housing
NDP	National Development Plan
NDPC	National Development Planning Commission
NEP	National Evaluation Plan
NEPF	National Evaluation Policy Framework
NES	National Evaluation System
NESSAP	National Environmental Sanitation Strategy and Action Plan
NGO	Non-governmental organisation
NIMES	National Integrated Monitoring and Evaluation Strategy
NLLAP	National Learning Alliance Platform
NPC	National Planning Commission
NPM	New Public Management
NPO	Non-profit organisation
NRT	Northern Rangeland Trust
NSFAS	National Student Financial Aid Scheme
NSNP	National School Nutrition Programme
NSO	National Statistics Office
NWG	National working group
OECD	Organisation for Economic Co-operation and Development
OPM	Office of the Prime Minister
PACE	Programme for Accessible Health Communication and Education, Uganda
PAG	*Programme d'Action du Gouvernement* (Government Programme of Action)

PASCiB	*Plateforme des Associations de la Société Civile du Bénin* (Network of Civil Society Associations of Benin)
PDE	Procuring and disposing entity
PDU	Procuring and disposing unit
PFM	Public financial management
PNIASAN	*Plan National d'Investissement pour l'Agriculture, la Sécurité Alimentaire et la Nutrition* (National Plan for Investment in Agriculture, Food Security and Nutrition)
PNOPPA	*Plateforme Nationale des Organisations de Paysans et de Producteurs Agricoles* (National Network of Small Farmer and Agricultural Producer Organisations)
PoA	Programme of Action
PPDA	Public Procurement and Disposal of Assets
PPDA	Public Procurement and Disposal of Assets Authority
PPH	Postpartum haemorrhage
PPMS	Public Procurement Management System
PRS	Parliamentary Research Services
PSDSA	*Plan Stratégique pour le Développement du Secteur Agricole* (Strategic Plan for the Development of the Agricultural Sector)
PSI	Population Service Initiative
PSO	*Plan Stratégique Opérationnel* (Strategic Operational Plan)
PSRSA	*Plan Stratégique pour la Relance du Secteur Agricole* (Strategic Plan for the Revival of the Agricultural Sector)
RCME	Research Coordination, Monitoring and Evaluation
REACH-PI	Regional East African Community Health Policy Initiative
RRS	Rapid Response Service
SAMEA	South African Monitoring and Evaluation Association
SAPS	South African Police Service
SDDAR	*Schéma Directeur du Développement Agricole et Rural* (Master Plan for the Agricultural and Rural Development Sector)
SEA	Strategic Environmental Assessment
SESIP	Strategic Environmental Sanitation Investment Plan
SNCA	*Stratégie Nationale de Conseil Agricole* (National Strategy for Agricultural Advice)
SNE	*Système National d'Evaluation* (National Evaluation System)
SNV	Netherlands Development Organisation
SR	Systematic review
TASU	Technical Administration Support Unit
TEHIP	Tanzania Essential Health Interventions Project
TNC	The Nature Conservancy
ToRs	Terms of reference
TWG	Technical working group
UBOS	Uganda Bureau of Statistics
UCIMB	*Union des Chambres Interdépartementales de Métiers du Bénin* (Union of Interdepartmental Chambers of Trade of Benin)

UEA	Uganda Evaluation Association
UNDP	United Nations Development Programme
UNICEF	United Nations Children's Fund
URA	Uganda Revenue Authority
USAID	United States Agency for International Development
VAC	Violence against children
VAW	Violence against women
VAWC	Violence against women and children
VEP	Victim Empowerment Programme
VHT	Village health team
WACIE	West African Network on Impact Evaluation
WAEMU	West African Economic and Monetary Union
WB	World Bank
WCMA	Wildlife Conservation and Management Act
WHO	World Health Organization
WSUP	Water and Sanitation for the Urban Poor
WWF	World Wildlife Fund

1 Introduction to the book

Ian Goldman and Mine Pabari

Summary

This introductory chapter outlines the rationale for this book on evidence-based policy making and practice in Africa and sets the scene for the chapters that follow. The book takes a policy-maker, not a researcher perspective, and is concerned with how the use of evidence by policy makers and practitioners (project/programme managers) can be supported. The book documents eight African experiences in using evidence, from Benin, Ghana, Uganda, Kenya, South Africa and the ECOWAS region (i.e. West Africa). The chapter gives a brief contextual overview of the five countries from which the case studies in the book are drawn, locating the cases within their context. The research methodology is based on case studies and a realist approach to evaluation research. The case studies cover evidence generated through evaluation, research, research synthesis and the involvement of civil society. However, the book does not focus on the evidence itself but on how interventions that promote use played out and how they influenced individuals, organisations and systems, building capability or motivation to use evidence, and creating opportunities to use evidence. The cases show how these led to policy outcomes. The chapter briefly introduces the analytical framework and outlines the structure of the book.

South Africa has had one of the highest rates of HIV/AIDS in the world. At an early stage of the pandemic, the then South African president refused to accept the evidence of the link between HIV and AIDS and that anti-retroviral (ARV) therapy was a solution. As a result, the rollout of ARVs was delayed, leading to the deaths of millions of people whose lives could have been prolonged with ARVs. With the rollout of ARVs, the percentage of deaths due to AIDS has fallen from 42.9% in 2006 to 23.4% in 2019, and life expectancy for men has risen from a low of 52.3 in 2006 to 61.5 today (Statistics South Africa, 2019).

Africa – a period of self-discovery

There is a sense of dynamism in Africa, with many countries having higher economic growth rates than developing countries elsewhere in the world (AfDB, 2019). African leaders today are determined to bring about meaningful change, and the African electorate is demanding more of its leaders and pushing harder for accountability.

African governments have a wealth of knowledge and experience to draw on, and there is much that the world can learn from Africa and that African countries can learn from one another. Rwanda and Ethiopia, for example, brought down the percentage of people living with HIV/AIDS from 9.5% and 4.7%, respectively to less than 0.5% in just under 20 years.[1] South Africa has a GDP more than 35 times that of Rwanda and four times that of Ethiopia.[2] Yet, in 2018, South Africa's incidence of HIV was at 8.7% while that of Rwanda sat at 0.5% and Ethiopia at 0.4%. What can be learned from the achievements of Rwanda and Ethiopia in their respective contexts?

African countries are grappling with increasingly complex policy challenges. Across the continent, governments are struggling to translate economic growth into opportunities for all citizens to prosper. From 2008 to 2018, Africa's combined GDP increased by nearly 40%. Yet, almost half its citizens 'live in one of the 25 countries where sustainable economic opportunity has declined in the last ten years' (The 2018 Ibrahim Index of African Governance, 2018). Concurrently, the repercussions of unsustainable growth on both present and future generations are increasingly apparent (AfDB, 2019; UNECA, 2018).

Enabling growth, improving the well-being of all, strengthening resilience to shocks and stabilising the integrity of the environment and natural resource base can only be achieved through a transformational shift in policy and practice, and so in the way we learn and make decisions.

This book is based on the premise that using evidence[3] contributes to improving development policies, programmes and practice. It responds to a central challenge: how can we better harness the wealth of evidence that is being generated in Africa to develop wisely and equitably under the diversity of conditions that we face?

Rationale for a book on evidence use

There is no shortage of data and information today with technology increasing access exponentially.

Evidence comes from multiple sources ranging from scientific research, evaluations, traditional/indigenous knowledge and administrative data to surveys of public opinion. To answer our development challenges, we need to be able to recognise and access evidence that is relevant, credible and robust. We need to know how to access existing evidence and when and how to commission and generate new evidence to fill the gaps. Equally important is our ability to navigate the political and social context to create opportunities to use this evidence in decision making, integrating the evidence with decision makers' and practitioners' knowledge, skills, experience, expertise and judgement.

The *use of evidence* is the focus of this book, and it was written to improve understanding of how using evidence can help inform and strengthen development policy, programmes and practice in Africa. We analyse the processes which support or inhibit evidence use rather than focusing on the sources of evidence or the evidence generation process, of which much has been written.

The book approaches evidence from the perspective of policy makers rather than researchers. It explores how African policy makers and development practitioners can apply interventions to promote the use of evidence to improve development outcomes and impacts. Practitioners may be government or NGO staff. This book should also be of value to knowledge brokers from both government and non-governmental organisations contributing to development outcomes as well as academics interested in the use of evidence.

There are debates as to whether to refer to 'evidence-based' or 'evidence-informed', 'policy making' or 'decision making', 'evidence-based policy making' (EBPM) or 'evidence-informed decision making' (EIDM) (e.g. Stewart et al., 2019). Banks (2018) quotes an Australian public servant as saying,

> some have interpreted the term EBPM so literally as to insist that the word 'based' be replaced by 'influenced', arguing that policy decisions are rarely based on evidence alone. That of course is true, but few using the term would have thought otherwise.

In this book we use EBPM and EIDM interchangeably, with a preference for evidence-informed policy and practice (EIPP). Our focus is around the relationship between evidence and change in its various forms – policy, development practice or beliefs, and world views.

Learning from African experiences of using evidence

The movement for evidence-based policy has been promoting the use of evidence to inform policy making and practice since the 1970s. The early work in this field was led by the health sector and took place primarily outside Africa. Since 2010, however, work on evidence-based policy making has been expanding in Africa. Most countries have national statistics agencies with the capacity to gather national data, although there are issues around the quality of the data (PARIS21, 2019). Most countries also have some form of national monitoring and evaluation (M&E) system, but usually they focus on monitoring, performance and accountability rather than evaluative thinking and learning (Porter and Goldman, 2013). Some countries, such as Benin, South Africa and Uganda have national evaluation systems and are systematically evaluating key policies and programmes (Goldman et al., 2018). There are numerous examples of evidence being systematically synthesised from multiple studies rather than relying on single studies, particularly in the health sector.

Countries are also investing in promoting evidence use. For example, Benin, South Africa and Uganda have offered advocacy courses to senior managers to stimulate demand for evidence. Evidence-related organisations and networks are emerging, ranging from the Centres for Learning on Evaluation and Results (CLEAR) in Anglophone and Francophone Africa to the Africa Evidence Network. Today, there are African examples of policy makers using evidence from evaluations and evidence synthesis, of experimentation in approaches to evaluation and evidence synthesis, and evidence use is being discussed in national and international platforms.

This book draws on the wealth of practice around evidence generation and use across Africa, giving voice to African experience. We use case studies to explore the experiences of organisations and individuals using evidence to inform development outcomes. We do so across multiple countries, sectors and sources of evidence including evaluations, research synthesis and citizen engagement. In doing so, the book recognises the importance of going beyond evidence to include the knowledge of actors, acknowledging local world views, values, practitioner and citizen experience and the tacit knowledge needed to judge whether an idea is relevant and how to adapt it to a local context (Martinuzzi and Sedlačko, 2017).

The cases are written by researchers and policy makers working together to explore evidence journeys with the aim of identifying the critical factors that enabled or hindered the use of evidence in the particular context. The authors do their best to 'tell an honest story', recognising that often the most important insights emerge from challenges and failures.

The book identifies and documents lessons from the participating African countries with the aim of sharing these with policy makers, practitioners and researchers across Africa and beyond, and contributing to building the networks and processes which help to promote the use of evidence on the African continent. In this way it seeks to support action-learning, giving a voice to policy makers directly involved in the evidence process and to the researchers of the cases. Videos and policy briefs have also been developed to provide diverse ways of conveying the lessons.

The research process

The research undertaken for this book used an analytical framework drawn from existing work on research impact (Langer et al., 2016) and work led from Latin America on the importance of policy context (Weyrauch et al., 2016). Further detail is given in Chapter 3. The methodology is based on a case study approach, relevant when 'how' or 'why' questions are being posed and where it is difficult to separate the phenomenon to be studied from the context (Yin, 1994). Case studies were identified from countries linked to the Twende Mbele programme, a partnership of African governments focusing on using M&E to inform change.[4] These partners enabled ready access to policy makers and the potential to use the book itself as a change intervention in these countries.[5] The case studies include good examples of evidence use, from a variety of evidence sources and a range of sectors.

Research tools included document review, interviews with key stakeholders, participant observation[6] and, in some cases, workshops or focus groups, using similar checklists. The authors were asked to follow a similar structure in writing up the cases, and policy makers were involved in writing each of the cases. The editors then turned the cases into chapters, which were reviewed by the authors. The chapters document and analyse these examples of generating and using evidence, how these have or have not informed policy and practice and draw out what facilitated or inhibited the use of evidence, and the lessons from this experience for Africa.

Introduction to the case studies

Eight case studies are presented, from five countries plus the ECOWAS region (the Economic Community of West African States). Benin, South Africa and Uganda have a national evaluation system in place and are demonstrating the use of evaluation in decision making. Kenya and Ghana have draft M&E policies in place, with Kenya's awaiting approval from Cabinet. All the countries have universities and think tanks conducting research as well as national statistical organisations. In some cases such as Uganda, Kenya and South Africa, parliamentarians are starting to request evidence. In the case of Uganda, the use of evidence for large-scale projects is mandatory and built into policy requirements.

This section provides a brief overview of the five case study countries and the cases selected, with the sixth covering the ECOWAS countries.

Kenya

Kenya's system of government is made up of national government and recently devolved local government units, known as counties. It has an active parliament with a research service and a Parliamentary Budget Office. Kenya has developed an M&E policy which has been awaiting approval from Cabinet for some time. The M&E Directorate in the Ministry of Finance and Planning is responsible for the national integrated M&E strategy (NIMES) as well as Kenya's Vision 2030 and its national economic recovery strategy. Other sources of evidence include the rapid results initiative (RRI), which is focused on monitoring project performance, an electronic national integrated M&E system (E-NIMES) and an electronic county integrated M&E system (E-CIMES), which facilitate real-time information sharing on project implementation. According to a diagnostic study carried out by CLEAR-AA on the status of national evaluation systems (NES) in Kenya (Khumalo, 2019), the introduction of NIMES significantly improved the role of M&E in policy formulation and implementation.

Kenya has an active National Bureau of Statistics and well-established universities and research institutes such as the African Population Health Research Centre, Kenya Institute for Public Policy Research and Analysis and the African Institute for Development Policy. These institutes play a key role in evidence generation, promote research synthesis, and are directly involved in training and support for EBPM. There is also a range of international research institutions based in Nairobi. However, persistent challenges hinder effective evidence use at multiple levels. These include inadequate resources and capacities and a weak evidence culture in the country as well as limited engagement of civil society and other non-state actors (Ibid.).

The Kenyan case in Chapter 10 focuses on the wildlife sector, a sector with a long history of polarised ideologies amongst its stakeholders. Specifically, it reflects on the role of a parliamentary committee which led the review of the Wildlife Conservation and Management Act 2013 through citizen engagement.

Uganda

Uganda has two levels of government, national and local, with two levels of local government, district and subcounty. Most services to citizens are run by local governments. The Office of the Prime Minister (OPM) is responsible for coordinating national-level monitoring and evaluation. The national integrated M&E strategy (NIMES) was launched in 2005/06 and the national M&E policy was passed by Cabinet in March 2013. A Government Evaluation Facility (GEF) was established in 2013 which oversees the management and use of evaluations. There is collaboration between state and non-state actors, with the Uganda Evaluation Association (UEA) working closely with government. The Uganda Parliament is a member of the African Parliamentarians' Network on Development Evaluation (APNODE) and has a parliamentary research office, a budget office and its own M&E office.

According to the NES diagnostic study carried out by CLEAR AA (David-Gnahoui, 2018), evaluations of large projects are mandatory and approximately 12% of the evaluations conducted by the time of the diagnostic study in 2018 had been commissioned and/or co-managed by government, with relatively high levels of quality. There are many organisations undertaking evaluation including consultants, universities, and think tanks like the Economic Policy Research Centre. The subject of Chapter 7 is an evaluation of the national public procurement system, undertaken relatively early in the national evaluation system.

Uganda has a well-established university sector – Makerere University is one of the highest-rated universities in Africa – and a range of think tanks such as the African Centre for Health & Social Transformation and the Institute for Public Policy Research. There are evidence users outside government such as the Civil Society Budget Advocacy Group (Obuku, 2018). Makerere University College of Health Sciences has had a programme promoting research synthesis and knowledge translation for some years, producing knowledge products for government (Nankya, 2016).

The second Ugandan case, discussed in Chapter 8, is a rapid research synthesis service in the health sector, situated in Makerere University. This is a pioneering service which has been synthesising existing research and testing out rapid models, where government gets a summary of existing health research within 28 days (Mijumbi-Deve et al., 2017). This is a model of great interest to Africa. Three mini-cases of evidence use are also discussed. One comes from national level and the other two are from decentralised district health services.

South Africa

South Africa is a semi-federal state, with semi-autonomous spheres of national, provincial and local government. Local government is divided into district and local municipality levels. Services to citizens such as education and health are run by provincial governments, and water and electricity services are run by municipalities. South Africa has well-established institutional arrangements for M&E at the national and provincial levels. Key at national level is the Department of Planning, Monitoring and Evaluation (DPME), which runs various monitoring systems, as well as the national evaluation system (NES), and evaluations are happening at national, provincial and departmental levels.

Research is widely used in government, which is also starting to use research synthesis and evidence mapping (Stewart et al., 2019). DPME, with the University of Cape Town, has run training for the top three levels of the public service in EBPM. The South African Monitoring and Evaluation Association (SAMEA) is actively providing a platform for multiple actors to engage around M&E. Another player in evaluation, not just in South Africa, is the Anglophone Centre for Learning on Evaluation and Results (CLEAR-AA), based at the University of the Witwatersrand.

Capacity for evidence supply, such as consultancies and research institutes, is considerably higher than in other countries in Africa. Research councils such as the Human Sciences Research Council conduct research, and there is a network of universities producing high-quality research. Research synthesis work is strong in the health sector, led by the South African Cochrane Centre and the Medical Research Council, and emerging in other sectors, with an important role played by the Africa Centre for Evidence at the University of Johannesburg. There is a South African network of five research centres committed to synthesising evidence for decision making (Stewart, Dayal, et al., 2019).

The two cases in this book from South Africa cover evaluations conducted within the national evaluation system. The first is of the evidence work of the Department of Basic Education (Chapter 5), highlighting a department which has been forward-thinking in developing its own evaluation and research capacity and was an early adopter of evaluations, as well as exploring use of evidence synthesis. The case looks at two evaluations, of a teacher bursary programme and the National School Nutrition Programme, and reflects on the journey of the department in promoting and using evidence, highlighting the role of an internal knowledge broker.

Chapter 6 is the second South African case, focusing on an evaluation of the state's response to violence against women and children, a very complex issue, where significant progress has been made in informing policy supported by a deep dialogue process.

Benin

Benin has two levels of governance, central and local government, the latter with a considerable degree of autonomy. It has a national evaluation policy in place, evaluation guidelines and a national evaluation board (Porter and Goldman, 2013). The Bureau of Public Policies, Evaluation and Government Action Analysis (BEPPAG), hosted by the General Secretariat of the Presidency, establishes and leads the national evaluation system and evaluation capacity development and ensures the use of evaluation in management.

Between 2007 and 2018, Benin carried out 17 national-level evaluations and has had an impressive record of uptake and use of evaluations to influence implementation. However, the NES diagnostic study showed that approximately 90% of the demand for evaluations came from donors. Evaluations are made available to the public through a database established in 2018[7] (Présidence du Bénin, n.d.). Ministries are required to send annual performance reports to the Supreme Court which are then published on approval and utilised in informing legislation.[8] Broadly, there is a strong level of competence amongst evaluation consultants in the country (though some specialised skills are lacking) as well as structures offering capacity-building in evaluation (David-Gnahoui, 2018). However, in spite of its institutional framework, evidence generation and use continues to be a significant challenge, particularly with regard to local supply and demand.

The case from Benin in Chapter 9 is an evaluation of its agriculture sector policy conducted in 2009, relatively early in the implementation of the evaluation system, and subsequent evolution of the policy process to involve producers, building on the evidence in the evaluation.

Ghana

Ghana has two levels of government, national and local (district assemblies), with an intermediate regional coordinating structure (regional coordination councils). Most services are run by national departments, but there has been an ongoing decentralisation programme transferring functions to districts and municipal structures.

M&E functions take place at the national level, with the Ministry of M&E responsible for priority flagship programmes and projects and the National Development Planning Commission (NDPC) responsible for planning and monitoring the national development plan and work in the sectors. A draft M&E Policy has been developed, but meanwhile the NDPC provides guidance for M&E activities, including manuals and guidelines. There is an active national statistical office: Ghana Statistical Service.

Evaluations usually take place in response to donor requirements and are carried out by external evaluators in private firms. Interest in evaluation is growing, with the Ghana M&E Forum playing an important role in promoting evaluation and evidence use (Amatoey et al., 2019). A diagnostic review carried out by CLEAR-AA found limited use of evaluation findings, due to limitations in time as well as competing interests (Ibid.). Sampong (2018) provides an example of one government agency, the Environmental Protection Agency, showing limited engagement of research institutions, fragmented evidence collection and uncoordinated research efforts.

There is a range of universities undertaking research and consultancy, notably institutes like the Ghana Institute for Management and Public Administration and the Institute of Statistical, Social and Economic Research at the University of Ghana. Research is usually commissioned with donor funding. Sampong (2018) suggests there is limited systematic collaboration between researchers and policy makers.

Ghana's use of evidence for decision making is still fairly nascent, and emphasis remains on performance management and compliance as opposed to the use of evaluations and other forms of evidence for learning and policy making. There is an active civil society which has produced some interesting tools for tracking government performance and the state of services. Chapter 11 focuses on two civil society tools for looking at performance of services at district level, focusing particularly on management of sanitation services.

ECOWAS

ECOWAS is a regional economic community covering 15 West African states and operates in parallel to the West African Monetary Union (WAMU). It has a primary role in legislation for taxation across the community. The last case (Chapter 12) focuses on a regional initiative through ECOWAS using research evidence and a well-facilitated process of dialogue at technical and political levels to increase tobacco taxation, with the aim of reducing tobacco consumption and increasing government revenue. The case tracks the journey to get a new directive on tobacco taxation adopted and the important role played by a West African research institution, CRES, in facilitating the process.

Introducing the analytical framework

The analytical framework is discussed in depth in Chapter 3. However, for those who do not wish to read this in any depth, a simplified version is given in Figure 1.1.

The theory of change which underlies the analytical framework is based on the following:

- The external and internal *context* is key to the design, operationalisation and success of any initiative. Therefore, each case is analysed in relation to the context.
- In different cases we see different levels of *demand* for evidence, which can be from policy makers, donors, researchers or civil society.
- Evidence is *generated* through a variety of types of evidence production.

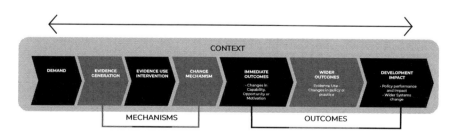

Figure 1.1 Simplified version of the analytical framework

Source: Author generated.

- Interventions to promote ownership, use and consensus around the findings occur prior to, as part of and after the evidence generation process. Other interventions promote the credibility of the evidence or wider access.
- These interventions trigger *change mechanisms* within individuals and organisations, which are critical to enabling use. Examples are making the evidence *accessible*, stakeholders *aware*, building *trust* in the evidence, or *institutionalising* the recommendations in some way.
- That should lead to an immediate outcome of strengthening the *capability* of stakeholders to use evidence, the *opportunity* to use the evidence in a particular setting, and the *motivation* for the evidence to be used.
- If that happens, then we may begin to see *changes in behaviour, policies and practice* at individual, organisational and wider system levels.
- The process is rarely linear and is usually iterative, and it may involve successive levels of evidence generation and use. Indeed, the triggers for change may come from different stages. For example, in Benin and South Africa, the need for theories of change in evaluations led to the introduction of theories of change for planning.

The cases seek to track the real pathway of change – what actually contributed to use of the evidence – so that we can learn how to do so better and more deliberately. To that end, the book draws out lessons emerging (Chapter 13) so that readers of the book can apply the learnings to their context – what use interventions might be likely to work and what change mechanisms need to be triggered to get the outcomes you want.

The flow of the book

The book essentially has three parts – four introductory chapters which introduce the topic, eight chapters presenting case studies, and a concluding chapter that provides an analytical reflection on the initial assumptions and how the understanding of evidence-based decision making prior to this research project was adjusted based on what has emerged from the case studies.

Following this introductory chapter, Chapter 2 discusses the evidence-based policy field. Chapter 3 provides an in-depth explanation of the analytical framework that guided the case study research carried out for this book. Chapter 4 looks at the context of three of the countries in relation to use of evidence, based on a M&E culture survey carried out by Twende Mbele in Benin, Uganda and South Africa in 2017.

Chapters 5 to 12 present specific cases, documenting and analysing examples of generating and using evidence and how the evidence did or did not inform policy and why. In doing so, factors facilitating or inhibiting the use of evidence and lessons going forward are identified and discussed. In each of these chapters, the focus is on the processes which support or inhibit evidence use rather than the type of evidence source, but the cases do include a variety of evidence sources ranging from evaluations to research synthesis to citizen engagement.

The final chapter of the book (Chapter 13) provides an overall picture of what has emerged across the cases; the lessons emerging from the case studies including a refined version of the analytical framework for evidence use, based on the experience from the case studies; and lessons emerging about how to promote evidence.

We hope you enjoy the read!

Notes

1 Incidence of HIV (per 1,000 uninfected population ages 15–49; World Bank, n.d.-b).
2 GDP (current USD; World Bank, n.d.-a).
3 According to Ciarney, 'evidence is assertion back by information' (Cairney, 2016). We discuss definitions around evidence further in Chapter 2.
4 www.twendembele.org
5 The cases are not projects of the Twende Mbele partnership itself, except for Chapter 3, which uses research funded by Twende Mbele into the performance culture in Uganda, Benin and South Africa.
6 A key method was participant observation, where the researcher or co-authors had been involved in the case. This provided access to detailed knowledge of the context, ready access to information, historical recall of events and insight into the background and motives with the possibility of a 'thick description' of the events that happened as well as a detailed picture of the context. A thick description is usually a lengthy description that captures the sense of actions as they occur. It places events in contexts that are understandable to the actors themselves.
7 Available at www.presidence.bj/évaluation-politiques-publiques.
8 Personal communication, Elias A.K. Segla, Spécialiste en gouvernance et évaluation des politiques publiques Présidence de la République du Bénin Bureau de l'Évaluation des Politiques Publiques et de l'Analyse de l'Action Gouvernementale.

References

The 2018 Ibrahim index of African governance: Key findings. 2018, November 7. Retrieved 17 August 2019, from Mo Ibrahim Foundation website: http://mo.ibrahim.foundation/news/2018/2018-ibrahim-index-african-governance-iiag-key-findings/
AfDB. 2019. *African economic outlook*. Abidjan, Côte d'Ivoire: African Development Bank.
Amatoey, C., Adaku, E. and Otoo, R.K. 2019, January. *Diagnostic report: Current status of the national evaluation system in Ghana*. CLEAR Anglophone Africa, Graduate School of Public and Development Management, University of the Witwatersrand.
Banks, G. 2018, November 30. *Whatever happened to 'evidence-based policymaking'?* Australian online magazine for public sector managers. Retrieved 26 March 2019, from The Mandarin, Australian online magazine for public sector managers website: www.themandarin.com.au/102083-whatever-happened-to-evidence-based-policymaking/
Cairney, P. 2016. *The politics of evidence-based policy making*. London: Palgrave Macmillan.
David-Gnahoui, E. 2018. *Etude diagnostique de l'offre et de la demande d'évaluation au Bénin*. Twende Mbele.
Goldman, I., Byamugisha, A., Gounou, A., Smith, L.R., Ntakumba, S., Lubanga, T., . . . Rot-Munstermann, K. 2018. The emergence of government evaluation systems in Africa: The case of Benin, Uganda and South Africa. *African Evaluation Journal*, 6(1), 11. https://doi.org/10.4102/aej.v6i1.253

Khumalo, L. 2019, January. *Diagnostic report: Current status of the national evaluation system in Kenya.* Centre for Learning on Evaluation and Results Anglophone Africa (CLEAR-AA). Faculty of Law, Commerce and Management, University of the Witwatersrand.

Langer, L., Tripney, J. and Gough, D. 2016, April. *The science of using science; researching the use of research evidence in decision-making.* EPPI-Centre, Social Science Research Unit, UCL Institute of Education, University College London EPPI Centre.

Martinuzzi, A. and Sedlačko, M. 2017. *Knowledge brokerage for sustainable development: Innovative tools for increasing research impact and evidence-based policy-making* (1st ed.). https://doi.org/10.4324/9781351285483

Mijumbi-Deve, R., Rosenbaum, S.E., Oxman, A.D., Lavis, J.N. and Sewankambo, N.K. 2017. Policymaker experiences with rapid response briefs to address health-system and technology questions in Uganda. *Health Research Policy and Systems*, 15(1), 37. https://doi.org/10.1186/s12961-017-0200-1

Nankya, D.E. 2016. *Evidence-informed decision-making landscape at Makerere University, College of Health Sciences, Uganda.* Retrieved from www.africaevidencenetwork.org/wp-content/uploads/2016/11/19-Nankya.pdf

Obuku, E. 2018. *Rapid landscape review map: A navigation guide to the R2P jungle in Uganda.* Retrieved from www.africaevidencenetwork.org/wp-content/uploads/2016/11/9.-Obuku-2018.pdf

PARIS21. 2019. *Statistical capacity development outlook.* Retrieved from https://paris21.org/sites/default/files/inline-files/Statistical%20Capacity%20Development%20Outlook%202019.pdf

Porter, S. and Goldman, I. 2013. A growing demand for monitoring and evaluation in Africa. *African Evaluation Journal*, 1(1). https://doi.org/10.4102/aej.v1i1.25

Présidence du Bénin. n.d. *Évaluation des politiques publiques.* Retrieved 17 April 2019, from Présidence du Bénin website: www.presidence.bj/evaluation-politiques-publiques

Sampong. 2018. *Evidence ecosystem map: Ghana Environmental Protection Agency.* Retrieved from www.africaevidencenetwork.org/wp-content/uploads/2016/11/13.-Sampong-2018.pdf

Statistics South Africa. 2019, July 29. *Mid year population estimates.* Statistics South Africa.

Stewart, R., Dayal, H., Langer, L. and van Rooyen, C. 2019. The evidence ecosystem in South Africa: Growing resilience and institutionalisation of evidence use. *Palgrave Communications*, 5(1), 90. https://doi.org/10.1057/s41599-019-0303-0

Stewart, R., Langer, L. and Erasmus, Y. 2019. An integrated model for increasing the use of evidence by decision-makers for improved development. *Development Southern Africa*, 36(5), 616–631. https://doi.org/10.1080/0376835X.2018.1543579

UNECA, 2018. *2018 Africa Sustainable Development Report: Towards a transformed and resilient continent*, Addis Ababa, United Nations Economic Commission for Africa, eISBN: 978-92-1-047600-3.

Weyrauch, V., Echt, L. and Suliman, S. 2016, May. *Knowledge into policy: Going beyond context matters.* Framework. Politics & Ideas and the International Network for the Availability of Scientific Publications.

World Bank. n.d.-a. GDP (current US$) – Rwanda, South Africa, Ethiopia | Data. Retrieved 1 November 2019, from World Bank Open Data website: https://data.worldbank.org/indicator/NY.GDP.MKTP.CD?locations=RW-ZA-ET

World Bank. n.d.-b. Incidence of HIV (per 1,000 uninfected population ages 15–49) – Rwanda, South Africa, Ethiopia | Data. Retrieved 1 November 2019, from World Bank Open Data website: https://data.worldbank.org/indicator/SH.HIV.INCD.ZS?locations=RW-ZA-ET

Yin, R. 1994. *Case study research: Design and methods.* London: Sage.

2 An introduction to evidence-informed policy and practice in Africa

Ian Goldman and Mine Pabari

Summary

This chapter introduces the theory around evidence and evidence-based policy making, otherwise referred to as evidence-informed policy and practice. The authors acknowledge that, in practice, policy makers use values, experience and political necessity as well as evidence to inform decisions, so they apply a limited or 'bounded rationality'. We discuss different types of evidence use, including instrumental, conceptual, symbolic and process use. An overview is given of the historical development of use of evidence, in Africa and internationally, from a focus on data to monitoring and evaluation to evaluation as a distinct discipline, and the move from single studies to research synthesis. The role of knowledge brokers is discussed, dealing with both the supply and demand for evidence. The authors emphasise the importance of creating an enabling environment for evidence use. This is introduced in this chapter and is a theme throughout the book.

Evidence matters, or does it?

All governments have to make choices about how to deploy their resources. In Africa, where resources are more limited and social problems are pressing, these choices are critical. Much has been written about how evidence can assist, for example, in demonstrating progress in implementing national plans, negotiating and designing large-scale investments and assisting in decision making (Parkhurst, 2017; Weiss, 1979).

Yet, in spite of the rhetoric around the importance of evidence, use of evidence for policy and practice remains challenging and somewhat elusive. A study of policy makers in South Africa found that while 45% of senior managers hoped to use evidence in decision making, only 9% reported being able to translate this intention into practice (Paine Cronin and Sadan, 2015). In Chapter 4 of this book, it is reported that between 40% and 50% of managers in Benin, Uganda and South Africa rarely or never use evaluation evidence. This situation is not just limited to Africa. Stewart et al. (2019) refer to several examples of evidence not being used: 85% of health research not being used internationally; in the Obama administration only 1% of government funding was informed by evidence (Bridgeland and Orszag, 2015); and, despite extensive spending on What Works Centres in the UK, only 4 out of 21 government departments were able to account for the status and whereabouts of their commissioned research evidence, let alone demonstrate that they were using it (Sedley, 2016). Evidence can also be used inappropriately, for example, to validate pre-existing viewpoints – sometimes referred to as policy-based evidence (Weatherall et al., 2018).

There is little research into African policy makers' use of evidence. A study carried out in South Africa in 2011 found that policy makers' primary source of evidence was informal rather than more rigorous sources of evidence (Paine Cronin and Sadan, 2015). A positive sign, however, was that officials across departments were unanimous about the need to improve the use of evidence in policy making.

In Chapter 1, it was pointed out that generating or acquiring high-quality evidence does not automatically lead to use. Attention, therefore, needs to be given to the processes and factors that enable use so that they can be more consciously promoted. That is the central focus of this book.

We explore how evidence use was promoted in eight different regional, national and subnational cases and how evidence use influenced the eventual policy outcomes. This chapter lays out the theoretical foundations for evidence-based policy and practice and how it is applied in Africa.

What do we mean by evidence and evidence use?

Policy making is grounded in theory, values, ideology and practice, and so it will always be subject to political contestation (Davies, 2011).

Chapter 1 refers to the debates as to whether we should refer to 'evidence-based' or 'evidence-influenced', 'policy making' or 'decision making', 'evidence-based policy making' (EBPM) or 'evidence-influenced decision making' (EIDM).

This book is based on the premise that policy decisions are not and cannot emanate solely from evidence – or even rational analysis! Such is the nature of humanity that emotions, politics, power, fear and many other factors play a central role in the directions we take and choices we make. In terms of using the words 'policy making' or 'decision making', Cairney (2016, p. 2) suggests that in practice, policy is 'the sum total of government action, from signals of intent to final outcome', i.e. actors make and deliver policy continuously.

We recognise that policies and practice are influenced by many factors of which evidence is a part, and so prefer 'informed'. We also feel that policy is important because it is the agreed guideline as to what is to be done (policies, legislation, plans, etc.), but that in the end it is what is actually done (i.e. implementation or practice) that matters. So while the different authors use EBPM and EIDM interchangeably, we have a preference for using evidence-informed policy and practice (EIPP).

Some definitions of the term 'evidence'

According to Cairney, 'evidence is an argument or assertion backed by information' (Car). Evidence is sometimes associated with rigorous quantitative scientific studies. However, evidence can take many forms and come from many *sources*, including:[1]

- *Statistical evidence* from surveys, official statistics and administrative data, each of which can indicate the size, nature and dynamics of the problem in hand;
- *Descriptive and experiential evidence* including experience and intuitive/ tacit knowledge from stakeholders which illuminate the nature, size and dynamics of a problem;
- Individual evaluations and research studies;
- *Research synthesis* including systematic reviews of evidence, meta-analyses and rapid evidence assessments;
- *Economic and econometric evidence* which refers to the cost benefit or cost-effectiveness of interventions;
- *Implementation evidence* indicating how similar policies have been successfully implemented and how barriers to successful implementation have been overcome;
- *Ethical evidence* in terms of questioning or understanding the ethical implications of a policy.

Davies (2013) defines *quantitative evidence* as data that meet the standards of:

- *Internal validity*: what is the extent to which the design and conduct of the study eliminate the possibility of bias?
- *Adequacy of reporting*: are the statistics adequate, and does the data support the findings?
- *External validity*: does the study have the potential to be extended to the wider world?

In this definition, the key qualities of evidence are independence, objectivity and verifiability. In contrast, *opinions* are statements and claims that do not meet the standards of evidence, as they are positional, subjective, partial (selective) and hard to verify.[2]

Qualitative evidence has an equally strong claim and a need for rigour. Spencer et al. (2003) suggest that qualitative evidence meets the tests of:

- *Contribution*: does the study advance wider knowledge or understanding about a policy?
- *Defensibility*: does the study provide an appropriate research strategy to address the evaluative questions posed?

- *Rigour*: how systematic and transparent are the collection, analysis and interpretation of qualitative data?
- *Credibility*: how well-founded and plausible are the arguments about the evidence generated?

The use of evidence involves policy makers and practitioners drawing on these different sources of evidence and linking them to their own experience and their local context when making choices of what and how to implement.

What do we mean by evidence use?

Humans have been refining scientific research methods over the centuries but have only recently turned their attention to methods for using research to inform policy. Weiss (1979) is the author of one of the earliest papers looking at research utilisation, which talks about a knowledge-driven versus problem-solving model. In a *researcher-focused model*, basic research leads to applied research, which is then developed and finally applied. In the *problem-solving model*,

> A problem exists, and a decision has to be made, information or understanding is lacking either to generate a solution to the problem or to select among alternative solutions, research provides the missing knowledge. With the gap filled, a decision is reached.
>
> (p. 427)

Weiss also distinguishes between research undertaken to *anticipate needs*, or the commissioning of evaluation or research to *address a knowledge gap*. Cairney (2016) points out the importance of understanding policy-making processes and the use of evidence within these complex and political processes in order to better understand which model might be most effective in a particular circumstance.

In this book, we apply the concepts of instrumental, conceptual, process and symbolic use. Johnson et al. (2009) define these terms in the following way. *Instrumental use* refers to instances where a specific action has been taken arising from an evaluation or research. *Conceptual use* refers to cases when no direct action has been taken but where people have greater understanding as a result of the evaluation. *Symbolic use* occurs when evidence is used to legitimise pre-existing views. We also consider the case of *positive symbolic use*, for example where the presence of an evaluation raised the profile of an issue.[3] Patton emphasises the importance of *process use*, the 'individual changes in thinking and behaviour and program or organizational changes in procedures and culture that occur among those involved in evaluation as a result of the learning that occurs during the evaluation process' (Patton, 1998, p. 225).[4] Apart from intended use, there may well also be *unintended uses*, which are as important to identify and learn from.

Evidence use will rarely be the result of a single study or piece of evidence changing the world but will rather be the result of multiple small steps. The larger changes can take many years to accumulate (Stewart et al., 2019), often through interactions between multiple agents (Weiss, 1979). The case studies in this book all highlight the multiple steps that took place, sometimes forward, sometimes backward.

When we talk about influencing policy makers – who are we influencing? Here, we draw on the definition used by Cairney: 'Policy-makers include elected and unelected civil servants, individuals and organisations who collectively make decisions' (Cairney, 2016, p. 2).

When can evidence be used?

Figure 2.1 is a policy/programme cycle developed for training in evidence-based policy and implementation in Africa. The cycle includes the stages of agenda setting, diagnosis, selection of intervention, planning/design, implementation,

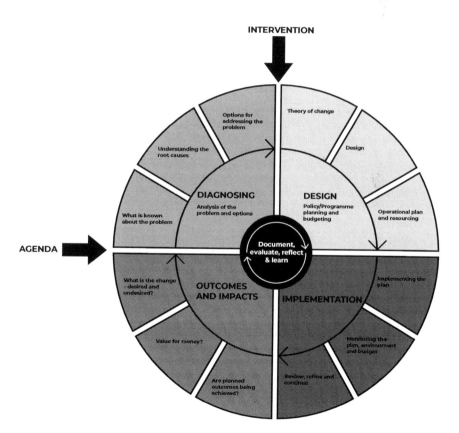

Figure 2.1 Policy/programme cycle used in training in Africa

Source: University of Cape Town; Department of Planning, Monitoring and Evaluation, South Africa.

evaluation and ongoing learning.[5] Evidence can (and should) be used at different stages of the policy cycle:

- Diagnosis (e.g. to establish the size or extent of a problem);
- Design of an intervention (e.g. in developing the theory of change, appropriate outcomes or appropriate indicators of scale or quality);
- During implementation to assess progress (e.g. as part of monitoring);
  To assess outcomes (e.g. the effectiveness of a solution).

How likely are policy makers to use evidence?

The reality of many development situations is the pervasiveness of 'wicked' emergent problems ranging from climate change to violence against women to migration, where simple answers do not work, solutions are unclear and the values of groups in society differ. We need to be realistic about what to expect from the use of evidence in this complex world where policy makers and practitioners are subject to multiple pressures, there are many different stakeholders and decisions often have to be made rapidly. In an idealistic rational view which Cairney refers to as *comprehensive rationality*, policy makers have clear priorities, gather and understand the relevant information and make informed choices. In a *bounded rationality model*, policy makers have unclear aims and limited information, and the rationale behind the choices they make is often not clear (Cairney, 2016).

If one looks at key features of comprehensive or bounded rationality within Africa, what does the evidence tell us? The research presented in Chapter 4 on the performance culture in Uganda, Benin and South Africa suggests that 50%–60% of managers are using evidence. However, around 40% of managers say departments do not champion monitoring and evaluation (M&E) and are not honest about performance; approximately 25% reject the accuracy of results that reflect negatively on their performance; and in around 30% of cases, learning is not documented to improve future results (refer to Table 4.3 in Chapter 4). This is clearly within the bounded rationality end of the spectrum.

Historical development of different forms of evidence

National statistics

Pre-colonial states which had a centralised administration and hierarchical organisation, such as the Shongai Empire in western Africa, the Luba kingdom in central Africa and the kingdoms of Buganda and Ankole in eastern Africa, must have had mechanisms for collecting, storing and using data. However, current national statistics offices (NSOs) originate from colonial governments. For example, Kenya's National Bureau of Statistics has its origins in 1925 when the colonial government appointed its first official statistician. The first population census in Kenya was undertaken in 1948, with the results published in 1952.[6]

Today, all African countries have national statistics offices and are gradually strengthening their capacities. A study carried out in 2014 by the Centre for Global Development and the African Population Health Research Centre states:

> Nowhere in the world is the need for better data more urgent than in Africa, where data quality is low and improvements are sluggish, despite investments from country, regional and international institutions to improve statistical systems and build capacity.
> (Center for Global Development and the African Population and Health Research Centre, 2014)

The Statistical Capacity Development Outlook 2019 indicates that countries in sub-Saharan Africa have performed relatively well in improving their capacities since 2009 (PARIS21, 2019). The same study identifies four main obstacles to data collection and use in Africa (Center for Global Development and The African Population and Health Research Center, 2014):

- *Limited autonomy and unstable budgets*: The majority of NSOs across Africa lack autonomy and do not manage their own budgets. Capacity and resource limitations are the most commonly cited reasons for the lack of progress in statistical capacities. This often results in a reliance on development partners and increases the vulnerability of data production and management to political and interest group pressures.
- *Lack of adequate incentives to produce accurate data*: Accuracy of data is a significant problem across the region. While technical capacities are one obstacle, politics and the uses of data can work against producing accurate data or create incentives to produce inaccurate data.
- *Dominance of donor priorities*: The larger proportion of funding for data gathering across many Africa countries comes from donor-driven initiatives. Therefore, NSOs and their individual staff often spend more time involved in donor-funded projects than in improving national statistics.
- *Access and usability of data*: There is often a reluctance or lack of capacity to generate useful data, manage data and ensure that it is easily and widely accessible for use.

Despite these challenges, NSOs are a primary source of data which is much used by policy makers. However often the data is not analysed to the depth that is possible and necessary for evidence use, and NSO data is not necessarily good for explaining *why* things are happening or whether interventions are working.

The development of monitoring and evaluation

Following the shock of the Second World War, in the 1940s the US and Europe implemented a variety of social programmes to address the challenges facing society. Many of these programmes were innovative and redistributive, with the

> **Box 2.1 Distinguishing between monitoring and evaluation**
>
> Monitoring helps managers and policymakers to understand what the money invested is producing and whether plans are being followed. Evaluation helps to establish what difference is being made, why the level of performance is being achieved, what is being learned from activities and whether and how to strengthen implementation of a programme or policy.
>
> (Porter and Goldman, 2013)

creation of welfare states and widescale social assistance for children. Governments looked for ways to assess whether the money was being well spent, and in 1949 in the US, performance budgeting emerged as a response. This was followed by 'management by objectives' and 'monitoring for results' in the 1960s (Parkhurst, 2017). Meanwhile, adoption of a logical framework approach in 1969 by the United States Agency for International Development (USAID) was a significant milestone in the monitoring, evaluation and evidence journey (see Box 2.1 for a definition of M&E). The logical framework approach included the development of a programme logic, with indicators at different levels of performance. This was widely adopted in the aid industry in the 1970s and is still widely used – one of the drivers for monitoring as well as evaluation in the developing world.

During the 1980s, the advent of New Public Management (NPM) led to a focus on separating the commissioner of a service from the deliverer of a service, the creation of agencies and the resultant need for performance control, including through public service agreements, with monitoring of key performance indicators (Ranson and Stewart, 1994; Mouton et al., 2014). In the 1990s, the Government Results and Performance Act of 1993 in the US provided for the establishment of strategic planning and performance measurement and for a widespread assessment of government performance.

In Africa, a network of evaluation practitioners was established in east Africa as early as 1977, supported by UNICEF. This network comprised the national evaluation associations of six countries.[7] The imposition of structural adjustment programmes in the 1980s and 1990s, and the adoption of NPM frameworks, were important influences in the development of evidence use in Africa. Management frameworks and economic models necessitated the establishment of mechanisms to strengthen results orientation, transparency and accountability. This, in turn, stimulated a demand for M&E (Basheka and Byamugisha, 2015; University of the Witwatersrand, 2012). Evidence use in Africa during this period was primarily driven by external influences from former colonial countries (Mouton et al., 2014).

In the 1990s, the newly established Expert Group on Evaluation, established by the Development Assistance Committee of the OECD, together with multiple donors and financing institutions, convened two pivotal pan-African forums to raise awareness of and identify African evaluation needs and capabilities, with the support of multiple international donors and financing institutions.[8] These forums led to the creation of the African Evaluation Association (AfrEA), formed in 1999 as an umbrella organisation for African evaluators across the continent.

Howard White refers to this period, with its focus on a results agenda and on measurement and monitoring, as *wave one* of the evidence revolution (White, 2019b; see also Figure 2.4).

Across multiple countries over the last 10 to 15 years, national M&E systems and processes have been established to respond to increasing pressures to demonstrate performance, accountability and transparency – key elements underpinning good governance. The development of these systems has taken place in very different ways across the different countries, but the process accelerated generally in the 2000s. For example, Benin started an evaluation system in 2007, while Uganda and South Africa started theirs in 2011.

In addition to evaluation networks and associations, a number of regional initiatives exist. These regional initiatives were established to support countries in strengthening M&E and evidence-based decision making. Examples include AfrEA, Twende Mbele,[9] the African Evidence Network (AEN), the African Parliamentarians Network on Development Evaluation (APNODE) and the West African Capacity-building on Impact Evaluation (WACIE).

The emergence of evaluation as distinct from monitoring

The use of evaluation, with its focus on independent, objective and credible assessments of performance and reasons for under-performance, was already well established in the US, Australia and Canada by the 1980s. As mentioned earlier, the first moves to focus on evaluation in Africa were as early as 1977. Since then the discipline of evaluations has expanded dramatically in Africa. The Centre for Learning and Evaluation for Results for Anglophone Africa (CLEAR-AA), and the Centre for Research on Evaluation, Science and Technology (CREST) at the University of Stellenbosch in South Africa, undertook a search for African evaluations between 2005 and 2015 in 12 countries and came up with 2,635 evaluations (Blaser Mapitsa and Khumalo, 2018).[10] Taking just one country as an example, the Campbell Collaboration[11] worked with Uganda's Office of the Prime Minister to search for evaluations and found a total of over 500 evaluations since the year 2000 (White, 2019**a**).

A limitation of conventional M&E work is how to identify causal links and attribution of effects to interventions. To address this, the use of impact evaluations (IEs) using randomised controlled trials grew in the mid-1990s (Banerjee, 2016), in what White (2019b) refers to as the *second wave* of the evidence revolution. We would rather describe the development of evaluation more generally as the *second wave*, with impact evaluation as the *third wave*. Key organisations were created in the 2000s to support impact evaluations such as the International Initiative for Impact Evaluation (3ie) in 2008[12] and the Abdul Latif Jameel Poverty Action Lab (J-PAL).[13]

The expansion of evaluation can also be seen in the increasing numbers of impact evaluations. The IE repository of 3ie shows the number of completed impact evaluations per year, rising from less than 10 in 1995 to around 50 in 2003, 100 in 2008, and over 500 in 2012, having levelled off since then. IEs focused on health, nutrition and population account for around half of these, followed by education, social protection, and agriculture and rural development. Africa is well represented in terms of the geographical areas in which these IEs were conducted, with over 300 in each of South Africa, Kenya and Uganda, 50–99 in Tanzania, Nigeria, Ghana, Zambia and Zimbabwe, and 21–49 in Mali, DRC and Mozambique, with few in the remaining countries (Sabet and Brown, 2018).

From single studies to research synthesis

As it became clearer that single studies on a topic can be misleading, a new field of research has emerged known as evidence synthesis which seeks to summarise and synthesise the findings from multiple studies on the same topic. White (2019**b**) refers to this as the *third wave* of the evidence revolution (we would use fourth). The science is most established in the health sector with systematic reviews (SRs) and the development of standard methodologies and protocols to try and eliminate bias in the research process.

Evidence synthesis has taken longer to emerge in international development. The main sponsors have been 3ie, the Cochrane Collaboration (which houses a database of SRs in health care) and the Campbell Collaboration (which produces and disseminates SRs in the social, educational and behavioural areas). To date, 3ie has been supporting and cataloguing SRs, evidence maps and other synthesis products, notably outside the health field, and has a repository of these. The 3ie repository demonstrates a similar steady increase in SRs as with IEs, with fewer than ten completed SRs before 2006, rising to over 100 in 2016 (White, 2019b). As of 6 March 2019, the total number of SRs in the 3ie database was 691, of which 337 were in health.[14]

What about SRs in Africa? The Cochrane Library contains the health SRs registered with it, of which 169 have the word 'Africa' in their abstract. Once again there is a rising trend, with 5–8 per year between 2009 and 2012, rising to 23 in 2017.[15] This indicates a fairly steady progression in Africa. A search on the 3ie systematic review database carried out while writing this chapter yielded 180 out of 691 SRs with the word Africa, of which 72 were in health.

In terms of capacity to conduct and use SRs, the African Centre for Evidence (ACE), which is located at the University of Johannesburg, conducted a survey of its Africa Evidence Network members in 2017 and obtained 177 responses from 18 African countries. Sixty-five percent (112/173) of respondents had participated in at least one evidence map, systematic review, review of systematic reviews or other form of synthesis. This shows growing evidence synthesis capacity across Africa, with the strongest capacity in South Africa and within the health sector. This ACE study also identified factors affecting the use of evidence synthesis (Stewart et al., 2017). Common factors included the following:

1. Capacity, collaboration and support
2. Access to literature and data
3. Need for clear questions and guidelines
4. Time availability
5. Funding availability.

Focusing on the demand for evidence

The previous sections have focused on some of the drivers for evidence from NSOs, M&E and research synthesis. We now consider the *demand* from policy makers, which is needed if evidence is to be used.

Demand for evidence in relation to government policy and programmes can come from a number of sources:

- *Ministers*, wanting to know how best to achieve a manifesto commitment, or wanting to monitor rollout (e.g. a commitment to meet targets for development infrastructure, such as schools);
- *Parliamentary committees* and the parliamentary research services that serve them, whether to promote their oversight of specific departments, to review progress with a national plan, or to review budget allocations;
- *Senior managers* in the public service, seeking to make policy choices, decide on implementation strategies, or decide where budgets should be reprioritised;
- *Managers* of programmes and services who need information to adjust their programming;
- *Civil society* seeking to hold government to account;
- *Sector think tanks* seeking to strengthen their knowledge and awareness of what government is doing.

Government ministers have manifesto commitments to fulfil (the agenda in Figure 2.1), but many factors influence what they want to do and how they intend to do it. There is more chance of evidence being used if it is readily available at the time when choices need to be made, hence the development of evidence maps. Evidence maps, sometimes called evidence gap maps, were developed by 3ie and are being used by the Department of Planning, Monitoring and Evaluation (DPME) in South Africa to build the evidence base for a sector or topic, which can then be drawn on rapidly as needed.[16] The case study from Uganda on the Makerere Rapid Response Service in Health (Chapter 8) provides an example of using existing research to provide rapid synthesis reports for government.

There is also an emerging demand for evidence from *parliamentary committees* and their support services, which include parliamentary researchers and libraries. South Africa and Uganda both provide M&E information, including evaluation reports, to Parliament (Department of Planning, Monitoring and Evaluation (DPME), 2018; Goldman et al., 2018). In South Africa, for the first time, an evaluation has been initiated that was specifically requested by a parliamentary committee, where the Standing Committee on Public Accounts requested an evaluation of scholar transport (Department of Planning, Monitoring and Evaluation (DPME), 2018).

Through participation in APNODE, some parliaments have established parliamentary groups focused on EBPM. For example, Kenya's Parliamentary Caucus on Evidence-Informed Oversight and Decision Making was established in 2015. The Caucus has implemented evidence dialogue forums focused on specific topics related to evidence generation and use.

Examples of *senior managers* requesting evaluations are found in the cases of South Africa's Department of Basic Education (Chapter 5), an evaluation of violence against women and children in South Africa (Chapter 6), an evaluation of procurement policy in Uganda (Chapter 7) and of agriculture in Benin (Chapter 9). The Makerere Rapid Response Service is an example of a national ministry of health and district offices of health requesting specific evidence, as are the evidence maps being produced by DPME. The South African system also encourages government departments to propose evaluations for the National Evaluation Plan and to propose evaluations within their departments (Goldman et al., 2015). ACE has also worked with South African government departments to develop evidence maps and undertake systematic reviews.

Some countries, such as Benin and Uganda, have been more successful at involving *civil society* in the evaluation system, while South Africa has been less successful (Goldman et al., 2018). NGOs and foundations also commission evaluations. Porter and Feinstein (2014) identified some key think tanks in five African countries and their involvement with evaluation. An important initiative has been the Think Tank Initiative, which has sought to strengthen think tanks and their contribution to the policy process. A recent evaluation of the African think tanks found that

> across the region, national think tanks tested are generally seen as performing well with regards to having knowledge of the policy-making process, having quality research and researchers, as well as solid regional knowledge. Areas for improvement are fairly consistent across the region, with gender empowerment/equality research, having adequate infrastructure to function effectively, and partnering with non-government policy actors topping the list.
> (Globescan, 2018, p. 7)

However, these think tanks are fragile, and an earlier study suggests that 30% are highly vulnerable, and an additional 25%–30% are extremely fragile, with a serious risk of disappearing, given unstable funding, staff turnover and brain drain (Muyangwa et al., 2017).

Role of donors

Many countries in Africa receive donor funding for government programmes, which may contribute a major part of national budgets. For example, 'about

93% of Malawi's nutrition financing is from donors, with government providing only 7.3 percent' (Khunga, 2018). This dependence on donor funding is true for many of the lower-income countries in Africa, while less true for middle-income countries like Kenya, Ghana, Botswana or South Africa. Donors influence the development agenda by, for example, controlling what programmes get funded, and by insisting on following their own systems rather than building country systems. Many of these programmes are evaluated, and so donors then also become key in funding evidence generation. There are times when this can adversely influence use of evidence – for example, in the case of the review of Uganda's procurement regulations (Chapter 7), concerns were raised about donor influence having an adverse effect on ownership of the review and review findings.

Donors are also key in funding work on EIDM/EIPP, as in the Hewlett Foundation funding this book, Twende Mbele and 3ie. Similarly, the UK's Department for International Development (DFID) has been an anchor donor for 3ie and Twende Mbele; has funded M&E work in DPME and in Uganda's Office of the Prime Minister; and has funded the BCURE (Building Capacity to Use Research Evidence) project, which helped ACE and AEN to develop.

Mediating supply and demand for evidence – the role of knowledge brokering

Use of evidence can be seen as a link between supply and demand for evidence. However, the link is neither seamless nor automatic and requires thoughtful mediation. Figure 2.2 shows a model developed in South Africa. The elements

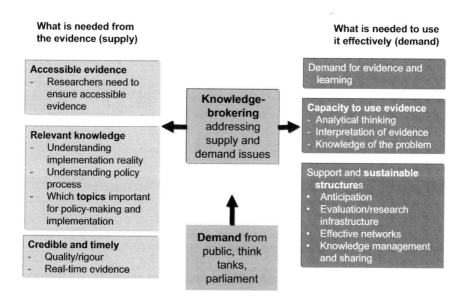

Figure 2.2 Supply, demand and knowledge brokering for evidence

Source: Ian Goldman.

include the supply of appropriate evidence, demand and capacity to use the evidence, and the knowledge linkage and translation to stimulate and support both the supply and demand for evidence, which involves all these roles. This is discussed further in Chapter 3.

The type of supply and demand differs in each country. Figure 2.3 (from Segone, n.d.b) categorises countries based on the quality and trustworthiness of their evidence, as well as the policy environment. The figure shows four categories: evidence demand-constrained countries where the evidence is good but demand is weak (evidence-influenced), vicious circle countries where the quality of evidence is poor and demand poor (opinion-based), evidence-supply-constrained countries where demand is good but supply low (evidence-influenced), and virtuous circle countries, which he refers to as evidence-based, where supply and demand are high.

Figure 2.3 shows the role of an evidence broker or knowledge broker. White (2019**b**) refers to knowledge brokering as *wave four* (we would use wave five) of

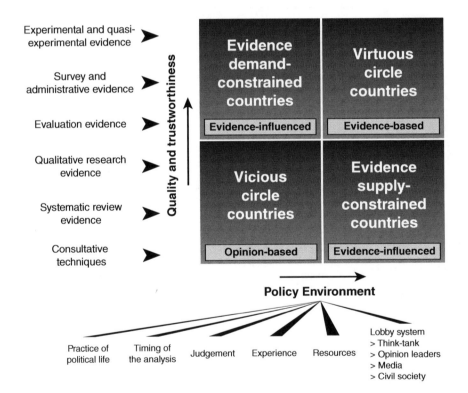

Figure 2.3 Different evidence: policy dynamics

Source: Segone, n.d.a; open access.

the evidence revolution. Martinuzzi and Sedlacko (2017) discuss the role of the knowledge broker, suggesting three different dimensions:

- The development, transfer and translation of knowledge, in which case knowledge brokers act as *knowledge managers*;
- Development of knowledge-based networks, in which knowledge brokers act as *linkage agents*;
- Development of capacity to produce and use policy-relevant knowledge, in which knowledge brokers act as *capacity builders*.

In the cases in this book we see examples of these different roles:

- *Knowledge managers* who often play multiple roles as transmitters, interpreters and synthesisers of information. An example in this book is the Parliamentary Research Unit[17] in Kenya, which was central to brokering supply and demand between civil society and the government (Chapter 10).
- *Linkage agents*: the national evaluation units in Benin, Uganda and South Africa support development of an evaluation agenda, commission the evaluations, ensure policy makers buy in to these, ensure the quality of the evaluation process and then undertake the knowledge translation of the products at the end, ensuring they end up in the policy space (Goldman et al., 2018). The case of the Department of Basic Education in South Africa and the Ugandan procurement case (Chapter 5 and 7) are examples of this.
- *Capacity builders*: Goldman et al. (2018) point out the development of capacity development elements in the evaluation systems in Benin, Uganda and South Africa.

White (2019b) differentiates the levels of curation and interpretation of data in knowledge brokering (see Figure 2.4). An example of high levels of interpretation and curation of data is the Educational Endowment Foundation in the UK, which synthesises evidence and turns it into toolkits of practical recommendations which it supplies to schools. There are similar examples in South Africa and Uganda of synthesis, at least at the evidence map level, but most countries are at the level of single studies, or SRs. Langer and Weyrauch discuss the knowledge translation process further in Chapter 3.

Supporting an enabling environment for evidence

Governance of evidence systems

Evidence can easily be politicised by the cherry-picking of favoured evidence (White, 2019b). In addition, social value can be obscured through the supposed technical rigour of evidence. Evidence inclusion or exclusion is often based on the content expertise of the policy maker and the active policy area interests

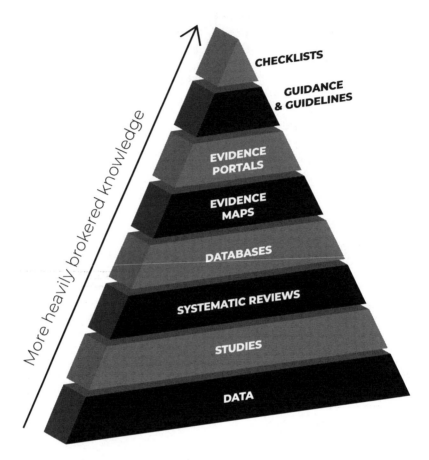

Figure 2.4 Levels of knowledge brokering
Source: White, 2019**b** [Permissions – Creative Commons].

of senior managers (Davies, 2011). In a challenging paper titled 'How to Beat Science and Influence People', Weatherall et al. (2018) suggest that

> biased production, which does not involve fabricating results, is a successful strategy for misleading the public. And in many cases, biased production is itself less effective than selective sharing, even though it involves more direct and explicit interventions on the production of science.
>
> (p. 3)

We need to move beyond the notion that evidence quality is in itself a greater good to supporting the *ecosystem which supports evidence*, so that rigorous, systematic and technically valid pieces of evidence are used within decision-making processes that are inclusive of, representative of and accountable to the multiple social interests of the population served (Parkhurst, 2017, p. 8). Parkhurst (2017) calls this the good governance of evidence. He suggests eight principles (pp. 161–162) which could add significant value to policy making in Africa; these are discussed further in Chapter 3.

Establishing evidence ecosystems

So what could an evidence ecosystem involve? Stewart et al. (2019, pp. 3–4) refer to an evidence ecosystem as 'a system reflecting the formal and informal linkages and interactions between different actors (and their capacities and resources) involved in the production, translation, and use of evidence'. A key feature of some of the evidence systems that have been established is the many components that are needed to make the overall ecosystem work. These range from governance and management of the system overall, knowledge broker roles, building relationships between suppliers and users, resourcing the system, building capacity to both supply and use evidence, quality assurance functions such as setting standards and providing guidelines, and planning for the evidence needed each year (for example, see Goldman et al., 2018). We come back to this in Chapter 13, looking at elements of the enabling environment which can be seen in the different cases.

In conclusion

There is limited data available on how evidence is actually used by policy makers and practitioners in Africa. The contribution of this book is in its in-depth cases of evidence use and the factors which have supported or inhibited use, using a behavioural change lens. This chapter defines some of the concepts we use in the book and provides an overview of the state of evidence production and use in Africa. We clarify that use of evidence will only be one factor that governments consider in their decisions and actions.

Overall, there is an increasing supply of evidence in Africa ranging from evaluations to research synthesis. While capacity in Africa is increasing, supply continues to be dominated by international players, primarily due to donor policies and preferences from which much of the demand for evidence originates, particularly in the form of evaluations. However, demand for evidence by governments is on the increase and is gradually being institutionalised in both the executive arm of government and legislatures. Civil society and think tanks are using evidence to hold government to account, and this has been institutionalised in the reporting on progress against the UN Sustainable Development Goals. An important knowledge broker role is emerging, of units with an understanding of the content, the evidence generation process and the ability to reach policy makers.

Chapter 3 takes these basic concepts and looks at the evidence relating to what works to stimulate use of evidence. Chapter 3 also presents the analytical framework that has been used to inform the case studies that are presented in Chapters 5 to 12.

Notes

1 Adapted from Davies (2011, p2).
2 Phillip Davies, in training materials used in training of senior managers in evidence, 2013–2018, University of Cape Town.
3 An example of this is an evaluation of nutrition interventions for children under 5 in South Africa, which helped to raise the profile of the challenge of malnutrition. In 2017, 27% of children under 5 experienced stunted growth.
4 Forss describes five different types of process use: learning to learn; developing networks; creating shared understanding; strengthening the project; and boosting morale (Forss et al., 2002).
5 This cycle is derived from training materials on evidence used in a range of settings, including the University of Cape Town/DPME course for senior managers.
6 www.knbs.or.ke/history-of-knbs/
7 Today, there are 40 Voluntary Organizations for Professional Evaluation (VOPEs) across Africa who are members of AfrEA (Adeline Sibanda, former chair of AfrEA, personal communication, August 2019).
8 The first was convened in May 1990 in Abidjan with the support of DAC/OECD Expert Group on Aid Evaluation and the African Development Bank (AfDB). A second forum was convened in November 1998 with the support of AfDB, the World Bank, the United Nations Development Programme (UNDP) and agencies of international cooperation of Denmark, Norway, Switzerland and Sweden.
9 A programme established to establish partnerships between countries to develop and implement M&E systems that improve government performance and impact on citizens. For more information, see www.twendembele.org.
10 The database aims to capture academic journal articles, conference presentations, evaluation reports, terms of reference, and other documents clearly related to evaluation, between the years of 2005 and 2015. Only open access articles and reports were considered due to the need for the resultant database to be open access.
11 An international research network that produces policy-relevant evidence syntheses. https://campbellcollaboration.org/.
12 Ian Goldman is a commissioner of 3ie.
13 J-PAL is a global research centre working to reduce poverty by ensuring that policy is informed by scientific evidence, focusing in particular on the use of randomised impact evaluations.
14 www.3ieimpact.org/search/site?search=&f%5B0%5D=category%3Asystematic_review&t%5B0%5D=systematic_review&sort_by=search_api_relevance, accessed 21 March 2019.
15 Own search from Cochrane library.
16 DPME has developed four evidence maps to date – on human settlements, early grade maths, the role of a developmental state, and the National Spatial Development Framework/Spatial Transformation. DPME has also initiated an evidence map on land reform to support a presidential advisory panel (Harsha Dayal, personal communication, 20 February 2019).
17 Parliamentary research units are interesting knowledge-brokering entities in that they often play multiple roles as 'transmitters, interpreters and synthesisers of information', depending on the capacity of the units. In some countries, dedicated units have been

established to provide specialised information and analysis to members of Parliament (Draman et al., 2017). Key factors identified as influencing the effectiveness of these units include the following (Ibid.):

- Resources: Levels and skills of research staff, access to adequate budgetary resources, linkages with external research institutes and access to existing research.
- Leadership and support for research within parliaments: A key obstacle is the high level of turnover of members of Parliament (MPs), particularly in Africa where, typically, 60% to 75% of MPs do not win re-election. In addition, the attitude of MPs towards evidence and research has a strong bearing on the research units, and MPs' education and awareness.
- Timing and ability to plan: Research units often struggle to anticipate key issues and plan in advance, as legislative calendars are often released with very short time frames.
- Institutional structures and processes: Including quality assurance mechanisms for evidence as well as modalities for interdepartmental collaboration and coordination.

References

Banerjee, A.V. 2016. *The influence of randomized controlled trials on development economics research and on development policy*. Presented at the State of Economics, The State of the World.

Basheka, B.C. and Byamugisha, A. 2015. The state of monitoring and evaluation (M&E) as a discipline in Africa. *Africa Journal of Public Affairs*, 8, 21.

Blaser Mapitsa, C. and Khumalo, L. 2018. Diagnosing monitoring and evaluation capacity in Africa. *African Evaluation Journal*, 6. https://doi.org/10.4102/aej.v6i1.255

Bridgeland, J. and Orszag, P. July/August 2013. Can government play money ball? *The Atlantic*. https://www.theatlantic.com/magazine/archive/2013/07/can-government-play-moneyball/309389/, accessed 20 March 2020.

Cairney, P. 2016. *The politics of evidence-based policy making*. London: Palgrave Macmillan.

Center for Global Development, The African Population and Health Research Center. 2014. *Delivering on the data revolution in Sub-Saharan Africa*. Final Report of the Data for Africa Development Working Group.

Davies, P. 2011. Evidence-Based Policy-Making (EBPM): Enhancing the use of evidence and knowledge in policy making. PSPPD Policy Brief 1, available at www.psppdknowledgerepository.org, accessed 30 November 2019.

Davies, P. 2013. Evidence vs opinion, lecture notes at course on Evidence-Based Policymaking, UCT/Department of Planning M&E.

Department of Planning, Monitoring and Evaluation (DPME). 2018. *Report on the evaluation of the national evaluation system*. Summary report.

Draman, R., Titriku, A., Lampo, I., Hayter, E. and Holden, K. 2017. *Evidence in African Parliaments*. Oxford: INASP, available at https://agora-parl.org/sites/default/files/evidence_in_african_parliaments.pdf, accessed 20 March 2020.

Forss, K., Rebien, C.C. and Carlsson, J. 2002. Process use of evaluations: Types of use that precede lessons learned and feedback. *Evaluation*, 8, 29–45. https://doi.org/10.1177/1358902002008001515

Globescan. 2018. *Think tank initiative 2018 policy community survey final report on Africa*. Think Tank Initiative.

Goldman, I., Byamugisha, A., Gounou, A., Smith, L.R., Ntakumba, S., Lubanga, T., Sossou, D. and Rot-Munstermann, K. 2018. The emergence of government evaluation systems in Africa: The case of Benin, Uganda and South Africa. *African Evaluation Journal*, 6, 11. https://doi.org/10.4102/aej.v6i1.253

Goldman, I., Mathe, J.E., Jacob, C., Hercules, A., Amisi, M., Buthelezi, T., Narsee, H., Ntakumba, S. and Sadan, M. 2015. Developing South Africa's national evaluation policy and system: First lessons learned. *African Evaluation Journal*, 3, 9.

Johnson, K., Greenseid, L.O., Toal, S.A., King, J.A., Lawrenz, F. and Volkov, B. 2009. Research on evaluation use: A review of the empirical literature from 1986 to 2005. *American Journal of Evaluation*, 30, 377–410. https://doi.org/10.1177/1098214009341660

Khunga, S. 2018. Health budget at donors' mercy. *The Nation Online*. Retrieved 3 July 2019, from https://mwnation.com/health-budget-at-donors-mercy/.

Martinuzzi, A. and Sedlacko, M. 2017. *Knowledge brokerage for sustainable development: Innovative tools for increasing research impact and evidence-based policy-making*. London: Routledge.

Mouton, C., Rabie, B., Coning, C. de and Cloete, F. 2014. Historical development and practice of evaluation. In *Evaluation Management in South Africa and Africa*. Stellenbosch: SUN MeDIA.

Muyangwa, J.M., Signé, L. and Monde, M. 2017. *The crisis of African think tanks: Challenges and solutions*. Brookings. Retrieved 14 November 2019, from www.brookings.edu/blog/africa-in-focus/2017/12/13/the-crisis-of-african-think-tanks-challenges-and-solutions/.

Paine Cronin, G. and Sadan, M. 2015. Use of evidence in policy making in South Africa: An exploratory study of attitudes of senior government officials. *African Evaluation Journal*, 3. https://doi.org/10.4102/aej.v3i1.145

PARIS21. 2019. Statistical capacity development outlook.

Parkhurst, J.O. 2017. *The politics of evidence: From evidence-based policy to the good governance of evidence*. London and New York: Routledge, Taylor & Francis Group.

Patton, M.Q. 1998. Discovering process use. *Evaluation*, 4, 225–233. https://doi.org/10.1177/13563899822208437

Porter, S. and Feinstein, O. 2014. *Demand for and supply of evaluations in selected Sub-Saharan African countries*. CLEAR Anglophone Africa.

Porter, S. and Goldman, I. 2013. A growing demand for monitoring and evaluation in Africa. *African Evaluation Journal*, 1. https://doi.org/10.4102/aej.v1i1.25

Ranson, S. and Stewart, J. 1994. *Management for the public domain*. London: Macmillan Education UK. https://doi.org/10.1007/978-1-349-23787-6

Sabet, S.M. and Brown, A.N. 2018. Is impact evaluation still on the rise? The new trends in 2010–2015. *Journal of Development Effectiveness*, 10, 291–304. https://doi.org/10.1080/19439342.2018.1483414

Sedley, S. 2016. *Missing evidence: An inquiry into the delayed publication of government*. Commissioned Research.

Segone, M. n.d.a. *Bridging the gap: The role of monitoring and evaluation in evidence-based policymaking*. Geneva: UNICEF.

Segone, M. n.d.b. Enhancing evidence-based policy making through country-led monitoring and evaluation systems. In *Country-led monitoring and evaluation systems*. Evaluation Working Papers. UNICEF, pp. 17–31.

Spencer, L., Ritchie, J., Lewis, J., and Dillon, L. August 2003. National Centre for Social Research (www.natcen.ac.uk), ISBN 07115 04465 8.

Stewart, R., Dayal, H., Langer, L. and Carina, van R. 2019. The evidence ecosystem in South Africa: Growing resilience and institutionalisation of evidence use. *Palgrave Communications*, 5, 1–12. https://doi.org/10.1057/s41599-019-0303-0

Stewart, R., Nduku, P. and Langer, L. 2017. *Capacity in Africa: The results of a survey on support for and production of evidence maps and evidence syntheses, including systematic reviews*. Johannesburg: Africa Centre for Evidence.

University of the Witwatersrand. 2012. *Exploratory case studies*. A collection of case studies facilitated by the CLEAR initiative – WITS, African Monitoring and Evaluation Systems. Graduate School of Public and Development Management, University of the Witwatersrand, Johannesburg.

Weatherall, J.O., O'Connor, C. and Bruner, J. 2018. How to beat science and influence people: Policy makers and propaganda in epistemic networks. arXiv:1801.01239 [physics].

Weiss, C.H. 1979. The many meanings of research utilization. *Public Administration Review*, 39, 426–431. https://doi.org/10.2307/3109916

White, H. 2019a. *The four waves of the evidence revolution: Supporting better policy and practice, presentation at Uganda Evaluation Week, February 2019*.

White, H. 2019b. The twenty-first century experimenting society: The four waves of the evidence revolution. *Palgrave Communications*, 5, 47. https://doi.org/10.1057/s41599-019-0253-6

3 Using evidence in Africa

A framework to assess what works, how and why

Laurenz Langer and Vanesa Weyrauch[1]

Summary

This chapter presents an analytical framework for investigating the effectiveness of interventions aiming to support the use of evidence in policy and practice (i.e. evidence-informed decision making (EIDM)). The analytical framework draws on two existing conceptual tools to research and understand EIDM: the Science of Using Science framework (Langer et al., 2016a) and the Context Matters framework (Weyrauch et al., 2016). It aims to present an inductive analytical tool that can be adapted and applied by decision makers, researchers and knowledge brokers to explore evidence use interventions at all stages of development – from conceptualisation and planning to implementation to evaluation of interventions. It does so by providing a structured approach to categorising evidence use interventions through a mechanism typology, and to categorising evidence use outcomes by applying a behaviour change lens. Contextual factors influencing evidence use are structured and organised too. Practitioners of EIDM are thus provided with a versatile conceptual device that can be applied in investigating different facets of the process of using evidence to inform decisions.

Introduction

This chapter introduces an inductive analytical framework for conceptualising evidence use interventions and investigating their potential effects. The framework draws on existing conceptual tools for researching evidence-informed decision making (EIDM) and is aimed at supporting decision makers, researchers and knowledge brokers in exploring evidence use interventions. It does not constitute a deductive or normative framework outlining what or how interventions *should* lead to positive impacts on decision makers' use of evidence. The framework is intended as a versatile analytical device that can be adapted and used as an iterative lens to support the conceptualisation, implementation and evaluation of evidence use interventions.

This analytical framework was used to guide the research for and analysis of the case studies in this book. The insights and lessons emerging from the case studies were used to further refine this framework, as discussed in Chapter 13.

This chapter starts by explaining why there is a need for a new analytical framework to conceptualise evidence use interventions and their potential effects.

It then discusses existing frameworks and analytical tools. The proposed analytical framework is then presented and illustrated in detail. The chapter concludes with thoughts on the potential application and limitations of the framework.

How an analytical framework can support EIDM research and practice

There is now a considerable body of research evaluating the effectiveness of strategies promoting EIDM/EBPM. Different types of evidence use strategies have been evaluated, focusing, for example on the impact of individual evidence champions, communities of practice or structural changes in organisational management and supervision structures. This growing number of evaluations covers multiple sectors such as health care, education, social work and international development and includes different users of evidence at a practice and policy level.

The same trend can be observed at a research synthesis level with multiple reviews attempting to bring together the results of these primary evaluations to understand what works in supporting research use (e.g. Moore et al., 2011). However, individual reviews differ in their conclusions. For example, while Yoost and colleagues' (2015) meta-analysis found that a multifaceted intervention on nurses' use of evidence (e.g. educational meetings and use of a mentor) had no effect, Hines and peers' (2015) systematic review identified interactive or activity-based learning to be effective in supporting nurses' evidence use. It is thus a challenge to generalise the findings of these reviews of what works to increase research use and to assess the patterns and directions of effects in the body of evidence.

In addition, it is challenging to compare and contrast different evidence use interventions across contexts as there is no agreed-on typology to categorise such interventions. For example, the intervention of using *mentoring* to support decision makers' use of evidence has been described as an intervention to support relationship-building and social influence by some commentators (e.g. Jordaan et al., 2018), whereas others see it primarily as a training approach (e.g. Yoost et al., 2015). Another difficulty is that interventions to support evidence use within government are rarely reported and discussed within the wider academic debates on EIDM. This fragmented state of conceptualisation of evidence use interventions challenges a transfer of knowledge across contexts. For example, decision makers in one country might not be aware of similar EIDM interventions and approaches in another country because they are reported and framed differently.

This characteristic of a fragmented evidence base for what works to support and institutionalise EIDM prevails in Africa too. As has happened internationally, Africa has seen a range of different evidence use interventions covering a spectrum of approaches. Examples are capacity-building programmes such as the Building Capacity to Use Research Evidence Programme (BCURE), to rapid response services such as pioneered by the Africa Centre for Rapid Evidence Synthesis, to high-level inter-governmental partnerships such as the Twende Mbele initiative, and continental evidence networks such as the Africa Evidence Network.

A particular feature of these approaches is that a comparatively large number of interventions and instruments are driven by African governments themselves. This includes for example South Africa's National Evaluation System (Goldman, 2014) and Kenya's parliamentary evidence-based policy-making caucus.

Many of these interventions in different countries hold large potential for synergies and cross-learning, but the reality is that most EIDM interventions and most cross-learning is confined to national, and often sectoral, silos (AEN, 2019). This situation is not confined to the African evidence ecosystem. We therefore propose an analytical framework to explore evidence use interventions in Africa, in order to:

1 Structure the available research and tacit knowledge on EIDM in a consistent manner;
2 Identify patterns in this overall evidence base;
3 Support cross-learning and collaboration around synergies of different interventions and approaches promoting evidence use.

The analytical framework was tested and further refined through the research and cross-learning presented within this book.

Existing frameworks and analytical tools for evidence use interventions

In order to systematically report on and review the effectiveness of strategies for evidence use, we require a detailed conceptual framework to categorise such interventions. This framework needs to be applicable to a diverse range of contexts, types of EIDM interventions and programmes so that it can guide their comparative analysis and investigation. At the highest level, there are three types of conceptual frameworks and models in EIDM: 1) supply-side frameworks and models; 2) demand-side frameworks and models, and 3) practice-informed frameworks and theories of change. Each is briefly discussed in the following subsections.

Supply-side framework and models

The first coherent academic theories about the use and systematic contribution of evidence to government policies can be traced back to the 1970s. Drawing on a decade of work on research use in the US government's fight against poverty, Carol Weiss developed a coherent theory of research use (Weiss, 1979). Various research has since refined Weiss's initial models, with the most important advancements being the development of the two-communities theory of knowledge utilisation (Caplan, 1979), the supply-and-demand model (Landry et al., 2001) and the producer-push and user-pull model (Stone, 2002), all of which are related. Essentially all three posit that researchers and policy makers are two different professional 'tribes' with their own conventions, practices and thought-models. This leads to a disconnect which needs to be bridged through active interventions, akin to learning each other's languages. Landry et al. (2001) adds to this basic framework the notion of *supplying* research and *demanding* research to open up the two-communities model to other groups such as civil society organisations and practitioners who can either supply or demand research too.

However, the idea that there are two distinct communities that need to be bridged or in which evidence needs to be pushed from one side into action or use on the other side seems a rather linear understanding of research use that assumes a passive user ready to consume evidence. This leaves little room for the co-construction and co-creation of knowledge (Stewart et al., 2017; Dayal, 2016) and gives a simplistic view of the realities facing policy makers and practitioners – the so-called demand side.

Demand-side frameworks and models

More recent reviews of models of evidence use criticise their strong emphasis on the supply of evidence and abstract academic definitions of use (Newman et al., 2013; Langer et al., 2017). This has led to a more inclusive theory of evidence use in which users can be co-producers of knowledge and evidence rather than mere consumers (e.g. Oliver, 2012). Policy makers and practitioners are active protagonists seeking evidence to inform their practice rather than passive recipients of research, and in the process they create demand that drives evidence generation and use. Stewart and peers (2017) argue that this shift in the conceptualisation of evidence use can be traced in a shift in language too. For example, while early conceptions described evidence use as a linear process of academics producing and pushing evidence to rational policy makers who merely take up this evidence, recent conceptions of evidence use describe an organic system spanning producers and users of evidence, and intermediates, as well as a range of other factors.

The terms 'evidence system' or 'evidence ecosystem' (Goldman, 2014; Stewart et al., 2019) reflect well the shifting consensus relating to systemic models for evidence use. However, while individual attempts have been made to conceptualise and visualise the essential elements of an evidence ecosystem and their interactions (e.g. Shepherd, 2014; AEN, 2018), there is no agreed definition of what constitutes an evidence ecosystem or how it can be developed and maintained. The monitoring and evaluation (M&E) sector in Africa has arguably moved the furthest ahead within Africa, having established national evaluation systems driving both the supply and demand for evidence. Countries such as South Africa, Uganda, Ghana, Benin and Zimbabwe have made explicit attempts to build senior managers' awareness of the importance of evidence, and so to stimulate demand. In addition, they have been actively sharing lessons across these systems to work towards scaling and institutionalisation across the continent (Goldman et al., 2018).

This recent focus on the demand side of evidence use seems justified given the relative paucity of work in EIDM explicitly focusing on decision makers (Langer et al., 2016; Newman et al., 2013). In particular, in the context of a strong public sector interest in understanding what works to make policy and practice processes more receptive to the use of evidence, it does not seem justified to apply a rigid supply-side model to conceptualise evidence use (Dayal, 2016; Langer et al., 2017). There is now an increasing range of demand-side mechanisms and activities proposed by public service sector organisations, such as capacity-building for civil servants,[2] evidence-informed guidelines[3] and policy proposals requiring an accompanying review of evidence. Further, research and practice relating to these demand-side mechanisms is supported by a range of national governments, which has led to a third theoretical frontier: developing empirical frameworks and theories of change for the practice of evidence use.[4]

Practice-informed frameworks and theories of change

A last set of theories and models of EIDM does not so much aim to outline overall meta-theories of how evidence can be used by policy makers. Rather, a range of scholars has started to develop more micro-level theories of change relating to how evidence can be used in particular contexts using different interventions. Examples are the linkages and exchange model (Lomas, 2000); the context, evidence, and links model (Crewe and Young, 2002); the knowledge to action framework (Graham and Tetroe, 2009); and Parkhurst's good governance of evidence model (Parkhurst, 2017).

The good governance of evidence model is of particular interest as it deep-dives into the institutional structures of evidence use. The model proposes a more holistic understanding in which EIDM advocates strive for good governance of evidence rather than 'good' use by individual decision makers.

As part of a more empirically informed understanding of EIDM, scholars have also attempted to better understand contextual variables such as barriers to, and facilitators of, evidence use, either through individual case studies (e.g. Uneke et al., 2011), primary research on decision makers' perception of evidence and its use (e.g. Cronin and Sadan, 2015) or systematic reviews of such factors (Oliver et al., 2014).

This empirical work on barriers and facilitators is further complemented by a rich body of knowledge on the role of context in influencing the use of evidence (Cairney, 2016; Crewe and Young, 2002; Shaxson et al., 2015; Weyrauch et al., 2016). Paul Cairney's work in particular highlights the importance of political factors in the use of evidence. In 2016, the learning from this work on the role of context was formalised into the Context Matters framework (Weyrauch et al., 2016), which unpacks the importance and nature of context and its interaction with evidence use.

This work on context does not focus directly on interventions to support research use (which is within an organisation's control), but rather on the factors and variables that affect use. It asks which factors interventions need to be sensitive to and work towards addressing. As a result, the work informs the design of evidence use interventions and can be used to assess how an intervention interacts with different contexts that can affect the use of evidence. However, it does not assess the effectiveness and causal impact of evidence use interventions. This last contribution is provided by an existing body of work focusing on assessing what works to support evidence use.

As earlier mentioned, there have been a number of evaluations of the effectiveness of interventions aiming to support policy makers' use of evidence.

Langer and colleagues' (2016) systematic review of reviews identified 36 existing reviews of primary evaluations of evidence use interventions, covering 129 primary evaluations. A key challenge in the synthesis of this large primary evidence base is to identify groups of homogenous interventions to understand which of them work (or don't work) to support evidence use, how and why. A framework is required to group and categorise these interventions in order to be able to aggregate their results and synthesise findings across contexts.

A range of scholars has developed frameworks and typologies of evidence use interventions, including Nutley et al. (2007) and Gough et.al. (2011). However, despite this range of existing typologies, there is no agreed overarching theory of how to categorise evidence use interventions. Further, none of the aforementioned work attempts to unpack the outcomes of research use. This means there is an absence of conceptual work on how to categorise and define different types and measures of evidence use. Aside from Carol Weiss's 1979 definition of different types of use, Dobbins and colleagues' (2009) Global EIDM index and 3ie's evidence use categorisation, little conceptual guidance is available on how to consistently define and measure evidence use.

In summary, there is a large body of conceptual and empirical research aiming to understand the practice of evidence use. This body of work has produced a range of conceptual models and frameworks, but there is no agreed analytical tool to assess evidence use interventions in practice. In order to guide the assessment of different EIDM initiatives in a range of African countries, we therefore set out to develop an analytical framework that is fit for purpose to explore these initiatives.

Developing an analytical framework for comparative analysis

To develop our analytical framework, we adapt the framework for evidence use interventions developed by Langer and colleagues (2016) and supplement this with an analytical tool to understand contextual factors shaping the impact of evidence use interventions (Weyrauch et al., 2016). More information on the methodological development of Langer and colleagues' (2016) and Weyrauch et al.'s (2016) framework can be found in the respective publications.

Applying an analytical lens for evidence use strategies and outcomes: the Science of Using Science project

Langer et al.'s (2016) framework was developed as part of the Science of Using Science project,[5] a systematic review of what works to support the use of research evidence by decision makers. The framework consists of two core components: (1) a *mechanism* typology to structure research use strategies and activities and (2) a *behaviour change* typology to structure research use outcomes. It thereby contributes a structured analytical lens for categorising and analysing different applied activities to support the use of evidence and assessing whether these have been effective in changing behaviour.

In order to group research use strategies and activities, (e.g. capacity-building in evidence use, research communication, rapid response services), Langer and colleagues focus on the underlying mechanisms of change of these activities. Mechanisms of change are defined as the processes by which evidence use might be achieved within a given strategy or activity. For example, a networking event for decision makers and researchers might support research use by developing *trusted relationships* and ongoing *interaction* and exchange between the two groups. Relationships and interactions in this example would then be the underlying mechanism of change of the activity of hosting a networking event.

Langer et al. (2016) formulated a list of six mechanisms underlying research use interventions, which is presented in Table 3.1.[6] As introduced earlier, this list builds on existing work by the authors, in particular Gough et al. (2011). Building on the first conceptual foundation and taxonomies for evidence use interventions by Walter et al. (2003) and Nutley et al. (2007), Gough et al. (2011) refined an initial concise list of mechanisms as part of the Evidence Informed Policy in Education in Europe project. The Science of Using Science project then further adapted and developed these mechanisms resulting in the final six mechanisms.

The six mechanisms are structured using a numerical list and abbreviation (M1–M6) for the purpose of accessibility. This structure does not reflect a

Table 3.1 Evidence use mechanisms

Mechanism	Description	Example of linked activity
Awareness (M1)	Building awareness of, and positive attitudes towards, EIDM.	• Social marketing of the norm to use evidence • Awareness-raising campaigns
Agree (M2)	Building mutual understanding and agreement on policy-relevant questions and the kind of evidence needed to answer them.	• Co-production approaches between researchers and government staff • Steering committees
Access (M3)	Providing communication of, and convenient access to, evidence.	• Knowledge repositories • Communication campaigns and strategies
Interact (M4)	Interaction between decision makers and researchers to build trusted relationships, collaborate and gain exposure to a different type of social influence.	• Knowledge brokers • Networks and communities of practice
Ability (M5)	Supporting decision makers in developing skills in accessing and making sense of evidence.	• Capacity-building (e.g. workshops and formal training courses) • Mentoring programmes
Institutionalising / formalising (M6)	Influencing decision-making structures and processes.	• Secondments • Embedded support (e.g. knowledge brokers)

hierarchical order of the mechanisms, and each mechanism is assumed to be of equal importance in supporting decision makers' use of research. For each mechanism, illustrative examples of corresponding evidence use activities and interventions are provided in the right-hand column.

In order to structure evidence use outcomes, Langer and colleagues conceptualised evidence use as a form of behaviour change, that is for decision makers to increase their use of research evidence requires a change in their behaviour. Examples of evidence use include decision makers introducing evidence during policy debates, accessing and interpreting diagnostic evidence when developing a policy proposal or integrating evaluation results into programme design. Using this conceptualisation of evidence use as behaviour change, Langer et al. adopt an existing framework for characterising and designing behaviour change interventions developed by Michie et al. (2011).

Based on a review of existing frameworks for conceptualising behaviour change, Michie et al. (2011) propose a 'behaviour system', which assumes behaviour change to result from the interplay of three essential conditions: capability, opportunity, and motivation, which they termed the COM-B system. Behaviour change interventions work through changing one or more of these conditions. Langer and colleagues follow this conceptualisation of behaviour change in their framework for evidence use outcomes and retain Michie et al.'s definition of capability, opportunity and motivation.

Langer and colleagues' final framework then merges their six mechanisms for structuring evidence use interventions with the COM-B system for structuring behaviour change outcomes (Figure 3.1). As Figure 3.1 indicates, all evidence

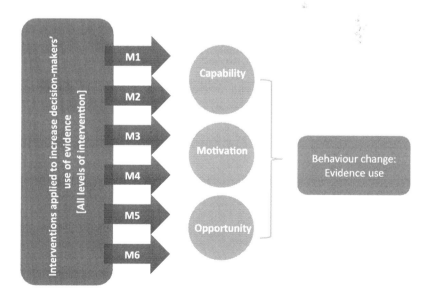

Figure 3.1 Science of Using Science conceptual framework

Source: Langer et al. (2016).

use interventions are categorised according to the six mechanisms of change. It is these mechanisms that are assumed to be the unit of analysis in applied strategies and activities to support decision makers' use of evidence

Each of the six mechanisms (M1–M6) then works through one or more of the three COM-B components in order to effect decision makers' behaviour in relation to evidence use. This leaves the COM-B components to serve as intermediate outcomes representing the capability, opportunity and motivation to use evidence. The final outcome of evidence use is defined as a type of behaviour change of decision makers. Behaviour change in terms of evidence use may occur at different levels including individual behaviour, immediate organisational context (e.g. where people work), broader organisational context (e.g. local government) or wider national and international context.

Developing an analytical lens for the context in which evidence use activities are implemented: the Context Matters framework

Evidence use activities are not implemented in a vacuum but are highly dependent on the context of implementation. The role of context and how it shapes the use of evidence has been discussed widely in the literature on EIDM (e.g. Nutley et al., 2007; Parkhurst, 2016; Cairney, 2016), but context is often merely acknowledged as a large and general barrier or facilitator when describing the effectiveness or ineffectiveness of an intervention. In order to understand context in a more holistic and structured manner and to detect and understand the best entry points to improve the use of knowledge in a public agency, Weyrauch et al. (2016) developed an interactive and participatory tool: the Context Matters framework. This tool is a lens for understanding and acting upon internal and external factors of the context that may influence the use of evidence within an organisation.

The framework focuses specifically on the production and use of research in government institutions. Context in this tool refers to the specific environment in which people try to get research evidence and knowledge into practice. In its most simplistic form, the term includes the physical environment in which practice takes place but also encompasses the relationships and processes that go beyond this physical environment and enable change as a consequence. As with Langer and colleagues' framework for intervention and outcomes, the explicit aim of the Context Matters framework is to structure and systematise different patterns of how context influences evidence production and use in order to gain a consistent analytical lens.

Weyrauch's framework comprises six facets or 'dimensions' of context that systematically influence the use of evidence by decision makers, as presented in Table 3.2.[7] These six dimensions fall into two categories: external and internal. The first two external dimensions (in grey) are (1) the macro-context and (2) intra-and inter-relationships with state and non-state agents. The four internal dimensions are (3) culture; (4) organisational capacity; (5) management and processes; and (6) core resources. Table 3.2 provides an overview of the key definitions of each of these six dimensions.

Table 3.2 Dimensions of context according to the Context Matters framework

Dimension of context	Description	Sub-dimensions
1 Macro-context	Overarching forces at the national level that establish the 'bigger picture' in which policy is made and, consequently, how research can or cannot inform it. This includes the political, economic, social and cultural factors that surround the policy-making institution and in which it is embedded.	• Usual large factors acknowledged in literature (extent of political, academic and media freedom, etc.) • Popular pressure for change • Crises and transitions • Degree of power distribution in the political system • Prevailing policy narratives • Discretional decision making and corruption • Strategic planning culture • Consultation and participation in policy processes • Knowledge regime
2 Intra- and inter-institutional linkages	Refers to the relationships between related government agencies. Inter-institutional linkages refer to an agency's interaction with other knowledge users and producers (such as universities, NGOs or think tanks) which can affect or be affected by policy design and implementation.	• Flow of information between jurisdictions and levels • Capacity to use evidence among different sections and departments • Support from governmental agencies that produce data and research • Coordination among agencies • Policy domains • Relationships with other state agencies for policy design and implementation • Existence and types of policy forums and epistemic communities • Formal channels of interaction with researchers and research institutions • Number and type of civil society actors involved in decision processes, and degree of vested interests • Status of consensus on the policy base
3 Culture	All organisations have a culture. This is a set of values and assumptions that are generally accepted by those within the organisation as 'the norm'.	• Values and beliefs • Openness to change and innovation • Incentives • Motivations
4 Organisational capacity	An organisation's ability to use its resources effectively to achieve its aims – in this case, to design and implement public policies. It includes human resources and the legal framework that determines how resources can or cannot be used.	• Leadership • Senior management • Human resources • Legal capacity

(Continued)

Table 3.2 (Continued)

Dimension of context	Description	Sub-dimensions
5 Management and processes	How an institution organises its daily work to achieve its mission and goals, from planning to implementation and evaluation.	• Degree of systematic planning • Existing formal processes to access and use evidence in policy making • Positions, including division of work and roles and responsibilities • Communications processes • Monitoring and evaluation
6 Other resources	Key resources that affect how an organisation systematically gathers and uses evidence, including its budget and technology.	• Budget committed to research • Technology • Existence of a knowledge infrastructure • Time availability

The links between these dimensions of context are various and changing. For example, a restrictive macro-context will limit the room for change in most of the internal context dimensions. However, Weyrauch and colleagues stress that there are a number of sub-dimensions of the six main facets that can positively shape the overall contextual environment. These sub-dimensions refer to (1) leadership of EIDM by individual decision makers; (2) organisational culture as a key determinant of effective management processes for EIDM; and (3) staff incentives and motivation to use evidence.

In sum, the Context Matters framework aims to help decision makers better assess the contexts in which they operate and, based on careful assessment, detect where the potential for change may be greater and barriers more significant. It can thereby serve as an effective analytical lens to unpack already implemented evidence use strategies as well as plan new ones in government departments and provide a coherent structure to organise and describe how context affected or may affect these activities.

Developing a combined analytical framework: synergies between the Science of Using Science and Context Matters

In a last step, we merged the Science of Using Science's framework for unpacking evidence use interventions and outcomes with the Context Matters framework to create a tool to explore variables affecting decision makers' evidence use. Figure 3.2 outlines the combined analytical framework.

The combined analytical framework explores the evidence process from generation through to potential development impact. Each section in the framework presents an independent element that can be unpacked in more detail. The framework starts with the *demand for evidence*, which is assumed to be a key contextual feature that affects the production of evidence, the applied evidence use intervention, its underlying change mechanism, and the intermediate changes.

Using evidence in Africa 45

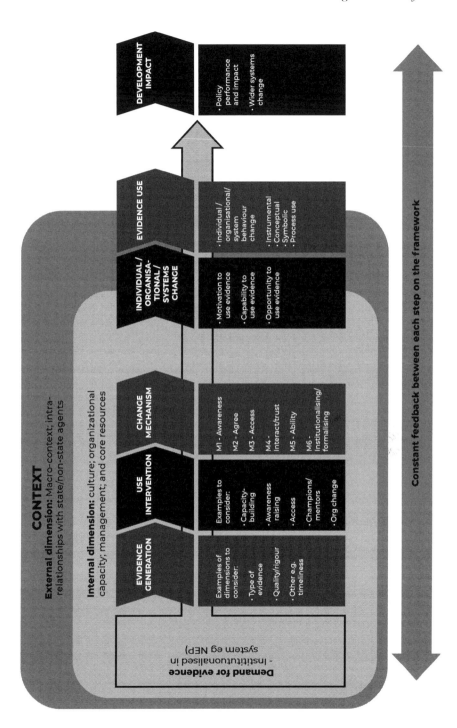

Figure 3.2 Combined analytical framework
Source: Langer et al. (2020).

The demand for evidence refers to decision makers' and evidence users' pull for evidence. This user pull is deliberately the starting point of the framework and reflects a more government-focused rather than researcher-focused application of the framework. It suggests that efforts to increase the use of evidence ideally start with an in-depth understanding of the demand for such evidence and its existing use. The framework is thus firmly demand-led.

The second section of the framework refers to the production or supply of evidence (*evidence generation*). There is a range of factors to be considered when assessing the nature of evidence generation. Three key aspects related to the supply of evidence include quality, type and evidence claim. First, the *quality* of the evidence is likely to strongly affect its use. We would caution against a narrow interpretation of quality as methodological rigour and instead refer to quality and relevance to a policy context (Parkhurst, 2016). Second, the *type* of evidence matters; different types of evidence answer different questions and thus can inform different policy decisions. Third, the specific *evidence claim* and the standard of evidence needs to be assessed. Policy decisions should be informed by strong bodies of evidence that support specific evidence claims and comply with explicit standards of evidence set by decision-making bodies (Gough and White, 2018).

The third section of the framework investigates *evidence use interventions*. This refers to any programme, instrument, strategy or activity that is a deliberate and tangible input to support the use of evidence. The term 'intervention' indicates that a deliberate and tangible effort is made to intervene in the status quo in order to effect change in relation to evidence use. As outlined earlier, there is a plethora of evidence use interventions, and the Science of Using Science review alone identified 121. The analytical framework only provides a few selected examples of such interventions.

Given the diversity and complexity of evidence use interventions, section 4 of the framework suggests that these work through six underlying mechanisms of change (M1–M6). This assumes that one can understand a given intervention through a change mechanism lens rather than investigating the interventions as a whole. For example, an EIDM mentoring programme would be assessed by unpacking its relevant mechanisms of change, which could include: *ability* (M5) as mentors might support a technical skill such as critical appraisal capacity; *interaction* (M4) as mentors and mentees assumingly connect and build a trusted relationship; and *access* (M3) as mentors might support mentees in accessing academic databases or linking them to sources of evidence. Most evidence use interventions are likely to employ a range of mechanisms, and it is often the precise interplay of different mechanisms that unlocks change.

Section 5 of the framework then moves from the intervention side to the outcome side, that is the use of evidence by decision makers. It assumes that intervention outcomes can be observed at an individual, organisational and systems level. For instance, the mentoring example discussed could support either an individual decision maker or the organisation that she works for, or both, depending on the content of the mentoring as well as the seniority of the mentee. This immediate or intermediate outcome of the evidence use intervention can be broken down into supporting *capability* to use evidence, *motivation* to use evidence, and *opportunity* to use evidence. To illustrate these, examples of these immediate outcomes are provided in Table 3.3.

Keeping to the EIDM mentoring example, we would then investigate how different mechanisms of change (e.g. ability, interact, access) have affected the three intermediate outcomes of capability, motivation, and opportunity to use evidence. For example, interaction with an EIDM mentor might motivate a mentee to pursue evidence by decreasing the person's isolation and providing encouragement and support. Likewise, the mentoring might provide the individual with technical EIDM skills, such as appraising a piece of evidence.

Section 6 of the framework then explores whether these intermediate outcomes did translate into actual *use of evidence*. It is important to note that the framework does not prescribe what constitutes a meaningful or 'positive' use of evidence. For example the sought-after instrumental use of evidence that directly leads to a more evidence-informed decision or action is but one (and rare) form of use.

In the last step (section 7), the framework encourages an investigation into whether the actual use of evidence did translate into *changes in policy performance or wider systems change*.[8] There is no guarantee that an evidence-informed policy or programme leads to better socio-economic outcomes or that an organisational structure receptive to the use of evidence leads to improved organisational performance. Similarly, some interventions might have the power to effect systemic change across decision-making sectors (e.g. the National Evaluation System in South Africa). However, caution must be applied when investigating this last step on the framework.

The *context* in which this process takes place – from evidence generation to designing an evidence intervention, effecting change related to evidence use and policy impact, is indicated by the two overarching boxes that embed the

Table 3.3 Immediate outcomes

Immediate outcome	Individual change	Organisational change	Systems change
Capability to use evidence	• Skills to search for evidence	• Access to databases	• Diverse supply of training and capacity support around evidence use
Opportunity to use evidence	• Timely access to relevant evidence	• Organisational processes that create a space for evidence (e.g. submission standards, performance appraisal)	• Investment in tailored evidence systems
Motivation to use evidence	• Awareness of the value of evidence use	• Organisational norms support the use of evidence	• Investment in diverse evidence networks advocating for the use of evidence

EIDM process. As per the Context Matters framework, the context is divided into an external dimension and an internal dimension. The external dimension is indicated in a darker shade and comprises (1) the *macro-context* and (2) *intra- and inter-relationships* with state and non-state agents. Both these variables are external to an evidence use intervention and cannot be significantly affected by it; they depend on larger forces and a myriad of external actors. However, certain evidence use interventions and mechanisms could alter external contexts, for example, by forging strategic alliances and networks between different actors in the evidence ecosystem. An illustration of this is how the Ghanaian Environmental Protection Agency decided to act upon opportunities to collaborate with a wider range of stakeholders, including promoting more citizen engagement to revive multi-stakeholder networks (INASP, 2018).

The four internal dimensions of context (lighter shade) can be more directly affected by an evidence use intervention. These four dimensions are (3) *culture*, (4) *organisational capacity*, (5) *management and processes* and (6) *core resources*. These internal dimensions only extend across the first five sections of the framework until the intermediate outcomes, while the external dimensions extend until the sixth section, which is the final outcome of evidence use. This differentiation aims to capture that the internal dimensions of context usually are changed through the intervention itself. For example, an intervention might actively build evidence champions to change the organisational culture around evidence use.

Yet both dimensions of context have a bearing on the demand for evidence, its generation, the identification of relevant intervention approaches and change mechanisms as well as the intermediate evidence use outcomes. While both dimensions of context affect the demand for evidence, demand for evidence is primarily driven by internal context dimensions such as organisational culture and capacity; for this reason, the demand for evidence box is shaded similarly to the internal context dimensions.

Last, none of the context boxes extend to the development impact itself, as it is assumed that a different set of contexts, not linked to the EIDM intervention itself, affects these outcomes, which relate to the particular sector itself. For example, while macro-contexts such as the prevailing political climate affect the nature of the EIDM process, a completely different set of macro-factors determines whether a particular sectoral policy has positive socio-economic impacts (e.g. economic growth, social cohesion), and these factors are not linked to the EIDM process at all.

The framework acknowledges that in practice the flow of the suggested sections is not linear. There are multiple feedback loops between evidence generation and interventions and between intermediate outcomes and demand for evidence, and between all spheres of the context and the facets of the evidence use interventions and outcomes. The arrow at the bottom of the diagram serves as a placeholder to visualise these multiple interactions and feedback loops between all parts of the framework.

Intended application and limitations of the analytical framework

The intent of the analytical framework is to provide a consistent conceptual lens to analyse what happened in the diverse case studies of EIDM in Africa that have been collected in this volume. The consistent use of the framework as a guide and lens for analysis allows for the structured identification of transferable lessons learned and facilitates a synthesis of the insights and knowledge generated by the diverse case studies.

It is crucial to stress that the framework does not aim to reflect or prescribe how evidence use *should* take place;[9] neither does it prescribe how evidence use interventions *should* be analysed. It is intended as an analytical lens with different conceptual devices, which EIDM practitioners and scholars can apply as best fits their context. In some circumstances, the COM evidence use structure might help an analysis, whereas in others, it might be the dimensions of context; each conceptual device of the framework can be applied in its own right. The framework can therefore best be regarded as a starting point to guide EIDM research and practice and not does not constitute a static blueprint or one-size-fits-all device. We hope that EIDM scholars and practitioners will apply the framework in this inductive spirit and adapt its structure and application.

This analytical framework naturally has a number of limitations. First, it is not meant to describe or capture a holistic evidence ecosystem. It does not reflect all of the actors involved in evidence production and use and how they interact; neither does it facilitate sectoral assessments. Second, the framework is not well suited to inform diagnostic studies on EIDM such as perceptions of evidence use. It is designed for, and most useful for, thinking through and planning, implementing and evaluating tangible evidence use interventions. As a result, it best fits contexts where there is an existing practice of EIDM and an intention to promote evidence use, or at least a familiarity with the notion of evidence use. Third, the framework is not focused on the processes of evidence production. It approaches EIDM from a policy-maker and practitioner perspective with a strong focus on the demand side. As a result, it is most applicable to evidence users aiming to systematise the practice of EIDM, organisations that have an interest in strengthening their use of evidence, and organisations and teams working towards supporting decision makers in their use of evidence. Fourth, as with all analytical frameworks, the conceptual and analytical devices are necessarily aggregated and abstracted. This comes at the expense of detail relating to certain concepts. For example, the framework does not provide sub-frameworks and analytical tools for specific interventions such as EIDM capacity-building, even though these are widely available. Likewise, Michie et al.'s original COM-B framework goes into more detail on how to support behaviour change. Users of the framework are encouraged to complement it with more granular analytical tools for specific evidence use interventions, mechanisms and outcomes where relevant. Fifth, and last, the framework is only partially empirically informed. Both the Context Matters framework and the Science of Using Science framework have been developed based on decision makers' feedback and experiences and have been applied and adapted in an EIDM practice context since their publication. However, this combined analytical framework has not been applied in practice before and is open to adaption following the experience of the case study authors using it. Some proposed changes are included in Chapter 13.

Conclusion

This chapter presents an analytical framework for investigating the effectiveness of interventions aiming to support the use of evidence in policy and practice. The analytical framework draws on two existing conceptual tools to research and understand EIDM: the Science of Using Science framework (Langer et al., 2016) and the Context Matters framework (Weyrauch et al., 2016) and has been developed through a dialogue between the authors of the two frameworks and the researchers involved in this book, many of whom come from a policy background. It aims to present an inductive analytical tool that can be adapted and applied by decision makers, researchers, and knowledge brokers to explore evidence use interventions at all stages of development: from conceptualisation and planning to implementation and evaluation of interventions.

Notes

1 Laurenz Langer developed the manuscript for this chapter. Laurenz is a co-author of the Science of Using Science report, which was part of a wider project led by David Gough and Janice Tripney from the UCL EPPI-Center and who share intellectual ownership of the Science of Using Science framework applied in this chapter. Vanesa Weyrauch read, reviewed, and commented on the chapter. She is the lead investigator of the Context Matters framework, jointly developed by INASP and Politics&Ideas. The co-editors Ian Goldman and Mine Pabari have supported the development of the combined conceptual framework.
2 www.mandelaschool.uct.ac.za/gsdpp/courses/evidence_based_policy_making_implementation
3 www.afidep.org/index.html
4 www.dpme.gov.za/keyfocusareas/Socio%20Economic%20Impact%20Assessment%20System/Pages/default.aspx
5 https://eppi.ioe.ac.uk/cms/Default.aspx?tabid=3504
6 Note that there are two semantic changes in Table 3.1. In Langer et al.'s initial framework work, M3 was labelled as 'Communication & access' and M5 as 'Skills'. Following stakeholder feedback, we have adapted the labels of these two mechanisms for the purpose of this research project.
7 With an interactive version of the framework provided online: http://cm.politicsandideas.org/homepage-old.
8 It should also be noted that evidence use does not necessarily lead to any policy changes. An evidence-based decision could be to do nothing and remain with the status quo.

9 While applicable to all sections of the framework, this non-normative framing applies strongly to the last impact section of the framework as few individual evidence use interventions will be able to target and achieve impact at this scale.

References

Africa Evidence Network. 2018. *African evidence ecosystem maps.* Retrieved from https://aen-website.azurewebsites.net/en/learning-space/

Africa Evidence Network. 2019. *A geo-map of EIDM organization in Africa.* Retrieved from www.google.com/maps/d/u/0/viewer?mid=1j7yA9hfXnUio7WaRA2Ha2f4Ihr4Knng P&ll=7.062733884621437%2C14.946899331250052&z=3

Cairney, P. 2016. *The politics of evidence-based policy making.* New York: Springer.

Caplan, N. 1979. The two-communities theory and knowledge utilization. *The American Behavioral Scientist,* 22(3), 459–471.

Crewe, E. and Young, M.J. 2002. *Bridging research and policy: Context, evidence and links.* London: Overseas Development Institute.

Cronin, G. and Sadan, M. 2015. Use of evidence in policy making in South Africa: An exploratory study of attitudes of senior government officials. *African Evaluation Journal,* 3(1), 10–20.

Dayal, H. 2016. *Using evidence to reflect on South Africa's 20 years of democracy – Insights from within the policy space.* Knowledge Sector Initiative Working Paper 7.

Dobbins, M., Hanna, S.E., Ciliska, D., Manske, S., Cameron, R., Mercer, S.L., O'Mara, L., DeCorby, K. and Robeson, P. 2009. A randomized controlled trial evaluating the impact of knowledge translation and exchange strategies. *Implementation Science,* 4(1), 61.

Goldman, I. 2014. *Using evidence by government in South Africa.* Retrieved from www.africaevidencenetwork.org/wp-content/uploads/2014/12/Using-Evidence-by-Government-in-South-Africa.pdf

Goldman, I., et al. 2018. The emergence of government evaluation systems in Africa: The case of Benin, Uganda and South Africa. *African Evaluation Journal,* 6(1), 1–11.

Gough, D., Tripney, J., Kenny, C. and Buk-Berge, E. 2011. *Evidence informed policy in education in Europe: EIPEE final project report.* London: EPPI-Centre, Social Science Research Unit, Institute of Education, University of London.

Gough, D. and White, H. 2018. *Evidence standards and evidence claims in web based research portals.* London: Centre for Homelessness Impact.

Graham, I.D. and Tetroe, J.M. 2009. Getting evidence into policy and practice: Perspective of a health research funder. *Journal of Canadian Academy Child Adolescence Psychiatry,* 18, 46–50.

Hines, S., Ramsbotham, J. and Coyer, F. 2015. The effectiveness of interventions for improving the research literacy of nurses: A systematic review. *Worldviews on Evidence-Based Nursing,* 12(5), 265–272.

INASP. 2018. *Context Matters Framework case study: Supporting organizational change to improve the use of evidence in environmental protection in Ghana.* Retrieved from www.inasp.info/publications/context-matters-ghana

Jordaan, S., et al. 2018. Reflections on mentoring experiences for evidence-informed decision-making in South Africa and Malawi. *Development in Practice,* 28(4), 456–467.

Landry, R., Amara, N. and Lamari, M. 2001. Utilization of social science research knowledge in Canada. *Research Policy,* 30(2), 333–349.

Langer, L., Erasmus, Y., Tannous, N. and Stewart, R. 2017. How stakeholder engagement has led us to reconsider definitions of rigour in systematic reviews. *Environmental Evidence*, 6(20).

Langer, L., Tripney, J. and Gough, D. 2016. *The science of using science. Researching the use of research evidence in decision-making.* Technical Report. London: EPPI-Center, Social Science Research Unit, UCL Institute of Education.

Langer, L., Goldman, I. and Pabari, M. 2020. Analytical framework used to guide case study research. In *Using evidence for policy and practice—Lessons from Africa*. Routledge, Taylor & Francis Group.

Lomas, J. 2000. Using linkage and exchange to move research into policy at a Canadian Foundation. *Health Affairs,* 19(3), 236.

Michie, S., van Stralen, M.M. and West, R. 2011. The behaviour change wheel: A new method for characterising and designing behaviour change interventions. *Implementation Science*, 6(1), 42.

Moore, G., Redman, S., Haines, M. and Todd, A. 2011. What works to increase the use of research in population health policy and programmes: A review. *Evidence & Policy: A Journal of Research, Debate and Practice*, 7(3), 277–305.

Newman, K., Capillo, A., Famurewa, A., Nath, C. and Siyanbola, W. 2013. *What is the evidence on evidence-informed policy making?* Lessons from the International Conference on Evidence-Informed Policy Making. Oxford: INASP.

Nutley, S.M., Walter, I. and Davies, H.T. 2007. *Using evidence: How research can inform public services*. Bristol, UK: Policy Press.

Oliver, K., Innvar, S., Lorenc, T., Woodman, J. and Thomas, J. 2014. A systematic review of barriers to and facilitators of the use of evidence by policymakers. *BMC Health Services Research,* 14(1), 1.

Oliver, S. 2012. Making a difference with systematic reviews. In Gough, D., Oliver, S. and Thomas, J. (eds.), *An introduction to systematic reviews*. London: Sage.

Parkhurst, J.O. 2017. *The politics of evidence: From evidence-based policy to the good governance of evidence*. Abingdon: Routledge.

Shaxon et al. 2015. *Evidence-informed policymaking in practice: an overview from South Africa's Department of Environmental Affairs*. Republic of South Africa: Department of Environmental Affairs.

Shepherd, J. 2014 *How to achieve more effective services: The evidence ecosystem*. Cardiff: What Works Network.

Stewart, R., Dayal, H. and Langer, L. 2017. Terminology and tensions within evidence-informed decision-making in South Africa over a 15-year period. *Research for All*, 1(2), 252–264.

Stewart, R., Dayal, H., Langer, L. and van Rooyen, C. 2019. The evidence ecosystem in South Africa: Growing resilience and institutionalisation of evidence use. *Palgrave Communications*, 5(1), 1–12.

Stone, D. 2002. Using knowledge: The dilemmas of 'bridging research and policy. *Compare*, 32(3), 285–296.

Uneke, C.J., Ezeoha, A.E., Ndukwe, C.D., Oyibo, P.G., Onwe, F., Igbinedion, E.B. and Chukwu, P.N. 2011. Individual and organisational capacity for evidence use in policy making in Nigeria: An exploratory study of the perceptions of Nigeria health policy makers. *Evidence & Policy,* 7(3), 251–276.

Walter, I., Nutley, S. and Davies, H. 2003. Developing a taxonomy of interventions used to increase the impacts of research. Research Unit for Research Utilisation, ESRC Network for Evidence Based Policy and Practice.

Weiss, C.H. 1979. The many meanings of research utilization. *Public Administration Review*, 39(5), 426–431.
Weyrauch, V., Echt, L. and Suliman, S. 2016. *Knowledge into policy: Going beyond context matters*. Retrieved from www.politicsandideas.org/wp-content/uploads/2016/07/Going-beyond-context-matters-Framework_PI.compressed.pdf
Yost, J., et al. 2015. The effectiveness of knowledge translation interventions for promoting evidence-informed decision-making among nurses in tertiary care: A systematic review and meta-analysis. *Implementation Science*, 10(1), 98.

4 Mere compliance or learning – M&E culture in the public service of Benin, Uganda and South Africa

Ian Goldman, Wole Olaleye, Stanley Sixolile Ntakumba, Mokgoropo Makgaba and Cara Waller

Summary

This chapter builds on research on the performance monitoring and evaluation (M&E)culture in Benin, Uganda and South Africa conducted through the Twende Mbele African M&E partnership, which is presented here to provide a context for the cases in the book. The research was conducted on approximately five national departments per country and 368 managers were interviewed: 149 from Benin, 127 from South Africa, and 92 from Uganda. We see a mixed picture and many similarities in the three countries. Overall, all three have significant planning and monitoring systems and an established evaluation system. Around half of managers are seen to be using evidence from M&E, with evaluations used particularly in an ex-post role rather than during the life of interventions. The effect of each country's national evaluation system is recognised. However, there is also evidence of negative behaviour, using reports to conceal information, not interrogating the cause of failure. The survey is itself a baseline for Twende Mbele and the trends in these figures will be interesting.

Introduction

Background

Many countries in Africa are using M&E as part of their efforts to improve performance of the public sector (Porter and Goldman, 2013). Three pioneer countries in establishing government-led national evaluation systems (NES) are Uganda, Benin and South Africa (SA), which have been working together since 2012 to share experience around M&E. Since 2016, this has been formalised through the Twende Mbele African government +M&E partnership. One of Twende Mbele's projects was a survey of the state of performance M&E culture in national departments in the three countries. This chapter draws on this research and other literature to critically analyse the context for using evidence in African governments, building on the analytical framework guiding this book in Chapter 3, particularly the component on context drawn from Politics and Ideas (Weyrauch et al., n.d.).

Prior to this study there was little systematic empirical information on M&E culture within the public sector in Africa. Despite evidence suggesting that

M&E is gaining political recognition in the public sector, its ability to influence the efficacy of policies, projects, programmes and interventions remains unclear.

The purpose of the research was to assess the state of performance M&E culture in the three participating governments by seeing how each country's various M&E systems interact to improve performance and accountability, with a specific focus on policy, approach, concepts, framework and organisational arrangements in the public sector.[1] Initial interviews were conducted with 14 managers and used to help design the survey. A representative probability sample size of 490 senior managers was selected from across 22 national departments and ministries. In total, 368 managers were interviewed: 149 from Benin, 127 from South Africa, and 92 from Uganda. A survey instrument was administered either in a face-to-face interview or the questions were answered in writing and submitted electronically. The interviews were conducted using in-country researchers in either French or English. Quantitative responses were analysed using Stata.

This chapter also draws on wider literature from the three countries and highlights some of the barriers and facilitators to a performance culture.

What is a M&E culture that promotes performance?

> Culture conveys a sense of identity to employees, provides unwritten and, often, unspoken guidelines on how to get along in an organisation.... An organisational culture is reflected by what is valued, the dominant leadership styles, symbols, the procedures, routines, and the definition of success that make an organisation unique.
> (Cameron and Quinn, 1999, pp. 2–3)

The cultures of monitoring and evaluation are distinct. Monitoring involves tracking what has been planned, while evaluation is a systematic and rigorous analysis of interventions to assess and strengthen their performance. A monitoring culture is often closely linked to compliance with reporting requirements, while evaluation is usually more linked to a learning culture (Goldman et al., 2018). Mayne (2010, p. 6) describes an organisation with an evaluative culture as one that:

> deliberately seeks out empirical information to learn how to better manage its programs and services, and thereby improve its performance.... [It] is this evidence-seeking behaviour that characterises an evaluative culture and distinguishes it from a more general learning culture.

M&E culture is composed of perception, underlying assumptions, beliefs and values, reflected in the degree of support by senior management, people's behaviour and institutional practices, and embedded in policies, guidelines, tools and procedures (Mayne, 2010). For an organisation to establish a culture that goes beyond monitoring to promote the use of M&E evidence, it must have a system in place to use what may be critical evaluative information for learning and improvement. An organisation with a strong evaluative culture is likely to use empirical information to influence policy making and implementation.

In this chapter we define M&E culture as a 'shared set of ideas, values, beliefs and practices at an organisational level about M&E's role, functions and practice,

56 Ian Goldman et al.

and use of the knowledge generated for managing, reporting, learning and accountability and to improve performance'.

How organisational context contributes to M&E use – an emerging analytical framework

There are few empirical studies on M&E culture in Africa published in peer-reviewed journals. Much of the information is in the form of grey literature, which is difficult to access, hence the importance of this research undertaken in Benin, Uganda and South Africa. We also draw from other sources including research in South Africa (Paine et al., 2015, Umlaw and Chitepo, 2015), Ethiopia (Rogger and Somani, 2018) and Nigeria (Uneke et al., 2011).

The analytical framework for the book, presented in Chapter 3, identifies the following elements around the organisational context: macro-context, organisational capacity, management and processes, culture, intra- and inter-institutional linkages and other resources. The first two elements are external, and the remaining four are internal to the organisation.

The survey did not cover many questions in relation to the first two dimensions, macro-context and inter-institutional relationships, and so we primarily use other sources for this information.

We discuss the findings in relation to the elements of this framework, indicate the enabling and hindering factors identified in the research and from other sources, and conclude.

Findings

Macro-context

Weyrauch et al. (2016) see the macro-context as the over-arching forces that establish the 'bigger picture' in which policy is made, including political, economic, social and cultural systems, and, consequently, how research can or cannot inform it.

Development of the M&E systems in each country is discussed by the three country champions in Goldman et al. (2018). *Political will* was a factor in the development of all three national M&E systems, for example, in South Africa in 2010 (Phillips et al., 2014). In all three cases a structure for championing M&E was established either in the Presidency or Office of the Prime Minister (OPM), thus making it easier to oversee sectoral ministries (see Table 4.1). This provided high level *leadership/champions*, both at a technical (head of department) and a political (minister) level, championing M&E systems within their respective organisations and governments. This was mentioned by interview respondents as an important strength (Table 4.6).

Particular *transitions* and events have provided pressure for change and to establish M&E systems, as well as to undermine them. In Benin and South Africa, leadership changes have meant that the strength of national champions has varied, while there has been stronger continuity in Uganda. In Benin this has been due particularly to changes in the presidency and shifts of the location

Table 4.1 The situation with regard to evaluation/M&E units in each country

Components	South Africa	Benin	Uganda
Institutional champion	DPME in the presidency	Office for Evaluation of Public Policies and Actions, Benin (BEPPAG) in presidency	Department of M&E with Government Evaluation Facility in OPM
Evaluation and/or M&E units in line ministries	All national and provincial departments have M&E units. Sector M&E units link vertically	All line ministries have their own M&E system that links to the Ministry of Planning	M&E policy recommended creation of M&E units. Office of Prime Minister (OPM) is working with Ministry of Public Service to establish M&E units
Evaluation and/or M&E units at decentralised levels	All provinces have M&E units, but connection between national and provincial M&E is not systematic, except within some sectors.	All municipalities have M&E units, but these are not connected to national ones	M&E function is performed under district planning units. Efforts underway to have specific evaluation staff

Source: Goldman et al. (2018), p. 8.

between a ministry and presidency, while in South Africa it is changes in leadership of the M&E champion. These changes also play out at the sectoral level and can have major impacts on performance.

> I was doing M&E of local government in 2008/09 and another Minister came and he dismantled the M&E branch which was responsible for overseeing the work of the sector country-wide ... he did not understand their role and saw them as people who are there to merely write up reports.... That led to a collapse of a very strong M&E system which has not been yet been revived.
> (SA respondent 5)

None of the countries yet has *legislation* for overarching M&E, although Benin and South Africa have been drafting legislation. All three have *policies* for M&E (Uganda) or evaluation (Benin and South Africa), and sector laws often include M&E roles.

Besides leading the M&E function, if a government-wide M&E system is desired it must be *mainstreamed* within the public sector through transversal policies, systems and coordination mechanisms. All national departments in Benin and South Africa have M&E units, and these are being established in Uganda, as shown in Table 4.1. However, in all three countries, around 50% of respondents said these units had little influence (Table 4.3). Some respondents indicated that M&E units had most influence when they were located in the office of the head of department/ministry, as in the South African Department of Trade and Industry.

Intra- and inter-institutional linkages

According to Weyrauch et al. (2016, p. 35),

> Two particular types of relationship exert significant influence over how knowledge interacts (or not) with policy. One is related to *internal relationships* between the government institution and other related government agencies. The second one relates to *interaction with relevant users and producers of knowledge* who can affect or be affected by policy design and implementation.

Factors that influence evidence use include formal channels of interaction between policy makers and researchers, policy forums, and involvement of civil society in policy processes. Some of these relationships can be seen in the level of the degree of coordination within government, the degree of communication between stakeholders, and then the degree to which performance information is used by wider stakeholders for *accountability of government*. We explore these in turn in the following subsections.

Coordination

Coordination is seen to be necessary when 'an outcome can only be improved or attained through coordinated government action, and when the benefits . . . outweigh the costs. . . . But coordination takes time, resources and energy, so it needs to be carefully planned and focused to be effective' (New Zealand State Services Commission, 2008 quoted in DPME (2014, p. 13).

Government departments working in silos appear to be universal. One of the reasons for the gap between government's stated intentions and the reality of government services experienced by citizens is poor coordination (Gregory, 2006). An evaluation of the interdepartmental cluster system in South Africa concluded that

> the structures are not optimally meeting their roles and mandates. . . . only 50% (of respondents) felt that the quality of decisions was good, and only 32% that there was good accountability for implementing cluster decisions. . . . On average only 6% of clusters' time was spent unblocking implementation, while 32% was spent on reporting.
>
> (DPME, 2014)

Cultural issues including leadership, skills and incentive systems are key to achieving coordination.

All three countries have created coordination structures to support evaluation systems: in Benin the National Council for Evaluation, in Uganda the

National Evaluation Board, and in South Africa an M&E Forum and National Evaluation Technical Working Group. These provide oversight and support the system, and they are involved in selection of priority evaluations (Goldman et al., 2018). However, coordination is difficult.

In the three countries there are also different organisations with roles related to M&E, and reporting to these organisations was found to cause confusion and fatigue. Duplicate reporting requirements strengthen malicious compliance, as energy is directed to compliance reporting and not for learning and continuous improvement.

In Uganda and Benin there are much higher levels of *involvement of civil society* in M&E systems, with civil society and donors represented on M&E coordination structures, whereas in South Africa involvement of civil society is weak (DPME, 2018).

Communication with stakeholders

The Mo Ibrahim index (2018) on access to public information shows South Africa scoring high, Uganda midway, and Benin very low and falling. In the research, around 60% of respondents replied that evaluation reports were shared with only 45%–53% of respondents, indicating that websites were used to share evaluation reports. There are attempts to make available performance information, for example all three countries have a public repository for evaluation reports.[2] There is a much lower use of other communication mechanisms with the public.

In general, the resources involved in communicating with the public and wider stakeholders are limited. One of the recommendations in the evaluation of South Africa's national evaluation system (NES) was

> to allocate significant resources for evaluation communication, both financial and human. This will ensure full value is obtained from the investment currently being made, and that stakeholders are aware of the findings. This will also help to build trust in government.
>
> (DPME, 2018, p. xii)

Stakeholders use performance information to hold government accountable

All three countries have systems for wider accountability of government to stakeholders. In the Mo Ibrahim index, South Africa scores highly in Africa in access to records, accountability and sanctions for abuse of office. Benin and Uganda are in the middle of African countries (Mo Ibrahim Foundation)[3]. Uganda publishes an Annual Performance Report for government and a Local Government Performance Assessment.[4] In South Africa, departments produce annual reports that are on departments' websites, but these are produced for compliance purposes and to report to Parliament rather than communicating with wider stakeholders. Parliamentary committees 'scrutinised all our performance reports on a quarterly (basis) and there are even follow-ups on whether evaluation recommendations have been implemented and that must be done in writing through the presentation' (SA respondent 1). In Uganda and Benin, the reliance on donors for programme support and evaluations has benefits in terms of creating demand for performance information that is used for accountability but presents risks in terms of creating parallel reporting systems to both donor agencies and central bodies such as the OPM.

Culture

In all three countries, respondents felt that *learning is documented* and *used* to improve results and changes are implemented for that purpose (around 71% of managers) (Table 4.2). One of the challenges is how organisations respond to negative findings. Respondents from all three countries indicated that negative findings are reflected on, learning is documented and used to improve future results, and changes are implemented. Only in around 25%–30% of cases do managers reject the findings and are reluctant to change (Table 4.2).

Some civil servants look at the M&E function as a punitive function. Thus 62.7% of respondents in Uganda said that responsible officials are sanctioned for poor performance – much higher than in Benin or South Africa (Table 4.2). Around half of the managers suggested that stringent bureaucratic *hierarchies* make it difficult to openly discuss performance, managers fearing admitting mistakes and managers never/rarely championing M&E (Table 4.3). These tend to indicate more closed organisational cultures. Of concern is that Benin indicates that 26.9% of the respondents say that results are ignored.

The fear of making mistakes can be seen in that half of managers said, 'problems are never/rarely treated as an opportunity for learning and improvement'.

> If there is a budget cut, you will find that some entities will first think about cutting M&E because [they] don't appreciate the importance of M&E in their work. There are some civil servants who look at M&E function as witch-hunting and they would not like to be associated with such a function.
> (Uganda respondent 3)

Table 4.2 Perceived responses when the ministry/department's performance is *below* expectation

How likely are the following:	% of respondents saying always/often		
	SA	Benin	Uganda
Results are ignored	10.6	26.9	8.0
Managers tend to reject the accuracy of results that are poor	23.1	24.9	22.7
Responsible official is sanctioned	33.7	28.9	62.7
Responsible official is required to explain and identify how results can be improved	72.1	69.8	80.0
Learning is documented and used to improve future results	69.3	72.5	70.7
Changes are implemented to improve results	71.2	69.8	74.7

Table 4.3 Values and culture barriers to effective use of evaluation in decision making, learning and accountability in your department

Are any of the following a barrier?	% of respondents saying always/often		
	SA	Benin	Uganda
No consistent demand for evaluation from ministers and management	23.1	28.2	32.0
Time pressure means decisions are often taken without proper diagnosis of the problem	42.3	44.3	41.3
Resistance from senior management to transparent decision-making processes	27.9	35.6	33.3
Senior management do not champion M&E and honesty about performance	41.4	40.3	34.7
Little respect for evidence-based decision making in the department	27.9	30.9	34.7
The hierarchy makes it difficult to openly and robustly discuss performance	38.5	40.3	42.7
Managers fear admitting mistakes or problems	54.8	49.0	46.7
Problems not treated as an opportunity for learning and improvement	40.4	45.0	46.7
M&E is regarded as the job of the M&E unit, not of all managers	54.8	63.8	54.7
M&E unit has little influence in the department	51.9	45.6	48.0
M&E is seen by management as policing and a way of controlling staff	44.2	43.0	37.3
The concealing of findings is a barrier to effective use of M&E	31.7	24.2	34.7
Concerns from managers about 'unhelpful' conclusions about policies' effectiveness	52.9	42.3	50.7

However, when performance was above expectations, 20%–30% of managers were perceived as taking personal credit for good performance rather than crediting the team.

Overall, the value of M&E to help improve organisational performance is recognised by around half of managers who are open to change, using evidence from evaluation, and using problems as opportunities for learning. However, the other half indicate stringent hierarchies, closed compliance cultures and lack of appreciation of learning from experience by management – a serious impediment to improvement.

In terms of respondent comments on strengths related to culture (Table 4.6), several respondents indicated that systems were in place and that governments were now able to provide evidence of performance. In terms of weaknesses it was suggested that in Benin, there is lack of ownership of evaluation at the national level and the M&E culture is still not strong, and in Uganda, lack of ownership of the M&E function, lack of feedback and slow decision making.

Organisational capacity

Weyrauch et al. (2016, p. 23) define organisational capacity as 'the ability of an organisation to use its resources to perform . . . to design and implement public policies. It includes human resources and the legal framework that determines how resources can or cannot be used'. In terms of this definition, both leadership and general human resource capabilities are deemed important alongside other aspects such as policy, legal capacity and internal communication mechanisms.

In 2018, CLEAR AA found that the central coordinating bodies for M&E and planning in Uganda have strong capacity and serve to provide guidance and support to national and local government institutions, while internal organisational capacity for M&E within other ministries is deemed to be quite weak compared to the external demands of central agencies. The evaluation of the South African NES also indicated that DPME played a critical role (DPME, 2018).

M&E units are well *staffed* with a mean of 8.47 posts (SA with 11.6 posts, Benin 6.3 and Uganda 10.6). In general, M&E is seen as the *role* of the M&E unit rather than of all managers (58.8% of respondents in SA, 63.8% in Benin and 54.7% in Uganda). This can mean M&E gets sidelined to M&E units. It is interesting that an outstanding ministry in Africa in terms of evaluation, the Western Cape Department of Agriculture in South Africa, deliberately did not set up an M&E unit but left M&E as a strategic function in the office of the head of department (Joyene Isaacs, head of department, personal communication).[5]

Some respondents indicated major concerns about the *capacity of M&E units* to do their jobs, for example to analyse and produce their own reports or to manage and undertake evaluations, with around 55% of managers indicating the capacity to conduct evaluations is weak.

Some of the capabilities in government needed to use evidence effectively include analytical thinking, the ability to interpret evidence and knowledge of the problem (adequate diagnosis). A smaller proportion say that managers do not have the *skills to understand and use evaluation recommendations* (33% in SA, 28% in Benin and 25% in Uganda) and having the management *skills to use evaluation results*. In practice, officials tend to use informal sources and trusted experts as sources of information rather than research, evaluation or research synthesis (Paine Cronin and Sadan, 2015). This is partly a skills issue, partly lack of staff to conduct research and generate evidence in government and also lack of awareness of the evidence that may already be available.[6]

Management and processes

Systems in place

Many of the survey respondents indicated that M&E systems are in place and are institutionalised and standardised (Table 4.6). Some of these are discussed in the following subsections.

Strategic planning

All three countries have national development plans monitored by government, civil society and development partners, with a national agency responsible for the national development plan. However, around 50% of respondents indicated that diagnosis of problems to inform planning happens rarely or never, confirmed in training of senior public managers conducted in the three countries.

Linking plans to individual performance

Performance agreements are a key link between ministry plans and individual performance. Respondents were asked whether 'departmental performance expectations as recorded in strategic and annual plans are linked to individual performance agreements'. There was seen to be a strong linkage in Uganda (72.0%) and South Africa (75.6%), but much weaker in Benin (42.9%). Only 10% said they did not know whether departmental performance objectives are linked to individual performance agreements.

Monitoring implementation

In all three countries departments/ministries have annual plans, with over 80% of respondents reporting that indicators are embedded in these plans and that reports reflect progress. All three countries undertake routine monitoring of performance. However, 45%–52% of respondents indicated the focus of M&E is on activities and outputs (what we do) rather than outcomes and impact (what we achieve), reinforcing a compliance approach rather than encouraging achievement of desired development results. Key sectors such as health and education generally have integrated M&E systems that cover the sector from service point to national levels.

Evaluation being undertaken

All three countries have national evaluation systems, with basic systems and some process of evaluations related to national priorities. Goldman et al. (2018) report on the characteristics of the different systems. While all three countries are undertaking evaluations, only around half of respondents in all three countries indicated that evaluation was always/often undertaken as a systematic research process (49.3% in Uganda, 47% in Benin, 41.4% in SA). Overall, respondents indicated that strengths around evaluation include implementation of the policy, systems in place and the ability to show evidence of government's performance. Weaknesses included capacity, budget and limited evidence of use of evaluation results (Table 4.6).

Timely information provided to decision makers

This question is answered indirectly in 'time pressure means decisions are often taken without proper diagnosis of the problem'. Around 41%–44% of respondents in all three countries indicated that this happens always or often. This suggests that there is a problem with key evidence being unavailable when needed to make decisions. 'The information gets to us but not on time and most times [it is] not clear. The information is not usually used to make decisions' (Benin respondent 2). There is a need to get more rapid information for decision making, and the Twende Mbele programme has an initiative to look at rapid evaluation to help address this.

Evidence used to inform decision making

The point of generating evidence is so that it is used to support policy making and implementation. On average, 61% of respondents felt that M&E evidence was always/often used (58.4% in Benin, 63.5% in SA and 64% in Uganda).

A respondent from South Africa expressed the power of the use of evaluation:

> We are one of the best countries in terms of business process outsourcing simply because we did an evaluation which made it easy to look at how we can improve on the design and implementation.
>
> (SA respondent 6)

This reflects a highly performing department that was an early adopter of evaluation in South Africa. However, other respondents indicated the challenge. A Ugandan respondent from the Office of the Prime Minister said:

> The challenge which (evaluation) shares with the government assessment process is the issue of limited use of the findings.... we are happy when we have at least 30% of the evaluation findings adopted.
>
> (Uganda respondent 2)

In Table 4.4 we see levels of over 60% in instrumental, conceptual, symbolic and process use. Around 45% of managers indicated they saw evidence of improvement in management practices as a result of using M&E evidence, either instrumental or process use.

Only rarely is evaluation evidence used through the entire programme cycle (8%–15% of respondents); in the majority of cases, the evidence is used when evaluations are completed (Table 4.5). Nevertheless, as shown in Table 4.4, around 60% of respondents did feel they learnt something during the evaluation process, rather than simply from findings and recommendations.

One of the challenges for use is that 30%–40% of respondents felt there were inadequate mechanisms for ensuring use (e.g. improvement plans), and that 25%–33% of managers do not have the skills to understand and use evaluation recommendations.

Table 4.4 How evaluation recommendations are used

How often are evaluation recommendations used to:	% of respondents saying always or often		
	SA	Benin	Uganda
Make changes in the policies (instrumental use)	63.5	62.4	61.3
Improve understanding of the intervention (process or conceptual use)	64.4	67.1	72.0
Give legitimacy to a course of action taken (symbolic use)	66.4	63.8	69.3
Enhance value derived from stakeholders' participation in the planning and implementation of evaluation (process use)	58.7	65.1	61.3

Table 4.5 Stage at which countries use evaluation evidence

When do you use evaluation evidence?	% of respondents saying always or often		
	SA	Benin	Uganda
Throughout planning, designing and implementation of programmes and projects	15.5	12.2	8.0
Once evaluation is completed	32.0	47.6	42.7

M&E evidence used to inform planning and budget

Respondents in all three countries indicated there were links between M&E, planning and the budget.

> There are officers in the ministry in charge of M&E system and they know about the results of the evaluation findings. They are also the ones that initiate the costing at the ministry level, and they prepare the budget of all ministries.
>
> (Benin respondent 1)

In Uganda, respondents indicated that OPM ensures that the recommendations from government assessment reports the previous year are the starting point for every departmental plan. Each sector develops a budget framework paper and OPM wants to see that these have addressed the previous year's recommendation and the percentage of the recommendation from the year that is addressed.

> (Uganda respondent 5)

In South Africa, respondents indicated that annual and quarterly reports do inform plans. Several indicated the need to use evidence to justify budgets, for example:

> these days when you go to National Treasury and you want money for a programme or policy they ask you . . . what has informed your case?
>
> (SA respondent 3)

However, DPME has only managed to use a simple system drawing from evaluation findings to inform the national budget process.[7] The need to improve this linkage led Twende Mbele in 2018 to support an international literature review on the experience of linking M&E with planning and budget, seeking to find tools from this to inform this function in the Twende partner countries. Good examples proved difficult to find.[8]

Other resources

We did not collect data to corroborate whether adequate budgets exist within departments/ministries for evaluation. However, respondents reported that inadequate resources in terms of both people and finance hamper M&E practice and use of evidence for policy and decision making (see Table 4.6).

The enablers and hindering factors to M&E use

Enablers

Some of the *enablers* related to values and culture which emerged relate to *political will* and the *demand* for M&E evidence. The decision to locate the M&E champion in a strong central office was an example of political will. It gave these departments authority, and within departments the M&E unit had most authority when located in the office of the head of department or ministry. Around 70% of respondents indicated there was demand for evidence from ministers and management and recognition of the importance of M&E and learning in around 50% of managers, so a base of potential champions to work with exists.

Other system-related enabling factors are that national systems are in place, so systems are institutionalised and standardised, which is important in systems mainly driven by compliance. When donors reinforce government M&E systems, as in Uganda, this is enabling (and disabling when not the case). In addition, M&E information being made public creates a valuable resource for wider society.

Hindering factors

There were a number of *cultural barriers* to M&E (Table 4.3). Turnover in leadership caused some disruption, leading to a desire for creating new systems

Table 4.6 Summary of strengths and weaknesses

Country	Element	Strengths	Challenges
Benin	Culture	Political will with introduction of evaluation in a ministry	Lack of ownership of evaluation at national level, M&E culture still not strong
	Systems	Some systems in place and institutionalised with some uniformity, e.g. National Evaluation Policy with tools to implement, e.g. guideline	Lack of sectoral evaluation plans
	HR		Turnover of staff and lack of institutional memory
			Inadequate capacity of stakeholders in evaluation. Lack of strong quality assessors
	Finance		Resources for evaluation
	Follow-up and use	Now able to provide evidence of the work we are doing. The other area is the issue around uniformity	Some recommendations not implementable, inadequate system to develop and follow-up recommendations
	Timeliness		Information gets to us late
Uganda	Culture		Some civil servants look at M&E as witch-hunting
			Lack of feedback. Sharing of information is not good
			Most stakeholders are not aware of existing policies and procedures
			Coordination issues at all levels of government (ministry/district)
			Slow decision-making process in the system
	System	Implemented more than 65% of the national M&E policy	(System) mostly geared towards monitoring and not evaluation
		Our department meets to discuss reports that we submit to OPM every six months	Poor systems in some places, e.g. some local governments still use paper systems
		Tools have been good	Joint agreements but government and donors still sometimes do their own thing
	HR	Implemented a lot of capacity development	Skills gap – very few staff. Need M&E posts in each ministry and local government
			Poor capacity and skills, with poor quality trainers in M&E
			Low salary and motivation of staff

(Continued)

Table 4.6 (Continued)

Country	Element	Strengths	Challenges
	Finance		No clear budget for M&E and shortage of resources for evaluations
	Follow-up and use		Limited use of evaluation findings
	Data		UBOS statistics quality good and reliable
			Lot of admin data not credible leading to conflicting data
	Timeliness		UBOS statistics often comes very late
South Africa	Leadership	Much better when M&E function located in director general's office	
		M&E led from the presidency	
	Culture	Able to provide evidence of kind of work being done	
	System	Because led by government, more willing to use results	Evaluations not fully independent
		Degree of standardisation	Many frameworks not under one umbrella
		Evaluation become very strong. NES working very well. National evaluation policy framework, capacity building, and guidelines exist	Non-regulation is a weakness because some departments don't do evaluation. Evaluation after every programme should be compulsory
		Strength of what is done huge	Lack of good monitoring systems. Monitoring information not necessarily providing good performance reports against Annual Performance Plan
		Evaluation policy and guidelines	Don't work as well as they should with provinces on planning and M&E
			Evaluations done by departments separately from planning
	HR	Fully fledged evaluation team in DPME	Limited capacity of both policy makers and technical staff in the evaluation sector, with few service providers in the sector
			In government there are no evaluation people
			While called M&E, most of us are not strong in evaluations
			Need to develop more black evaluators
			Turnover, with new managers always starting something new

Country	Element	Strengths	Challenges
	Funding		Programme funding needs to include funds for evaluation
			Evaluation is costly
	Follow-up and use	Evaluations done of key programmes so that practices improve	Are managers using reports?
			Usage of evaluation information sometimes doesn't happen as you would want it to
	Timeliness		Evaluation takes time

Source: Interview respondents, baseline study.

and resulting in instability (especially South Africa). Around 50% of managers reported lack of ownership of M&E with M&E regarded as the job of the M&E unit, not of all managers; lack of respect for evidence-based decision making; and with around 40% saying senior managers are not championing M&E. The dominant culture is one of compliance and punitive, with a fear of making mistakes and so inhibiting learning.

In terms of systemic factors, we see five main areas:

- *Weaknesses in the public service* with limited capacity to undertake evaluations (55% of respondents), but a 25%–33% proportion saying that managers do not have the skills to understand and use evaluation recommendations, or management skills to use results. This is perpetuated by limited resources for M&E, and in particular evaluation (70% of respondents) as well as poor salaries and poorly motivated public servants.
- *Systems challenges* due to silos leading to separation of M&E from planning and budget (all three countries); duplication in reporting requirements and reporting fatigue (mentioned for SA); weak manual data systems in some locations, especially in rural areas, a contributor to poor quality administrative data (all).
- *Poor implementation*, either due to inadequate quality of evaluations (50% of respondents felt conclusions are often not helpful), or weaknesses in following up evaluations, either because there is no improvement plan system (e.g. Benin and Uganda) or because improvement plans are not followed up adequately, as in South Africa (DPME, 2018).
- Managers not seeing their role as *anticipating the evidence needs* of ministers or senior managers, and being required to provide evidence at the last minute, meaning decisions are taken without effective diagnosis because of time pressure.
- Donors sometimes operating *parallel systems* (all).
- *Involvement of civil society weak* in holding government to account, with civil society linkages weakest in South Africa.

Conclusions

Table 4.7 summarises the overall picture against the contextual elements identified at the beginning of this chapter, and the pattern for the three countries is surprisingly similar. What emerges is a mixed picture where, in these countries, the location of the driver of M&E gives it some authority. There appears to be significant demand for M&E evidence from ministers and senior managers and in around half of cases, respondents indicated there was a positive environment

Table 4.7 Summary of features of the context in Uganda, Benin and South Africa

Dimension of context	Summary
1 Macro-context (external)	In all three cases, there are powerful centre of government M&E roles. In some, these are a consequence of crises and transitions, which have also affected leadership. Role of donors is powerful in Uganda and Benin
2 Intra- and inter-institutional linkages (external)	Coordination is weak across government generally, stronger in M&E space
	Some transparency, and reports are shared. Much more work on communication needed
	Consultation with non-state actors weak in South Africa
	Performance information (e.g. evaluation reports) is used for wider accountability
3 Culture (internal)	High demand from ministers for evidence
	Half of managers are supportive of using evidence, but around half do not use problems for learning
	Historical evidence used more than real time
	Cultures still largely compliance driven
	Challenges with management attitudes, e.g. hierarchy that affects ability to take risks and learn
4 Organisational capacity (internal)	High-level political leadership in M&E. In a significant proportion of ministries the person responsible for M&E is high level. M&E units – the central unit and ministry units – are of significant size. There are limits to management's capacity and will to use evidence
5 Management and processes (internal)	All three have national development plans and monitor these. Benin is weak in linking performance agreements to the national and ministry plans
	Monitoring is done but largely for compliance and there is reporting fatigue
	All three have national evaluation systems
	Around 50% of managers use evidence, with >60% instrumental and conceptual use
	Basic communications occur, but not much wider media, which would broaden access
6 Other resources (internal)	Budgets for evaluation and research are limited
	Limited knowledge infrastructure, e.g. evaluation repositories
	Managers felt information system provides information needed

for evidence use; and 60%–70% reported that evidence from evaluations is used, with instrumental, conceptual, process and symbolic use emerging. This is fairly consistent across the three countries.

However, half of respondents indicated there was a negative attitude to M&E, with findings concealed, senior management not championing honesty about performance, little respect for evidence-based decision making, and managers fearing to admit mistakes. The hierarchy impedes learning and M&E is not seen as very influential.

This creates a mixed environment for learning, with a compliance culture still dominant. Some ministries are performing better, have stronger M&E systems, and use evidence, while others are very weak.

A high percentage of managers do not support M&E for learning because they lack the expertise and tools to deal with the M&E system, or because M&E may weaken their position and power in the organisation. Around 40% indicated the hierarchy made it difficult to discuss performance, and they feared admitting problems. This suggests it is autocratic management creating a punitive culture that impedes learning. In around a quarter of cases it appears that the skills to understand and use evaluation recommendations are a problem, and where culture is favourable, this may be easier to address through different capacity-strengthening interventions.

Compliance is clearly the dominant culture of the public service, and yet around half the managers believe that learning does happen. This is likely to ebb and flow, depending on the attitude and culture of top management. Autocratic managers are likely to promote compliance behaviour, as is a dominance of the auditor-general, with managers aiming for compliance rather than innovation. Some respondents indicated that evaluation is seen as a witch-hunt. Evaluation needs to be more widely understood and seen to be within a set of tools for adaptive management.

An action perspective

These three countries have a good base on which to build national evaluation systems that produce results to use for improvements. How can this be built on to reduce negative compliance behaviour? Several methods are suggested:

- Continuing to provide the message that evaluation is not intended to be punitive but for *continuous improvement*. This requires sustained approaches, and can be jeopardised by transitions.
- Providing *incentives* for using evaluations for learning, for example symbolic behaviour by politicians praising senior managers who learn and improve; focusing on Ministries of Finance requiring evidence to inform funding of new programmes; planning and performance management systems requiring managers to implement recommended changes; and donors using a learning mindset.

- Focusing on *champions* able to take evaluations forward in a learning manner.
- Building *coalitions* across departments to support M&E as part of adaptive management.
- Providing a range of evidence in a responsive way, so building up the perceived value of M&E, for example by having rapid methods as well as traditional evaluations.
- Sharing examples of *good practice*.
- *Training senior managers* in evidence, as has started in the three countries.
- Recognising that *autocratic management* has negative side effects and recruiting senior managers with more empowering management styles.
- Opening the evaluation process so that Parliament, the media and the public can bring pressure for improvements but handled carefully as it can increase fear of exposure from evaluation.

As Mayne (2010) says:

> Developing an evaluative culture . . . requires deliberate efforts by the organization and especially its senior managers to encourage, implement, and support such a culture. It needs to be clear to managers and staff that results information and evidence are valued and expected to be a regular part of planning, budgeting, implementation, and review.
>
> (Mayne, 2010, p. 22)

This chapter has sought to provide a picture of the context to evidence use in three of the five countries covered in the book. Overall, establishment of effective M&E systems is a component of creating a performance culture but is not enough. We see examples of systems, and 50% of managers indicate that evidence is valued and used. Using evidence must become part of how organisations work. But developing such a culture is not a short-term project. The evaluation of South Africa's NES concluded that establishing the NES is a 20-year project (DPME, 2018, p. xi), and these three countries have been implementing NES for 8–12 years – the reality is that developing M&E systems and culture that promote learning and use is an ongoing project.

Notes

1 National departments/ministries that formed part of the survey are President/Prime Minister's Office/Agriculture/Education/Finance/Health/Social Development/Planning and Economic Development/Labour, Public Administration and Social Affairs/Higher Education and Scientific Research/Secondary Education, Technical and Professional Training/Bureau of Evaluation of Public Policies and Analysis of Governmental Action of General Secretary of Presidency (BEPPAAG/SG-PR).
2 Uganda puts all the performance reports on the budget transparency initiative website (www.budget.go.ug), and South Africa also has online budget information for national and provincial government (www.treasury.gov.za), as well as a municipal budget website (https://municipaldata.treasury.gov.za/).

3 http://s.mo.ibrahim.foundation/u/2018/10/26211727/2018-IIAG-country-scorecards.zip?_ga=2.132075023.1604460325.1560161521-1633358436.1560161521
4 The most recent Annual Performance Report for government is September 2015, and for Local Government Performance Assessment is June 2018.
5 This department has done 22 evaluations (Dirk Troskie, personal communication).
6 For example, the African Evaluation Database (AFRED) of evaluations developed by CLEAR AA and CREST indicates 521 evaluations that at least partly cover Tanzania. In recently conducted training of senior Tanzanian officials, it was found that they were unaware that this resource exists. Similarly, in preparing an evidence map for Uganda, White (2019) found over 500 evaluations in Uganda.
7 A simple table has been developed using evaluation findings, recommendations, degree of implementation of the recommendations/improvement plans and the implications for the budget process.
8 The report is available at www.twendembele.org/wp-content/uploads/2018/11/Twende-Mbele-Report-Final-Nov-2018_Budgets-Planning2.pdf, accessed 17 August 2019.

References

Cameron, K.S. and Quinn, R.E. 1999. *Diagnosing and changing organizational culture*. Reading: Addison-Wesley.
DPME. 2014. *Impact and implementation evaluation of government coordination systems: Final Report: Policy Summary, Executive Summary and Short Report (Evaluation Report)*. Department of Performance Monitoring and Evaluation.
DPME. 2018. *Report on the evaluation of the national evaluation system: Summary report (Evaluation Summary Report)*. Department of Planning, Monitoring and Evaluation, Pretoria.
Goldman, I., Byamugisha, A., Gounou, A., Smith, L.R., Ntakumba, S., Lubanga, T., Sossou, D. and Rot-Munstermann, K. 2018. The emergence of government evaluation systems in Africa: The case of Benin, Uganda and South Africa. *African Evaluation Journal*, 6, 11. https://doi.org/10.4102/aej.v6i1.253
Gregory, R. 2006. Theoretical faith and practical works: De-autonomizing and joining-up in the New Zealand state sector, in Christensen, T. and Lægreid, P. (Eds), *Autonomy and regulation: Coping with agencies in the modern state*. London: Edward Elgar, pp. 137–161.
Mayne, J. 2010. Building an evaluative culture: The key to effective evaluation and results management. *The Canadian Journal of Program Evaluation*, 24, 1–30.
New Zealand State Services Commission. 2008. *Factors for successful coordination: Helping state agencies coordinate effectively*, available at: http://www.ssc.govt.nz/sites/all/files/Factors%20spreadsheet.pdf, accessed 23/05/2013
Paine Cronin, G. and Sadan, M. 2015. Use of evidence in policy making in South Africa: An exploratory study of attitudes of senior government officials. *African Evaluation Journal*, 3. https://doi.org/10.4102/aej.v3i1.145
Phillips, S., Goldman, I., Gasa, N., Akhalwaya, I. and Leon, B. 2014. A focus on M&E of results: An example from the Presidency, South Africa. *Journal of Development Effectiveness*, 6, 392–406. https://doi.org/10.1080/19439342.2014.966453
Porter, S. and Goldman, I. 2013. A growing demand for monitoring and evaluation in Africa. *African Evaluation Journal*, 1, 9. https://doi.org/10.4102/aej.v1i1.25
Rogger, D. and Somani, R. 2018. Hierarchy and information. Policy Research Working Paper 8644, World Bank, Washington, available at http://documents.worldbank.org/curated/en/474061541787560854/pdf/WPS8644.pdf, accessed 23/03/2020.
Umlaw, F. and Chitepo, N. 2015. State and use of monitoring and evaluation systems in national and provincial departments. *African Evaluation Journal*, 3. https://doi.org/10.4102/aej.v3i1.134

Uneke, C.J., Ezeoha, A.E., Ndukwe, C.D., Oyibo, P.G., Onwe, F., Igbinedion, E.B. and Chukwu, P.N. 2011. Individual and organisational capacity for evidence use in policy making in Nigeria: An exploratory study of the perceptions of Nigeria health policy makers. *Evidence & Policy,* 7, 251–276. https://doi.org/10.1332/174426411X591744

Weyrauch, V., Echt, L. and Suliman, S. n.d. Going beyond. *Context Matters*, 73.

Weyrauch, V., Echt, L. and Suliman, S. 2016. *Knowledge into policy: Going beyond context matters-framework.*

White, H. 2019. The twenty-first century experimenting society: the four waves of the evidence revolution. *Palgrave Communications*, 5, 47, https://doi.org/10.1057/s41599-019-0253-6

5 Using evaluations to inform policy and practice in a government department

The case of the Department of Basic Education in South Africa

*Nedson Pophiwa, Carol Nuga Deliwe,
Jabulani Mathe and Stephen Taylor*

Summary

South Africa's education sector has been very problematic with educational outcomes being less than desired. It has had to overcome the legacy of apartheid, and has struggled to create an effective educational system. The Department of Basic Education has been a pioneer department in the use of evaluations, research and data. Two of eight evaluations undertaken by the department are used as mini-cases of the use of evaluations: the Funza Lushaka Bursary Programme and the National School Nutrition Programme. A variety of instrumental, conceptual and process uses of the evaluations can be seen, supported by a range of use interventions undertaken internally by the department, supported through the mechanisms of the national evaluation system. The cases provide examples of evidence-informed policy and practice and how a government department can undertake evaluations effectively. They demonstrate the importance of an internal knowledge broker who is involved in the strategic discussions to champion and support evidence, as well as the usefulness of a national evaluation system providing key elements that encourage use.

Background

In 1994 the new government, led by the African National Congress, was faced with overcoming the legacy of discriminatory apartheid policies that deliberately provided poor quality education to black people.

The quality of basic education in South Africa has been a government priority since the advent of democracy in 1994. The new Department of Education (DoE) began crafting policy to transform, seek redress, and enable equity and quality education outcomes for all South Africans. Most people have participated in or experienced the education system and have strong views on the system's deficiencies and how to improve it. Tackling problems has required juggling popular ideas with scientific and evidence-informed approaches.

In 2010, the DoE was reorganised into two departments, the Department of Basic Education (DBE) and the Department of Higher Education and Training (DHET), to focus on the schooling and post-schooling sectors, respectively. The DBE is one of the stakeholders involved in establishing South Africa's national evaluation system (NES), and a pioneer in using evidence for policy and decision making.

This chapter examines the DBE's journey and looks at two mini-cases of the use of evaluations, the Funza Lushaka Bursary Programme (FLBP) for teachers, and the National School Nutrition Programme (NSNP), which were selected based on the importance of the programmes and the DBE's intention to use the products and outcomes of the evaluations in strengthening policy support and implementation. The chapter sets out lessons for the use of evaluations, and the factors enabling or hindering it in the DBE.

The methodology was guided by an analytical framework in Chapter 3 that informed the selection of research questions. Data collection methods included the review of published and unpublished documents such as annual reports, peer-reviewed journal articles, and evaluation reports. Semi-structured interviews were conducted between November 2018 and March 2019 with seven DBE officials, both senior policy makers, focusing on those managing the programmes in the two cases chosen (NSNP and FLBP), as well as monitoring and evaluation (M&E) officials from DBE and the Department of Planning, Monitoring and Evaluation (DPME). The involvement of key players in the process as co-authors provided the richness of participant observation. The chapter was drafted by a researcher, with key historical, structural and substantive contributions from the co-authors in DBE and DPME.

Overview of the sector and its evidence journey

Country context

South Africa is a constitutional democracy with a three-tier system of government: national, provincial and local. Education is shared between the national and provincial levels, with provincial having the responsibility for running the school system and national responsible for policy and functions such as teacher training and universities. There have been four education ministers since 1994, each bringing significant changes (Motala, 2015). The incumbent, Minister Motshekga, who has been in post since 2009, had oversight of the creation of the DBE and DHET from the original DoE.

South Africa's school education successes have been in providing universal access to educational opportunities for the majority of learners (97% participation for 7- to 15-year-olds, and 83% for 16- to 18-year olds); improving infrastructure; equalising resource allocation; providing free education to learners from poor households; and expanding the nutrition programme to about nine million learners (DBE, 2018b).

Despite South Africa's middle-income status and a large proportion of government spending on education, the major shortcoming is the quality of education outcomes, which can be seen in relation to our Southern African Development Community (SADC) neighbours. The main contributory factors to these deficiencies include: the lasting effects of intergenerational poverty;

low levels of language and cognitive skills of learners coming into the system; structural and accountability weaknesses in teaching, management and school support at district level; and low efficiency of conversion of resources into quality in government. Attempts to address school education challenges have been characterised by blame and a lack of accountability (National Planning Commission (NPC), 2012, p. 302). Despite a history of poor learning outcomes and performance, recent regional and international assessments for learners from poor households have shown improvements in education outcomes and quality in the foundation phases of schooling, albeit off a low base (Reddy et al., 2016).

The development of structures to use evidence in DBE

The DBE has a long tradition of using statistical evidence drawn from administrative data, official statistics on the population and special surveys. The educational planning system was developed from a need to understand the size and shape of the education system, and the first forays into evidence use were drawn from the first Schools Register of Needs, commissioned in 1996 to provide planning information on the distribution of resources and the extent of backlogs that the new government had to deal with. An Education Management Information System was created in 2001 to collect information on school-level resourcing, complementing information in the personnel administration system, followed by creation of a small Policy Support Unit to support system-wide planning, monitoring and evaluation and track medium- to long-range performance.

The Policy Support Unit set out to supplement the administrative data in the schooling system by motivating and advocating for education policy-relevant data in existing data collection, including those undertaken by Statistics South Africa. This allowed trends in provisioning of educational inputs, as captured in household surveys, to be analysed with provincial disaggregations from 2002 onwards. Deeper analysis was done of education data collected in demographic data. In its first decade, the unit focused on generating policy-relevant analyses and trends using in-house data and specially commissioned surveys. Econometric and other analyses of school performance were also possible using the end of school Grade 12[1] Senior Certificate Examination performance data and panel data provided by the National School Effectiveness Survey that was carried out over three years from 2007. This confirmed how little learning was happening in schools, even in the lower grades.

By 2010, the Policy Support Unit had been clustered with the unit responsible for short- to medium-term planning and monitoring and renamed the Research Coordination, Monitoring and Evaluation (RCME) Unit in the Strategic Planning, Research and Coordination Chief Directorate, with the former policy support director as head of the Chief Directorate. The new unit retained the functions of the Policy Support Unit and was now also responsible for intergovernmental coordination, strategic planning, research coordination, monitoring and evaluation. Its briefings, reports and analyses on policy-relevant trends were adopted in policy circles. Presentations by the director general and senior managers to oversight bodies and stakeholders increasingly included reference to data and trends rather than a recital of expenditure patterns, programme delivery and monitoring visits. Resolutions at ruling party conferences began to refer to this information.

By 2010, despite contestation around their use, national and international assessments of learning outcomes were used to identify the factors associated with the low levels of performance in schools. Between 2011 and 2014, Annual National Assessments (ANA) were implemented to measure learning outcomes at school level in maths and language from Grades 1 to 9. These created pressure for schools to account for learning performance and indicated what was expected in terms of learning outcomes at each grade. However, the assessments were abandoned in 2015 as burdensome, too frequent, and too focused on reporting and naming and shaming.[2] By 2018, despite the abrupt end of the ANA, long-standing participation in these assessments had illustrated progress in learning outcomes, albeit from a low base.

Despite resistance by unions, the tradition of tracking performance in the schooling system using evidence from different sources was strong and provided fertile ground for adopting an evaluative approach in policy analysis. By 2012, the National Development Plan (NDP) had been launched. The Basic Education Sector plan (developed in 2010) informed the education chapter of the NDP, along with a diagnostic review of the barriers to effective schooling and quality learning, and interventions designed to improve the quality of learning (NPC, 2011, 2012).

A textbook availability crisis in 2012 resulted in criticism of the political and administrative leadership of the national department and the minister responsible. The trauma of the crisis was felt in the whole system. There was heightened public and media scrutiny of the roles and responsibilities of provincial and national departments in service delivery, the monitoring systems and the data required to monitor progress. Information from household surveys was perceived by political and union-aligned stakeholders and the public as more independent than the education sector's administrative data, and so more credible.

The crisis was a turning point in the schooling system and galvanised the national and provincial departments responsible for basic education to work with experts to develop and document national standards and a national system for improving process management, capacity and monitoring of textbook provisioning, delivery and management.

Changes in the South African government-wide approaches to monitoring and evaluation were also critical in supporting DBE's momentum. A National Evaluation Policy Framework (NEPF) was approved by Cabinet in November 2011, with experts from DBE as co-authors (Davids et al., 2015, p. 1; Phillips et al., 2014). In its efforts to build a coalition to support the evaluation system, DPME established a cross-government Evaluation Technical Working Group (ETWG) 'as a sounding board and to be an advocate of the system' (Goldman et al., 2015, p. 3). DBE was among the early adopters and members of this ETWG as they had already undertaken evaluations.

Following adoption of the NEPF, in 2012 the national evaluation system (NES) was being designed. However, the harrowing and very public events of the textbook crisis in 2012 were fresh in the minds of policy makers and the context of implementing evaluations in the schooling system was politically charged. Too critical or public, and unfavourable evaluation findings could be shelved and not used. Too positive, and the media could dismiss the work as propaganda in a country with a healthy cynicism about service delivery. Faced with coordinating evaluations in the sector, the concerns in the DBE's evaluation unit were not only technical.

The unit adopted an improvement support approach, providing technical support and closely partnering the evaluating programme managers, with support from DPME. The M&E unit communicated the utility of evaluations in improving programme quality, effectiveness and efficiency. Drawing from the events that followed the textbook crisis, this improvement narrative resonated with programme managers and was used during and after the evaluation in discussions and debates, as well as in strategic events and presentations.

A range of programmes was identified for evaluation, with all programmes selected receiving large amounts of funding, ranging from early childhood development programmes to nutrition, initial teacher education bursaries, and the best ways of teaching reading. Six of the eight evaluations were implementation evaluations, partly because impact could not be determined due to the lack of data.

The NES required a number of systems to be established including Evaluation Steering Committees (ESCs), which included the custodian department and DPME, a commitment to publishing the evaluations as a deliberate accountability mechanism, development of a management response and implementation of improvement planning, with reports on progress for two years following approval of the report.

Starting evaluations under the national evaluation system

Prior to 2011, 'monitoring and evaluation' activities in DBE and its precursor had to a large extent been limited to monitoring and standard forms of reporting (Samuels et al., 2015, p. 3). Table 5.1 provides a list of the research and evaluations carried out from 2011. The first evaluation under the NES was of Early Childhood Development (ECD), undertaken with the Departments of Social Development and Basic Education and Health. This evaluation, reported in 2012, recommended that further evaluations should be undertaken on two components of ECD, namely an additional reception year of schooling (Grade R) and on nutrition interventions for children under five. In 2012/2013, an impact evaluation of the introduction of Grade R was carried out by a team of researchers from Stellenbosch University, building on the relatively good data that DBE had on learning outcomes from ANAs, and administrative data on registrations for Grade R.

With the stopping of ANA due to contestation from the main teacher union, DBE no longer had good data on learning outcomes and focused instead on implementation or impact evaluations of large programmes. The data was used to generate lessons to assist programme managers to improve their programmes.

Table 5.1 List of DBE's research and evaluations to date

Name	Type/purpose	Year
School Monitoring Survey	Survey of sector progress in achieving education mandate	2011/2012
Independent Workbook and Textbook Evaluation	Formative evaluation of a sample of approved DBE workbooks and textbooks	2011/2012
The Impact of the Introduction of Grade R★	Evaluation to estimate the effect of having attended Grade R on learning outcomes later in primary school	2012/2013
The Mind the Gap Impact Assessment	Randomised Control Trial to measure impact of study guides on performance	2012/2013
The Funza Lushaka Bursary Programme★	Implementation evaluation of FLBP Programme	2014–2016
The Early Grade Reading Study I North West★	Impact evaluation of three alternative teacher training interventions in Setswana using a randomised controlled trial method	2015–2018
The Early Grade Reading Study II★	Impact evaluation of two alternative teacher training interventions in English First Additional Language using a randomised controlled trial method	2016–2018 (2015 prep)
CAPS★	Implementation evaluation of the Curriculum Assessment Policy Statement (CAPS) system	2015–2017
NSNP★	Implementation evaluation of the National School Nutrition Programme (NSNP)	2014–2016

Note: ★Those in the National Evaluation Plan.

Evaluation buy-in was critical and the idea of improving implementation through evaluation was attractive for policy and practical purposes (Respondent 4). Once programme managers agreed to evaluations being conducted, it became easier for DBE to work with DPME to take evaluations forward.

Two evaluations are scrutinised in some detail in this chapter, both implemented as part of the National Evaluation Plan, and so in partnership with DPME. The chapter also mentions other evaluations and evidence that help to understand the contextual, institutional and cultural enablers or barriers to use of evidence in the educational policy space.

The evaluation of Funza Lushaka Bursary Programme (FLBP)

The FLBP was established in 2007 and provides full-cost bursaries to high-achieving students to undertake initial teacher education (ITE) programmes to become teachers in priority subjects such as maths, physical science and accounting and in foundation phase learning, and locations such as rural areas. It is a large-scale programme that reached 23,392 students during the period under evaluation (2007–2012), on average 15% of the total ITE enrolment over the period (DPME/DBE, 2016b). Owing to the importance of the programme and the need to motivate for its continued support by government, the head of the unit responsible for planning, monitoring, evaluation and research managed to convince key officials responsible for it to use the evaluation as an opportunity to improve implementation.

It was decided that the evaluation would be an implementation evaluation rather than an impact evaluation. The evaluation was procured by DPME and JET Educational Services was contracted to conduct it.

The overall findings were that the FLBP is performing well and is broadly effective (and cost-effective) in attracting high-achieving students who complete ITE programmes in good time and take up government-paid positions in public schools (DPME/DBE, 2016b). However, the evaluation identified inefficiencies in implementation with regard to supply and placement of educators at different levels of government. The final report, management response, and improvement plan to address the findings were approved by Cabinet in March 2017.

The improvement plan has been taken forward. 'The programme manager agreed with the recommendations and so he was eager to see those things put in place. In some of the other programmes it was more of a burden to be seen to be implementing the improvement plan' (Respondent 1).

There are different ways of understanding evidence use, and here we consider instrumental, conceptual, symbolic and process use as used by Johnson et al. (2009) and Patton (1998). This differentiation was discussed in Chapter 1.

In terms of use of the findings and recommendations, a key area was rethinking the selection criteria to target specific areas of teacher specialisation. Prior to the evaluation, students were simply told 'if you want to be a teacher, we will give you a bursary' (Respondent 2). The evaluation report recommended that DBE, with universities, should develop an effective system to monitor the priority areas that students have enrolled for and that subject areas should be fixed between application and selection (DPME/DBE, 2016a, p. 36). Since then, they have produced a set of guidelines and criteria for selection of students based on geographic and subject area and phases required by the FLBP policy, and become stricter as to who is selected as a beneficiary (instrumental use).

The ITE Directorate was able to use recommendations related to monitoring, tracking and data management to motivate for funding to modernise the information management system and successfully approached government for funding an online system that has been in use since October 2018 and has been an important building block to effectively managing information concerning the programme (Respondent 2) (instrumental use).

The evaluation recommended that the DBE, in collaboration with provincial education departments (PEDs), needs to strengthen methods for effective placement of graduating students. The ITE directorate has begun reporting not on administration of placement but on the utilisation of graduates in terms of where they are placed upon completion (Respondent 2) (instrumental use).

The process of undertaking the evaluation was very important in itself (process use) and led to considerable learning. For example, the theory of change workshop brought together officials from higher education institutions, the National Student Financial Aid Scheme (NSFAS), civil society groups, and provincial and national department officials to gain an understanding of key components of the bursary programme (conceptual use). This was an eye-opener for Respondent 2 because it was the first time he saw stakeholders with a common interest in implementation of the bursary programme come together to deliberate constructively on it.

Another example was the building of successful relationships. In October 2018, DBE held an indaba to open a dialogue on teacher professionalisation, teacher standards and school-based initial teacher education models. The success of this event was attributed to the collaborative nature of the Funza Lushaka evaluation: 'it wouldn't have happened smoothly if we hadn't collaborated in the Funza evaluation' (Respondent 2). Relationships that were established during the evaluation, especially the theory of change workshop, are said to have been a critical enabler for this event (DBE, 2018a) (process use).

There are examples of *unintended use*. Parliament became more interested in understanding how FLBP graduates are placed in specific targeted areas rather than the logistical, administrative data concerning how placement was managed (Respondent 2). The Directorate responsible for FLBP negotiated a partnership framework with roles and responsibilities/activities at all levels of government. The Directorate also used the findings on placement to obtain independent external advice on how the unit could improve its own efficiency, for example, a contract on how quickly graduates should be placed.

The evaluation of the National School Nutrition Programme

In a country with high levels of poverty and inequality such as South Africa where many children go to school without breakfast, the NSNP aims to improve the health and nutritional status of the poorest learners. It was initially a Primary School Nutrition Programme (PSNP) administered by the Department of Health, which provided learners at primary schools with at least one meal per day. In 2002 it was decided that the programme should be migrated from the Department of Health to the Department of Education and expanded to cover beyond Grade 7.

Following a 2006 survey, the need to expand the programme to secondary schools was confirmed. Quintile 5 are the best-off public schools and quintile 1 the poorest. The renamed National School Nutrition Programme was first implemented in quintile 1 secondary schools in April 2009, and was phased in to quintile 2 and 3 public secondary schools in April 2010 and 2011, respectively (NSNP Annual Report, 2009). NSNP has involved a large financial commitment from government (ZAR 5.3 billion by 2014) and reaches over nine million learners. Apart from feeding children at school, NSNP includes campaigns raising awareness on healthy eating and lifestyles among learners.

In thinking about the type of evaluation to assess the NSNP, DBE/DPME commissioned a scoping study in 2012 that revealed insufficient data for the impact to be assessed. The Steering Committee of the evaluation decided to shelve the idea of an impact evaluation. However, in 2014 Cabinet requested the DBE to undertake an evaluation of the NSNP. It was agreed to resuscitate the evaluation as an implementation evaluation, achievable with the information at hand. The evaluation was commissioned by the DPME and DBE and was conducted by JET Education Services.

The main purpose of the evaluation was to assess whether the NSNP is being implemented in a way that is likely to result in significant health and educational benefits to primary school learners and establish how to improve programme effectiveness. The evaluation report was approved in October 2016.

In the management response, the DBE agreed with 80% of the recommendations and indicated that some are already being implemented (DPME, 2017, p. 19). An improvement plan was developed and the report and improvement plan were approved by Cabinet.

The programme managers have continued to implement the improvement plan and report on progress. The NSNP evaluation was used instrumentally in effecting changes directly to the roll-out of the school nutrition programme. There also appears to be good buy-in from the PEDs to implement the recommendations, which 'is evidence that the evaluation study has strong potential to shape and influence implementation of the NSNP in the near future' (DPME, 2017, p. 19).

The recommendations included introducing individual targeting in certain provinces/schools in which not all learners eat the NSNP meals regularly, and income and poverty levels are mixed. Task teams have been set up with their *de facto* terms of reference the NSNP evaluation recommendations relevant to the theme of the task team (Personal communication, Ms K. Maroba, Department of Basic Education, 8 October 2019). One task team, set up to determine the targeting criteria to be used in addressing learner opt-outs, recommended that there should be set criteria for targeting meals provision according to learner needs as long as it is affordable (Respondent 4) (instrumental use).

A recommendation was that the NSNP guidelines should specify who the meals are intended for, how leftover meals and stock should be dealt with, with monitoring of implementation. The guidelines indicate that if the meals are intended to encourage social cohesion and be eaten together by learners, volunteer food handlers, teaching and administrative staff, the guidelines should indicate this and concomitant funding be made available. Within the improvement plan, DBE committed to revising its guidelines on meals and developing stock control and plans to manage learner food preferences, leftovers and wasted food. For example, the DBE had been required to make a submission to National Treasury for approval of soya from predetermined manufacturers through the centralised procurement system. In response, the DBE evaluated the quality of soya mince and developed a list of compliant manufacturers, which was then approved and circulated to PEDs at the end of 2017 to guide procurement decisions (instrumental use).

In addition, the Department set up a menu task team to consider alternatives to soya as a protein in meals, in consultation with nutrition experts. Finally, the DPME's Quality Assessment Report emphasised that the evaluation process deepened stakeholders' understanding of the NSNP activities, opportunities for better implementation, and utility (DPME, 2017, p. 19) (conceptual use).

The evaluation provided the DBE with a robust understanding of successes, barriers and inefficiencies in implementing the programme, and an overview of the perceptions, concerns and successes in its implementation. This information confirmed and strengthened the policy makers' hand in putting forward a plan of action for the NSNP long after the improvement planning and reporting process had expired.

Some conclusions on use

In both evaluations we see considerable levels of use, including the different types we are focusing on. In one of the planning workshops that shaped the focus of this chapter, one comment that stood out was that DBE is among the few departments to have 'institutionalised the use of evidence' generated from research and evaluations.

Use interventions undertaken and the change mechanisms

Key for this book is understanding how evidence use happened and the interventions undertaken to promote use. Table 5.2 summarises and elaborates on some of these, including those undertaken through DBE systems, and features of the NES that assisted in ensuring use.

Overall we can see that the Chief Directorate responsible for Planning, Research, Monitoring and Evaluation played a key role in championing the use of evaluations and in *knowledge brokering* with programme managers, senior management of DBE, DPME and the evaluation service provider. This complemented the technical work done by the Monitoring and Evaluation Unit. In general the work produced by the research and evaluation directorate has been taken more seriously over the years. There is a recognisable shift in the attitude of senior management, which acknowledges the importance of the evidence they are generating and using.

Different *forums* were important in widening awareness and ownership of the evaluation.

> Some of the meetings with senior people. . . . when I present they often rush, they have a massive agenda. They try to finish within a day. When you sit to present they say please try to summarise in five minutes. But recently they have been asking for more, I had lots of time. I was presenting in parliament yesterday. There is more of an interest in that kind of work on improving, what the research is saying. That's quite encouraging to see.
> (Respondent 1)

Ideally, organisations undertake evaluations at critical stages in the life cycle of interventions when important decisions need to be taken. *Timing of the evaluation* is therefore critical to facilitate use, while delays in finalising evaluations may prove to be a challenge as findings may be too late to incorporate findings during policy and programme reviews. Notwithstanding some delays, most recommendations from the two evaluations were still relevant for immediate use at the completion of the evaluation processes.

Three-quarters of all evaluation recommendations in basic education since 2013 have focused on promoting better internal operations rather than additional

Table 5.2 Use interventions and how these influenced use

Intervention	Effect and change mechanism activated
DBE systems	
Knowledge brokering role of Strategic Planning, Research and Coordination Chief Directorate	The unit 'marketed' itself to programme managers to help them see the value of improving implementation through evaluations, and identifying possible topics. It undertook internal communication to inform management and minister of the findings and recommendations
	Working with programme managers helped to build *awareness* in the Department of evaluations and findings, *trust* in the credibility of findings, and to ensure the *institutionalisation* of mechanisms to respond to the evaluation
Unit having technically strong members	This allowed DBE to play a strong role in the technical side of the evaluation, and increased the credibility and legitimacy of it within DBE, and so *trust* in the findings
Presenting and showcasing evaluation findings in different forums	The evaluations were presented at the Council of Education ministers, HeadCom of technical heads of education departments in provinces with national government, various interprovincial subcommittees, e.g. on teacher development; curriculum; planning and M&E. This helped to build *trust* in the evaluation results
Elements of NES	
Technical Working Group and Evaluation Steering Committee	TWG and ESC enabled co-development of all stages of the evaluation from formulation to finalisation. This facilitated *agreement*, *ownership* and *trust* between DPME and DBE and conviction in the usefulness of evaluation results
Developing theory of change with stakeholders	Helped to build common *understanding* of how the programme worked, valuable in itself, and interest by stakeholders in being part of the process
Validation workshop with stakeholders	This made stakeholders *aware* of the findings and then recommendations were developed in an *interactive* manner with them. This allowed stakeholders an opportunity to reflect on the recommendations and thereby *agree* and *own* them, and *trust* the results
Simple evaluation report	Improved *accessibility* helped with advocacy and dissemination of findings
Management response	The management response provided a *formal* mechanism whereby different departments had to acknowledge the recommendations and indicate those they *agreed/disagreed* with and why. It provided a way of *institutionalising* them

(*Continued*)

Table 5.2 (Continued)

Intervention	Effect and change mechanism activated
Improvement plan	This was developed for both evaluations and implemented closely with FLBP and NSNP. It also provided a *formal* mechanism for agreeing how to take forward and *institutionalise* recommendations
Quality assessment	Both evaluations were checked by the DPME through assessment of government evaluation reports to ensure credibility and *trust* in evaluation findings
Report public on DPME website	Once approved by Cabinet the reports were made available to the wider public on DBE and DPME websites. This helped in giving stakeholders *access* to the information, and *awareness* of the results
Approval by Cabinet	The Cabinet process was effective in getting people to take the evaluation results seriously and in generating momentum for follow-up actions. It also promoted *agreement* by Cabinet and *ownership* of the results
Role of DPME evaluation director	Provided technical assistance, guidance and logistical support for processes involved in evaluations, and a bridge to reporting to Cabinet

resources. In general, the evaluations completed in DBE, far from being compliance exercises, have been used for operational improvement and policy review.

The contextual factors supporting or hindering the use of evidence

Factors enabling use

Table 5.1 shows the increase in research and evaluations commissioned by the department in recent years, which reflects the *political will* to support independent evaluation, information and data. The minister has over the years demonstrated an appreciation for the need to use evidence in planning and policy making. The length of her tenure has ensured *stability in the leadership* of DBE as the macro-departmental focus has remained the same. This has allowed sufficient time for the department to implement policy changes over time, unlike during the frequent changes in minister prior to 2009. Another critical aspect that was mentioned in the interviews was that it is not only political will at the level of the minister or Director General (DG) that matters but also the backing of project managers in the DBE. Project and programme managers who buy in to evaluations and use of evidence can commit resources and energy towards the realisation of activities outlined by the evaluation recommendations. They can even lobby the department to shift its approach towards a specific aspect as a result of lessons they have learned from an evaluation.

Crises related to delivery of educational services, such as the 2012 textbook crisis, provided the impulse for the department to be prepared to consider changes. This crisis threw into relief the need for integrated information for monitoring and evaluation in the sector.

The Chief Directorate: Strategic Planning, Research and Coordination, which includes the Research and Evaluations Directorate, have been champions for evidence generation and use in DBE. They have played an important role in helping their peers who manage programmes and projects to appreciate the value of lessons from evaluations. They have access to strategic discussions in DBE and also provide a technically strong partner for DPME to work with on the evaluations, and they have played the knowledge broker role in DBE to maximise the likelihood of use.

> It's a bit fragile in that it's still a bit dependant on personalities. . . .There are two or three very competent staff members in the directorate who have a good understanding of evaluations. I guess with them that's a move slightly towards institutionalisation (as) those types of people would hopefully be retained in the Department, and may move to management over time. . . . part of our story has been the champions . . . without having to be pressurised into it or upskilled by DPME. . . . So it was fertile ground for the DPME to come and work in. But also maybe some of the juniors who are there now may become more senior in time. That's maybe a move in a direction of institutionalisation.
> (Respondent 1)

> As champions, they have been able to convince programme managers not to worry about negative evaluation findings but rather use the recommendations and lessons as to how they could strengthen the programme.
> (Respondent 2)

Officials in the DBE also valued the *facilitation of the DPME* in driving and leading the evaluation system and providing technical advice as well as the *presence of the NES*, which emphasises evaluation quality and use.

Barriers to use

Outside these two specific evaluations, impediments have arisen in the application of improvement plans where proposed activities have negative political implications, are inconsistent with the law, too expensive to implement, impractical, lack management support or require policy amendment and therefore are not enforceable. To ensure implementation, the improvement plans also need to be better linked to operational plans because that is how individuals are held to account (Respondent 1). The incorporation of improvement plan activities in the department's annual performance and operational plans is important to ensure that they are budgeted for and therefore implemented.

Mohohlwane (2018) explains potential *hesitation by managers in undertaking evaluations*, associated with uncertainty of the value of evaluations, concerns about underperformance and repercussions. She gives an example:

> A programme manager may be held accountable for the programme being evaluated, however, they may not have control of all the underlying

processes due to complexities in the structure, resourcing and the scale of programmes. These complexities include concurrent functions between national departments as well as the national and provincial education departments; funding that is received directly from National Treasury or Provincial Treasury to nine different Provincial Education Departments but accounted for nationally; and the number of schools in a programme.

Writing about the Grade R evaluation, Samuels et al. (2015) argue that one should not be naïve about the incentives facing government when conducting evaluations, because the results can point to significant problems and low impacts.

> In an environment where the media are likely to pick up on this and create negative press for the implementing department, this creates an incentive for government officials to resent an evaluation rather than embrace it so as to learn from it.
>
> Samuels et al. (2015, p. 9)

These observations suggest that DPME will need to find ways to assist partnering departments in communicating findings to the public and in ensuring that the process is constructive. With the NSNP, the report was leaked and the main television station wanted to do a feature on it.

Lessons for the country going forward

How did the context and intervention influence the use of evidence in DBE?

The realist analysis discussed in Chapter 1 suggests that in different contexts, particular interventions will result in varying outcomes. In the context of evidence use, interventions include an evidence generation process (e.g. an evaluation), use interventions adopted to try and promote use (e.g. evaluation steering committee), which influence certain behavioural mechanisms (access to information, building trust, etc.) and result in certain use outcomes (how evidence influences policy and practice). Understanding which mechanisms work within which context can help us understand conditions that increase the likelihood of research utilisation and therefore place us better to reproduce these.

The *context* in this case included the need for significant reforms and outcomes in education after huge financial resources had been committed and there was a need to demonstrate effectiveness. Multiple stakeholders at national and provincial levels are involved in implementation of educational programmes but with some confusion in roles. There is a history of using evidence in education, and there was a significant evidence champion, the Chief Directorate: Strategic Planning, Research and Coordination with a history of using evidence to support policy making. This was supported by a National

Evaluation System giving recognition to evaluation, and systems and support for implementation.

In terms of *evidence generation*, the department had internal capacity to generate evidence and used a variety of sources, including evaluations, research and administrative data.

We see a number of *use interventions* being applied, including *knowledge brokering* by the evidence champion Chief Directorate. This helped to identify areas to evaluate, and to maximise ownership of the findings and recommendations. The *systems* and *technical support* under the NES, with the focus on collaboration, contributed to ownership and learning through the process. The *quality assurance* systems were important in building the credibility of the evaluations, even where, as in NSNP, there was no budget to do as extensive a survey as the DBE would have liked. The *improvement plan* was an important step in trying to ensure use.

We see examples of these leading to building of *awareness, agreement/ownership* and *trust* in the findings and recommendations, and the *institutionalisation* of recommendations, which all help lead to individual, organisation and systems change. However, some managers remained sceptical and more institutionalisation of improvement plans in operational plans and departmental annual performance plans and budgets was needed.

We see a range of *outcomes* being achieved. In terms of individual change, in both processes we see stakeholders becoming committed to change, building their motivation to use the results of the evaluation, and use evaluation more generally. Organisationally, we see a developing capability in DBE with the Research, M&E Directorate having significant expertise in evaluation and strongly motivated to use evaluation, and a range of organisational changes directly emanating from the two evaluations.

The main lessons that emerge

Some of the lessons that emerge are:

- Having the same *leadership* for a relatively long period of time provides stability, which allows time for evidence to be generated and used to drive change.
- *Crises* can provide an opportunity for use of evidence – and developing an evidence base can provide the ability to respond quickly with evidence when need arises.
- With the increase in research and evaluations commissioned by the department, continuing *political will* to support independent evaluation, information and data is critical.
- Having an internal unit as *evidence champions*. In DBE they worked hard to promote appreciation of evidence, and to act as knowledge brokers linking evidence generation and use by policy makers and programme managers.

- Evidence was sometimes viewed negatively by programme managers and *advocacy* is required. The role of an internal champion is key in addressing this.
- The role of a *national evaluation system* and a national champion to drive, lead it and provide technical advice is necessary.
- The importance of an approach that supports *involvement of stakeholders* through the process, so that they own the product and process, for example, developing the theory of change with stakeholders, or recommendations developed in an iterative manner in a broader stakeholder validation workshop.
- The importance of perceived *legitimacy of the messengers*. In one evaluation, the choice of service provider was considered problematic as a renowned critic of government programmes was appointed in the competitive bidding process, possibly compromising the legitimacy of the results and findings.

Conclusions

The cases presented in this chapter are evaluations where the evidence and recommendations from the evaluations were used. Although there were reservations about evaluation initially, the knowledge broker role of the Chief Directorate was important in leading the use of evaluations. The constant need to reinforce the utility of the evaluations was a stumbling block but was overcome by consistently communicating the benefits. Both evaluations eventually strengthened the hand of the programme managers in reviewing and strengthening policy implementation, despite low levels of understanding about the need for evaluation by programme managers and initial reservations about the evaluations being public.

Overall, this chapter provides a picture of how a government department can undertake evaluations effectively, and the importance of an internal knowledge broker to champion and support this. It also shows the usefulness of a national evaluation system providing key elements that encourage use.

Notes

1 Final year of schooling.
2 For a history of the assessments, see Thulare (2018) and Nuga-Deliwe (2017).

References

Davids, M., Samuels, M-L., September, R., Moeng, T.L., Richter, L., Mabogoane, T.W., et al. 2015. The pilot evaluation for the National Evaluation System in South Africa – A diagnostic review of early childhood development. *African Evaluation Journal,* 3(1), Art. #141, 7 pages. http://dx.doi.org/10.4102/aej.v3i1.141

DBE. 2009. National School Nutrition Programme (NSNP) 2009/10. Annual Report. Department of Basic Education.

DBE. 2010. Curriculum news. Department of Basic Education. Pretoria.

DBE. 2018a, October. Teacher indaba evaluation report. Research Coordination, Monitoring & Evaluation Directorate. Department of Basic Education.

DBE. 2018b. General Household Survey (GHS): Focus on Schooling 2017. Department of Basic Education.

DPME. 2014. Evaluation guideline 2.2.6. How to develop an improvement plan to address evaluation recommendations. Department of Planning, Monitoring and Evaluation.

DPME. 2017. Report on the assessment of government evaluations – Implementation evaluation of the national school nutrition programme. Department of Planning, Monitoring and Evaluation.

DPME/DBE. 2016a. Implementation evaluation of the national school nutrition programme: Evaluation report. Department of Planning, Monitoring and Evaluation, and Department of Basic Education.

DPME/DBE. 2016b. Implementation evaluation of the Funza Lushaka Bursary Programme: Evaluation report. Department of Planning, Monitoring and Evaluation, and Department of Basic Education.

Goldman, I., Mathe, J.E., Jacob, C., Hercules, A., Amisi, M., Buthelezi, T., et al. 2015. Developing South Africa's national evaluation policy and system: First lessons learned. *African Evaluation Journal,* 3(1), 107, 9 pages. http://dx.doi. org/10.4102/aej.v3i1.107

Johnson, K., Greenseid, L.O., Toal, S.A., King, J.A., Lawrenz, F. and Volkov, B. 2009. Research on evaluation use: A review of the empirical literature from 1986 to 2005. *American Journal of Evaluation,* 30, 377–410. https://doi.org/10.1177/1098214009341660

Mohohlwane, N. 2018. Implementing evaluations: Successes and challenges from a DBE perspective, available at: https://www.zenexfoundation.org.za/programme/thought-leadership/m-e/item/363-implementing-evaluations-successes-and-challenges-from-a-dbe-perspective, accessed 15 March 2019

Motala, S. 2015. Equity, access and quality in basic education: A review. *Journal of Education,* 61.

National Planning Commission (NPC). 2012. *National development plan 2030: Our future – make it work.* Pretoria: Presidency of South Africa.

National Planning Commission, Diagnostic Overview. 2011. Retrieved 20 September 2018, from www.nationalplanningcommission.org.za/Downloads/diagnosticoverview.pdf

Nuga Deliwe, C.O. 2017. An analysis of the measurement of the progress in learning outcomes at country level: the case of South Africa. University of Wits, South Africa http://wiredspace.wits.ac.za/handle/10539/25944

OECD. 2008. Reviews of national policies for education: South Africa. *Reviews of National Policies for Education,* OECD Publishing, Paris, https://doi.org/10.1787/9789264053526-en.

Patton, M.Q. 1998. Discovering process use. *Evaluation,* 4, 225–233. https://doi.org/10.1177/13563899822208437

Phillips, S., Goldman, I., Gasa, N., Akhalwaya, I. and Leon, B. 2014. A focus on M&E of results: An example from the Presidency, South Africa. *Journal of Development Effectiveness,* 6, 392–406. https://doi.org/10.1080/19439342.2014.966453

Reddy, V., Visser, M., Winnaar, L., Arends, F., Juan, A. and Prinsloo, C.H. 2016. *TIMSS 2015: Highlights of mathematics and science achievement of grade 9 South African learners.* Pretoria: Human Sciences Research Council.

Samuels, M., Taylor, S., Shepherd, D., Van der Berg, S., Jacob, C., Deliwe, C.N., et al. 2015. Reflecting on an impact evaluation of the Grade R programme: Method, results and policy responses. *African Evaluation Journal,* 3b(1), Art. #139, 10 pages. http://dx.doi.org/10.4102/aej.v3i1.139

Thulare, T.D. 2018. A policy analysis of the annual national assessments in South Africa. In Wiseman, A.W. and Davidson, P.M. (eds.), *Cross-nationally comparative, evidence-based educational policymaking and reform* Emerald Publishing Limited, pp. 71–100. https://doi.org/10.1108/S1479-367920180000035004

6 Use of evidence in a complex social programme

Case of an evaluation of the state's response to violence against women and children in South Africa

Matodzi M. Amisi, Thabani Buthelezi and Siza Magangoe

Summary

This chapter focuses on the use of evidence from the Diagnostic Review of South Africa's response to violence against women and children (VAWC), carried out by the Department of Planning, Monitoring and Evaluation and Department of Social Development between 2014 and 2016. The Diagnostic Review provided evidence that government needed to develop a new plan for VAWC, increase the budget allocation for violence prevention and services and better coordinate VAWC responses, all of which is being taken forward in the National Strategic Plan for gender-based violence. Many of the interventions to promote the use of evaluations come from the national evaluation system, such as evaluation steering committees and improvement plans. These were found to have created ownership and likely use. The interventions were optimised through strong knowledge brokering by government evaluation units and creation of spaces for intersectoral dialogue to facilitate evidence use. The chapter adds to the knowledge base of factors that facilitate or inhibit evidence use in multi-sectoral complex interventions.

Introduction

Women and children in South Africa experience a very high level of different forms of violence including intimate partner violence, neglect, rape, femicide, child homicide and sexual assault. Research undertaken by South Africa's Medical Research Council reveals that 25% of women have experienced physical violence at some point in their lives (Gender Links and The Medical Research Council. 2010). Violence against children (VAC) shows the same trends, with studies finding that 1 in 3 children in South Africa have experienced some form of violence (Ward et al., 2018).

These high levels of violence have persisted despite significant investment by government, development partners, and civil society organisations (CSOs) in evidence generation, enacting policy, setting up institutions, allocating resources and delivering services aimed at reducing violence. This chapter uses the journey of the Diagnostic Review of South Africa's response to violence against women and children (VAWC) to understand facilitators and barriers to evidence use in public policy. The Diagnostic Review was carried out between 2014 and 2016 by South Africa's Departments of Planning Monitoring and Evaluation (DPME) and Social Development (DSD). The chapter also provides a snapshot of the operations of South Africa's national evaluation system (NES), in itself an important policy experiment in promoting the generation and use of evaluation evidence. Lessons shared in the chapter should improve uptake of research evidence in the VAWC sector in South Africa and offer insight and suggestions for improving uptake of evidence in other multi-sectoral interventions to address complex social problems.

The chapter draws from a case study carried out as part of a research project titled Evidence in Practice: Documenting and Sharing Lessons from Evidence-Informed Policy Making and Implementation in Africa. Data for the case study was collected between November 2018 and March 2019. The data comes from semi-structured interviews with 14 key informants, document review and participant observation. The main author was the evaluation lead from DPME on this project; the second author was chief of monitoring and evaluation (M&E) in DSD at the time the evaluation was done; and the third author led the policy process. Respondents were selected purposively because of their knowledge of the sector and known active participation in relevant policy and programme delivery. The case study used the framework described in Chapter 3 to guide data collection and analysis. In addition, the case applied the realist notion of change (outcomes) being the result of interaction between context and mechanism. Thus, the case study aimed to understand which evidence use interventions worked to produce which outcomes (decision/policy) and in which context.

Background: country, institutional and policy context

South Africa's democracy is nascent, established only in 1994 after many years of struggle against white minority rule. While the country has made significant investment in social protection, human development outcomes have not improved at the rate anticipated, partly due to social problems such as high levels of violence, decades of under-investment in human capital, poor nutrition and so forth. This has contributed to high levels of unemployment and underdevelopment. Seventy-six percent of the population, mostly black South Africans, live with the constant threat of poverty (World Bank, 2018). Family and household structures have also been strongly shaped by apartheid's restrictive labour migration policies which forced separation of migrant men from their families. While these policies were relaxed in the early 1990s and completely abolished after 1994, the result is that nuclear families are not the norm in South Africa, which impacts family dynamics and the ability of families to protect children. In fact, couples living with their own children make up only 19% of all households and 62% of children live in extended family arrangements (Hall and Mokomane, 2018, pp. 31–32), with single parent households representing 11% of households.

Though the constitution and government legislation are considered progressive, societal values are conservative. The 2016 Community Survey reports that more than 80% of the South African population is religious, with about 78% professing to be Christian, 4% practicing African religions and 2.6% being Muslim or Hindu (Statistics South Africa, 2016, p. 42). Patriarchy is embedded in the traditions, customs and values of most African cultures, and during apartheid it was state sanctioned, with white men having most rights and black women least rights and protection (Meer, 2016; Ademiluka, 2018). Others have argued that it is this confluence of deeply embedded patriarchy, religious conservatism, inequality, poverty, breakdown of the family and history of state-sanctioned violence under apartheid that has left South Africa battling with high levels of untreated trauma that is reproducing violence. The complexity makes responding to the problem so difficult (Lamb and Warton, 2011).

An important factor in South Africa's response to violence is government's configuration and capacity. The democratic political system of government at national, provincial and local level is a result of the 1994 consolidation of the apartheid state's racially fragmented administrations. Constitutional instructions allocate public service functions as either the exclusive mandate of national, provincial or local government or shared between spheres of government. Provincial and local governments are independent spheres of government and can determine their own priorities, develop plans and implement programmes (Amisi and Vawda, 2017), and they have varying capacity and resources (Chipkin and Meny-Gibert, 2011). This fragmentation diminishes government's ability to collaborate and deliver integrated services. This problem is experienced in government response to VAWC. For example, though most departments have done relatively well in delivering on their respective VAWC mandates, they have not effectively collaborated to optimise their cumulative effect enough to reduce the levels and effect of violence (DPME and DSD, 2016; Gould et al., 2019).

South Africa has a vibrant NGO sector and NGOs are critical to the country's response to VAWC. Nearly 40% of all registered NGOs operate in the social services sector (DPME and DSD, 2017). More than 90% of social welfare services, including VAWC services, are provided by NGOs (Barberton et al., 2018, quoted in Gould et al., 2019). Analysis done by National Treasury shows that government funding for social welfare services is low and NPOs experience up to a 71% funding gap (Barberton et al., 2018, p. i). In relation to NGOs, government is a policy maker, a regulator, a funder and, in some cases, a co-provider of services. The interplay of these different roles and funding challenges have caused conflict in the sector (DPME and DSD, 2017; Barberton et al., 2018) which also influences the flow of information between the government and CSOs.

The evolution of VAWC-related national policies

Over the years, the national policy landscape relating to VAWC has changed rapidly, reflecting a shift in paradigm and political leadership in the different ministries and the country. Figure 6.1 provides a visual representation of the policy timeline briefly introduced in preceding sections.

Evidence in a complex social programme 95

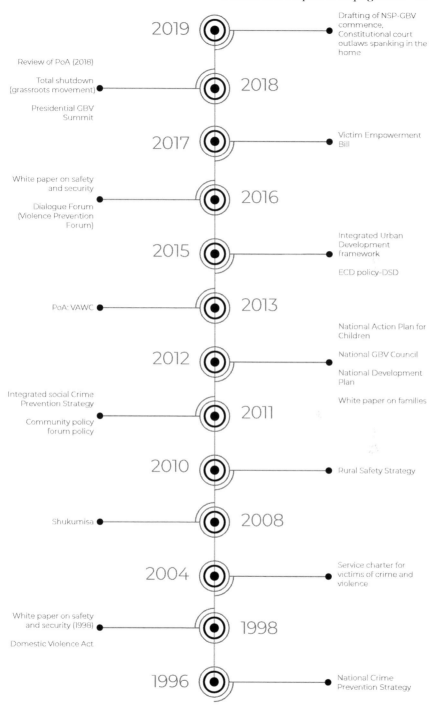

Figure 6.1 Timeline showing the evolution of VAWC-related national policy
Source: Author generated.

Though the timeline depicts a linear evolution of policy, in practice this has not been the case and it has been punctuated by changes in political leadership which, in most cases, have led to changes in policy direction. For example, Rauch (2000) argues that the shift in focus from crime prevention in the National Crime Prevention Strategy to crime combating was precipitated by a change in minister. One of the striking aspects of policy relating to VAWC is the difference in how criminal justice departments and social sector departments understand and respond to VAWC. Social sector departments are likely to see VAWC as a social problem that requires socio-economic interventions while criminal justice departments are likely to take a tough-on-crime approach (DPME and DSD, 2016). Attempts to address this policy disjuncture include the development of the Integrated Social Crime Prevention Strategy in 2011, led by DSD. More recently, the inter-ministerial committee (IMC) on VAWC, the Programme of Action on Violence against Women and Children (PoA:VAWC) and the White Paper on Safety and Security 2016 cover programmes from both criminal justice and social sector departments.

Identifying the need for evidence

A key element of the analytical framework on evidence use presented in Chapter 3 is the demand for evidence. This section explores the sources of the demand for evidence.

When the IMC on VAWC was established in 2010, it was tasked with investigating the root causes of VAWC and how to end all forms of violence against women and children. The South African government has a culture of commissioning evidence and so it was not surprising that when the IMC was established, they commissioned two studies to guide their work. One of the studies came to be known as the Diagnostic Review. DSD's evaluation unit recommended that the review be carried out as part of the National Evaluation Plan (NEP) implemented by the DPME and governed by South Africa's National Evaluation Policy Framework (NEPF). DPME's involvement would help because the evaluation required involvement of multiple departments. Secondly, the NEPF would ensure that the Diagnostic Review would be taken to Cabinet. Both the Evaluation and Policy Units in DSD viewed submission to Cabinet as a potential trigger for change, as Cabinet has the power to give direction/instructions to departments.

The Diagnostic Review was carried out at the demand of the potential evidence users in the IMC to answer an existing policy question, and with the participation of policy makers so they could be part of shaping the research process. Data from the interviews indicates this is not always the case for research in the sector. One respondent stated, 'there is almost an attitude amongst researchers, it is research for research sake, whether it finds practical application in government they do not seem to really care' (Respondent 8 – development partner). Another respondent said,

> I have been looking a lot at evidence on what work [is needed] to prevent VAWC. . . . The information is not helpful for implementers. The questions about costs, transferability, etc. are not answered. Without intending to do so, researchers fail policy makers because we don't answer the right questions.
> (Respondent 4 – think tank)

The role of development partners was important in the demand for evidence. Both the root cause analysis study and the Diagnostic Review were funded by UNICEF. This gave UNICEF some power in shaping the conceptualisation and use of the two studies, as we will show in the next sections.

The evaluation process

The NEPF directs all national evaluations to be managed by a technical working group (TWG) and evaluation steering committee (ESC). The TWG included DSD and UNICEF. The TWG developed the terms of reference (ToRs) and managed the evaluation, while the ESC, headed by the senior policy head from DSD oversaw the evaluation. For the Diagnostic Review, the technical committee for the IMC (IMC TTT) took on an additional role as the steering committee for the evaluation. Having these cross-government structures was important for the evaluation to incorporate what was happening in different subsectors and to have the support and ownership of the key departments.

It was difficult to attain consensus between the different departments on what the Diagnostic Review should cover, which showed unresolved policy dissonance in the sector. At the time of the evaluation, there were numerous discussions within the TWG and ESC (IMC TTT) about whether the problem is violence against women, gender-based violence (GBV) or violence against women and children. Framing the evaluation as responding to gender-based violence meant excluding violence against children, particularly forms of violence that are not gendered, such as spanking in the home, corporal punishment at schools and violence between children. The Children's Unit within DSD and UNICEF did not accept this proposal. The ESC did not approve separating women and children. Focusing on both VAW and VAC showed a recognition of the intersection between violence experienced by women and children. Thus, the decision about the evaluation focus was, in itself, signalling a policy position by government. The process to get consensus on the questions to be asked and the scope of the evaluation took some time; the ToRs went through 14 iterations from October 2013 to December 2013 before final approval by the ESC. The ability to broker a safe space for consensus building was an important role of the ESC.

The evaluation process was guided by the ESC. They substantively shaped the research process and the recommendations and approved the final report. This resulted in departments owning the recommendations but also the recommendations addressing key gaps in how government was responding to VAWC. The Diagnostic Review did not generate anything radically new but, as one of the respondents indicated, 'The difference was that this was done by government, and government itself was acknowledging these issues' (Respondent 4 – think tank).

Taking forward the findings

Following approval of the final report by the steering committee, the head of the steering committee formulates a *management response* to the recommendations and oversees the drafting of an *improvement plan* which spells out steps that will be taken to address the recommendations. In the current case, the plan was developed in a workshop with CSOs, government departments and development partners. The improvement plan was approved in April 2017 by the IMC TTT and was submitted for formal ratification by the head of the IMC TTT (director general of DSD) in July 2017.

The Diagnostic Review's findings were translated to messages for different target audiences. DPME, working together with DSD's policy and evaluation units, translated the evaluation report and improvement plan into a seven-page cabinet memorandum. Only key findings and recommendations were carefully selected by DSD and DPME to be presented in the memorandum. The memorandum was presented to different coordinating structures of government; firstly the cluster of director generals and then tabled at a Cabinet sub-committee. Because of the cross-cutting nature of VAWC, the Diagnostic Review was presented to both the social cluster and the criminal justice cluster and their respective Cabinet committees.

This process was carefully managed, balancing both political and technical pressures. The process took a year, with disagreements between departments leading departments to ask DPME to give them more time to interrogate the report and recommendations to units within departments who did not participate in the ESC but were affected by the recommendations. The *submission to Cabinet* made sure that heads of departments in the social and criminal justice sectors and all ministers were aware of the important findings and recommendations in the Diagnostic Review and that they were accountable for implementing the improvement plan. As with discussions in the ESC, the submission process offered space for senior managers and ministers to debate how government can improve its response to the problem. Approval by Cabinet was also the mechanism that enabled wider dissemination of the report. Under the National Evaluation System, once a report is approved by Cabinet without reservation, it can be made public and sent to Parliament.

As required by the NEPF, significant efforts were made to *share the results*. All important documents were placed on DPME and DSD websites, including the full report, the management response to the recommendations from the DSD, the improvement plan, and reports on progress against the improvement plan. This made the report easy to access by the sector. It also made government transparent in its learning, important in a sector fraught with mistrust and conflictual relationships between different stakeholders.

Two *policy briefs* were developed informed by the evaluation, one co-authored by DPME and DSD's evaluation and policy units, and one with the Institute for Security Studies and Save the Children South Africa. This co-production of policy briefs was intended to improve ownership and wider dissemination of results. The findings were also presented by government officials in DPME and DSD in more than ten different workshops and seminars, which familiarised the sector with the findings and recommendations of the evaluation and the resultant improvement plan. This showed ownership by government of the findings and commitment to addressing the issues identified, addressing a challenge in the sector where researchers often speak of failure by state agencies to respond, leading to further divisions/conflicts.

Internal government M&E units facilitated use of the Diagnostic Review through ongoing knowledge brokering within government and with external stakeholders. Within DSD the *evaluation unit* played an *internal knowledge broker role*, translating the research report into an internal communication memorandum to communicate to management of the department the findings and implications of the Diagnostic Review and the improvement plan. The unit also ensured that the minister was briefed before the presentation of the evaluation in Cabinet and the team presenting to Cabinet were aware of what is politically acceptable and what is not. DPME also played a strong knowledge broker role, working with DSD and other departments to make sure findings and lessons from the Diagnostic Review were integrated into the Programme of Action (PoA) on VAWC and its M&E framework. DPME continues to play an important role in the National Strategic Plan for GBV. As shown in the following comments, this role was influential:

> The respect given to DPME based on the pivotal role of the department and the mandate assigned to the department, and the level of work that the department did around the Diagnostic Review contributed to the buy in from departments. The push from DPME was very helpful. They did not come as big brother but gently guided the departments.
> (Respondent 1 – development partner)

> DPME is in the Presidency and this gave us some influence. It is the politics of being in the Presidency. The clout that came with being DPME, that is why we were able to enforce some of the work.
> (Respondent 2 – government)

Analysing use and the factors which contributed to use

This book seeks to contribute to an understanding of how evidence use can be promoted. In this section, we therefore first seek to understand the types of use that happened in the Diagnostic Review, and then unpack how the different use interventions and other factors contributed to, or inhibited, use.

Using the results of the Diagnostic Review

There are different ways of understanding use, and Chapters 1 and 2 discuss instrumental, conceptual, symbolic and process use. Instrumental use refers to cases where the recommendations are implemented, while conceptual use refers to cases where information provided through the research gives new insight and understanding that shapes the ways individuals and organisations do their work. Very often, organisations which track use of evaluations track responses to individual recommendations (i.e. instrumental use). As this chapter will show, in multi-sectoral complex interventions, conceptual use can be an important enabler for wider policy changes and remains important in EIDM.

Instrumental use of the Diagnostic Review

The following are some instrumental uses of the Diagnostic Review:

1. The Review of the PoA was informed by the results of the Diagnostic Review

    In 2017, DSD with the support of UNICEF started a process to review and develop a new PoA. This responded to the first recommendation of the Diagnostic Review. Though this process was paused pending the completion of the National Strategic Plan, the Diagnostic Review and other research studies were important sources in the revision process and in the NSP, as shown in the comment:

    The current PoA it is trying to embrace the evidence that was generated from the evaluation, the system-strengthening pillar was informed by the Diagnostic Review. The majority of issues [addressed in the PoA] came from there [Diagnostic Review], the coordination structure, the issue of information management, issue of social mobilisation.
    (Respondent 1 – development partner)

2. Bringing the voice of CSOs and provincial government to the revision of the PoA

    The revision of the PoA followed the process recommended by the Diagnostic Review, which emphasised the involvement of CSOs and provincial government. The ToRs advertised by UNICEF for a consultant to review the PoA specifically mentioned the need to consult with CSOs and provincial government in the review of the PoA. However, the way the involvement of CSOs was handled highlighted some limitations with tracking/measuring instrumental use of evaluation findings. DSD implemented several recommendations as articulated in the report, but without fully owning the intent underlying the recommendation. Therefore, the extent to which the implementation of the recommendation will change practice over time is not yet known.

3. Establishment of a coordinating structure for VAWC

    The Diagnostic Review recommended that a structure be established to coordinate the work of multiple departments responding to VAWC and that this structure must include NGOs. This was included in the revised PoA and in the Victim Empowerment Bill (2017), and was supported by DSD in the process of developing the National Strategic Plan for GBV.

4. Increase in the budget allocation for violence prevention

In 2018, National Treasury announced an additional budget allocation to provincial DSDs for VAWC programmes. The budget was increased by ZAR 206 million in the financial year 2018/19 while ZAR 309 million was added for the 2019/2020 financial year. This was a much-needed increase in strained budgets and addressed a big concern in the Review. The increase came as a result of a confluence of interventions. The Diagnostic Review found significant shortfalls in funding for response services. DSD used this finding in its budget proposal to National Treasury to motivate for additional budget allocation. However, this was only supported by National Treasury because other factors had influenced Treasury officials to believe that violence can be prevented, and that resources allocated for response services are inadequate, amongst others. This is shown in the next section.

Conceptual use

Respondents reported some cases of conceptual use. For example, UNICEF indicated that the evidence from the Diagnostic Review had been useful for informing other pieces of work they were doing, including the discussions that led to South Africa becoming a pathfinding[1] country for VAC.

> We are able to use this [Diagnostic Review] in our proposal for funding to shape the investment by other funders in South Africa in the area of GBV/VAC. And when we engaged with global partners we used the Diagnostic Review and root causes study to get support for work in South Africa. We also used the information when doing preparatory work for [the] Stockholm [conference] and in motivating for South Africa to be one of the pathfinder countries; the reports were shared with partners.
> (Respondent 1 – development partner)

The seeming openness to sharing the report and its findings helped create connections between government and CSOs and created space for more open conversations about why government interventions had not worked to address VAWC and what was needed to strengthen government response to VAWC.

> What was useful was that when it [Diagnostic Review] became public it became the basis of a conversation. And an honest conversation. The Diagnostic Review said tough things and in a way that did not sound blamey. The findings were hard and difficult but did not come across accusatory.
> (Respondent 4 – think tank)

The respondent from DPME also indicated how, beyond its specific recommendations, the Diagnostic Review had been used in preparation of the government's next Medium-Term Strategic Framework (MTSF). She, however, was cautious to claim victory in being able to influence the MTSF as the process was not yet complete.

Another conceptual use was enabling DPME to use evidence to respond to related issues arising. For example, the Diagnostic Review was very important when government had to respond to the Total Shutdown movement:

> When #TotalShutdown happened, we had material to help us respond. The Diagnostic Review shaped the government's input to the GBV summit held in November 2018. We had something to say and used it to push back against what lobbyists might be pushing for using research.
>
> (Respondent 2 – government)

What can we learn from the interventions that were implemented to promote use of the evidence from the Diagnostic Review and the resultant decisions it influenced? Table 6.1 presents use interventions and decisions influenced as stand-alone activities for ease of reading.

It is important to note that, though presented in Table 6.1 as stand-alone interventions, the way that the different use interventions worked to produce evidence use is not linear. In fact, the interventions interacted with one another and one action stimulated another in a snowball effect. The next section shows how these specific use interventions interacted with the wider context and with each other to facilitate uptake of evidence.

Enablers and inhibitors of evidence use in the VAWC sector

When commenting about barriers to evidence use, most respondents tended to reflect on trends they have observed in the sector more broadly rather than focusing on the Diagnostic Review. Therefore, the following analysis does not limit itself to the Diagnostic Review but includes experiences with other research and evaluation in the VAWC sector. It takes elements from the analytical framework relating to context, taken from Chapter 3. These are summarised in Table 6.2 and elaborated after the table.

The macro-context

An important barrier to uptake of research and full implementation of research findings that respondents raised and reflected on is the seeming disjuncture between the *values of individual public servants and those of researchers*. This was seen in contestations around the amendment of the constitution to decriminalise sexual relations between young children, discussions around the right to terminate pregnancy and, more recently, the criminalisation of spanking where religious communities applied for an appeal citing a religious right for parents to chastise their children:

> We are a conservative society, but our policies are very liberal. We have tried to impose policy on people who do not want it. We need to work closely with people who have to implement policies. Because if you are

Table 6.1 Interventions to promote use and their effect

Intervention	Effect
Elements of the NES	
Technical Working Group and Evaluation Steering Committee comprising key stakeholders	The interactions in the TWG and ESC facilitated co-development of evaluation elements, e.g. ToRs, collaboration and *trust* between DSD, DPME and UNICEF. They provided a safe space for meaningful dialogue. In this space the researchers could gain *understanding* of the policy world they are evaluating, and policy makers could be made more aware of the research process, inform the process and interrogate findings and analysis. The ESC was also useful in building consensus on problem definition.
Simple evaluation report	The full evaluation report was 206 pages long. The 1-page, 5-page and 25-page structure used for the summary report under the NES facilitated *accessibility* of the findings.
Management response	The management response provided a formal mechanism whereby the different departments had to *formally* acknowledge the recommendations.
Improvement plan	The improvement plan provided a plan *agreed* by all stakeholders for taking forward and *institutionalising* the recommendations.
Report public on DPME website	The availability of the report, improvement plan etc. created transparency and access and increased *commitment* from stakeholders.
Elements outside the NES	
Knowledge brokering role of departmental M&E unit	Internal communication made management and the minister of the department *aware* of the findings and recommendations and created an opportunity to potentially *agree/object* to what has been recommended. *Formal* approval authorises the evaluation unit to hold the department and individual units accountable for implementation of the research findings.
Knowledge brokering role of DPME	An important role was played by DPME as both a commissioner and knowledge broker in supporting the use of the Diagnostic Review up to two years after completion of the evaluation. This role in this evaluation went beyond the normal role that DPME evaluation directors played.
Process facilitation and relationship management	VAWC is predominantly experienced in black communities. However, lead researchers tend to be white, and this was the case with the Diagnostic Review. This has the potential to create tensions that inhibits uptake of findings. For the Diagnostic Review this was also an issue. The DPME project manager played a relationship management role, sensitising the research team to dynamics they should be aware of, including advising them to add experienced black researchers to the team. A more balanced team was well received and their work better received.

(*Continued*)

Table 6.1 (Continued)

Intervention	Effect
Spaces for ongoing dialogue in the sector	Presentation of the Diagnostic Review in sectoral spaces for ongoing intersectoral dialogue (led by CSOs) like the Dialogue Forum (now called Violence Prevention Forum) and Soul City Social Lab enabled difficult conversations between CSOs, government, development partners and academia about why interventions have not worked and how they can be strengthened, and strengthening partnerships between government and CSOs. This built trust and strengthened relationships which ensured that the revised PoA and the National Strategic Plan on GBV were informed by evidence.
Advocacy by CSOs	South African CSOs have a long history of advocacy for policy reforms. Some of the uses of the Diagnostic Review were influenced by, or enabled by, CSO advocacy. This includes CSOs in the Violence Prevention Forum and the Soul City Social Lab and Shukumisa Campaign.

Table 6.2 Summary of enabling factors and barriers from the context

Element of the context	Enabling factor	Inhibitor
Macro-context	Progressive legislation	Conservative values in the bureaucracy do not match progressive legislation
	Demand from policy makers for diagnostic review	Perception that in many cases research is shaped by researchers not policy makers and does not answer key implementation questions like cost
Intra- and inter-institutional linkages	Where these exist, good relationships between government and researchers	Interaction between researchers, government, NGOs etc. are often hostile, characterised by serious mistrust, power misuse, power dynamics, personality politics etc.
	Role of DPME in building trust and understanding between supplier and government users	Competition between departments limiting consensus in policy, collaboration and co-delivery of policy
	Multiple engagements reinforcing messages and relationships	Organisational silos within and across departments
Organisational capacity		Lack of time and capacity to absorb research
Linking research and other evidence	Research processes that give voice to the lived experiences of women and not just the voice of the researcher	Weakness in facilitating linkages between research and the experience of wider stakeholders

forced to implement a policy you do not believe in and goes against what you believe, who will you blame but the client. We have not been informed by what is going on the ground but what is coming from top down. We have imposed policies on populations who have not had a say on them.
(Respondent 9 – research institute)

Where research seems to be pushing for liberal positions or a position in policy does not accord with the values of those implementing it, the position is less likely to be taken on and does not significantly change the way services are provided. Kahan (2007) referred to this as identity protective cognition. People are more likely to use evidence in ways that are supported by their peer groups than to be guided by the fidelity of the evidence. Shared ideological and cultural commitments are likely to be intertwined with membership of communities (such as church, office, etc.) that furnish individuals with important bases of support. Most individuals will rarely form a contrary position to one held in institutions that provide them with important aspects that define their identity and social support.

The Diagnostic Review did not address any of the contentious issues in the sector. It focused on systems and how the government system was responding to the problem. Though it raised the issue of the beliefs and values of public servants, this was not a central issue of focus. Therefore, it was easier for different sectors and departments to agree on findings and recommendations.

Intra- and inter-institutional linkages

According to Weyrauch et al. (2016, p. 35),

> There are two particular types of relationships that exert significant influence over how knowledge interacts (or not) with policy. One is related to the internal relationships between the government institution and other related government agencies. The second one relates to interaction with relevant users and producers of knowledge who can affect or be affected by policy design and implementation.

In this case we reflect on relationships between government and researchers, and relationships within government.

Relationships between researchers and government or NGOs implementing programmes was cited as an important facilitator/barrier to evidence uptake. Some respondents argued that unrecognised and inadequately addressed trauma is seen in the behaviours of individual decision makers (both in government and NGOs) and in the nature of relations within the sector. Respondents reported that interactions between researchers, government and NGOs, and within government departments, are often hostile, characterised by serious mistrust, power misuse and personality politics hindering evidence-informed policy discussions in the sector.

Another important issue shaping relations in the sector is race. As already mentioned, researchers tend to be white and public service policy makers and implementers at national level are usually black, and specifically black Africans. This often raises issues of perceived cultural imposition and ideological differences between researchers and public servants or the communities they research.

> We (as white people) can't speak any of the African languages. It is seen as disrespectful in many settings; even communities have often raised the issue of race. We often experience people who are openly dismissive because we are white. You walk into a meeting and people look you up and down and comment in another language. You can anticipate that it is unlikely that they will listen to you, they will come back to you with some response about you not understanding the cultural context. Despite indicating our understanding of the culture, they will make some comments that refer to your otherness and your difference. This is fine, I recognise that I am a product of apartheid and that my otherness is an issue.
>
> (Respondent 11 – development specialist)

This played out in the Diagnostic Review and illustrates the importance of internal M&E units' key *knowledge broker* role. When KPMG was hired to carry out the work, there were reservations because the lead researcher was a white English woman who had recently relocated to South Africa, and the team was predominately white. There were questions about the ability of the team to understand the experiences of black women and communities. To overcome this issue, the DPME project manager, together with the Chief Director for M&E at DSD, advised KPMG to diversify their team and sensitised the research team to what is likely to trigger pushback from the ESC. As a result, KPMG added black sector experts to their team. Second, the project manager in DPME managed relations with the ESC, often having discussions outside of the official ESC meetings with senior officials in key departments to allay their fears about the research process or team. Most of the communication to external stakeholders was by DPME and DSD, not the evaluators. By doing this, the relationship between government and researchers was maintained, and despite some of the difficult findings that pointed at failures of government, the evaluation was not rejected by government.

The case study also showed how when a piece of evidence is completed it becomes part of an existing body of knowledge and moves between existing networks of people and institutions. Interviews revealed how often it was existing connections between individuals and *reinforcement* through different platforms that promoted ongoing conversations that were important enablers of use of the Diagnostic Review. The National Treasury respondent indicated that it was being part of ongoing dialogue with the sector through the CSO-led Dialogue Forum (now called the Violence Prevention Forum) that made all these different studies make sense, including the Diagnostic Review. The same official was part of a study tour to Uganda to see Ugandan models for violence prevention that had been effective. He stated the following: 'Going on the study tour broadened my perspective on interventions that are available to address violence. I looked at the interventions that are available in Uganda and see what we can learn' (Respondent 3 – government).

This is a good example of how a combination of factors often work together to influence the use of evidence. In this case, participation in an ongoing discussion with CSOs, government and academics and going on a study tour primed the official to be able to receive and use the information. Exposure of this Treasury official made it possible for the DSD's request for additional budget to be supported at a time when government was cutting budgets across the public service. Also, it highlights the importance of *spaces for dialogue* in evidence use, particularly in a sector where there are high levels of contestation, fragmentation, value-laden issues and so forth. Spaces for dialogue offer opportunities for sense making that can challenge strongly held beliefs, unlike other communication approaches. This can enhance interaction between different stakeholders, foster agreement with research evidence and motivate stakeholders to act on the evidence, key in promoting behaviour change.

Organisational silos and competition between departments was raised as a key challenge in the VAWC sector. VAWC programmes span many different policy domains that are the responsibility of different departments, and the silo mandates create artificial divisions within the VAWC sector that limit information flows. Respondents reported that collaboration is weak in the sector, and there is competition and conflictual relations between departments:

> A lot of the decision-making processes in government are based on politics and some form of competition and not on technical issues. That is the issue. It creates huge problems. Competition between departments, units, individuals and even within the same party. People do not get along and the right decisions do not get taken.
> (Respondent 7 – independent consultant)

This was also the experience of other respondents who argued that revision of the PoA was hampered by relationship issues between departments.

The fragmentation also happens *within departments* where it is possible to have different units working on different aspects of VAWC. In DSD, for example, there is the Children's Unit which works primarily through the lens of the child protection system; the Victim Empowerment Programme (VEP) unit is mostly guided by VEP policy; the Family Unit's work is shaped by the White Paper on Families; then there is the Social Crime Prevention Unit, amongst others. A respondent spoke of contestations within DSD where there was no agreement on some policy issues between the Children's Unit and the VEP Unit:

> During the revision of the PoA, the VEP chief director left the process. This created a power crisis. The two directorates are not working well together,

not taking decisions and not engaging with materials that are developed for the project.

(Respondent 2 – consultant)

The fact that VAWC is spread between so many units has been a problem. No one takes full responsibility for it in the department. You cannot hold any one unit for the improvement plan. I used to ask progress from one unit, and one day I was just told to go ask another unit. And that unit has not been responsive.

(Respondent 14 – government)

The different units in departments dealing with VAWC tend to relate to their subsector and the research that is produced in that subsector. This deepens policy fragmentation in the sector, as researchers in different subsectors are likely to push for certain reforms without being cognisant of how those reforms affect the entire policy area and therefore the achievement of broader policy outcomes (Gould et al., 2017). The ESC provided a platform to facilitate information sharing during the research process, and attempted to overcome these fragmentations.

Balancing different ways of knowing (grassroots knowledge and research evidence) in policy

Participants spoke about how despite instrumental implementation of the Diagnostic Review's recommendations, there were difficulties in balancing knowledge from empirical evidence with that from communities/CSOs that were consulted during the review of the PoA and planning the presidential GBV summit. Research was seen in some of the discussions as an elite indulgence which does not always represent the needs of survivors. Survivors of violence wanted certain actions (e.g. harsher punishment of perpetrators), which in some cases empirical evidence showed was not effective to address the problem.

Conclusions and lessons

How did the context and intervention influence the use of evidence?

A realist analysis suggests that in different contexts, interventions will result in varying outcomes (see Chapter 1). From a realist perspective, change cannot be solely attributed to the nature of an intervention as there are underlying causes of change that may not be directly observable (Pawson et al., 2005). Interventions (I) require mechanisms (M) which connect programmes to their outcomes (O) within certain contexts (C). In this case study, the intervention included an evidence-generation process (an evaluation) and interventions to promote use (e.g. communications), which influenced certain behavioural mechanisms (agreement, access to information, building trust, amongst others) and resulted in certain use outcomes (how the evidence influenced policy and practice). Understanding which mechanisms work within which context can help us understand conditions that increase the likelihood of research utilisation and therefore we can be better placed to reproduce these. Here we added to the realist Context–Mechanism–Outcome configuration, Interventions for evidence use.

In this case study we observe a number of interventions and mechanisms that appear to facilitate use of evidence (building on the analytical framework in Chapter 2):

1 In the context of interventions crossing organisational silos, the following are essential:

   • The formalised involvement of different organisations and stakeholders in the evidence-generation process (evidence generation). The participation of departments in the research process and on structures like the steering committee/IMC TTT was important to legitimise the research process and the outcomes. When departments pushed against the findings or recommendations on the grounds that their departments were not consulted, DSD and DPME could remind the departments of their participation in the research process.
   • Dissemination of findings with government formalised structures for coordination is essential. In this case study, these were the clusters and the IMC (inter-ministerial committee), which allowed different departments to interrogate the research and its implications for their departments (*use intervention*), in some cases suggesting changes to how the recommendation should be responded to.

2 In a sector where people hold strong opposing beliefs and where there is a history of conflict, oppression and subordination on the basis of race (or any other construct) (*context*), the following are very important:

   • The representativity of the evidence-generation team (evidence generation);
   • Wide dissemination of evidence led by government (use intervention);
   • Knowledge brokers that can facilitate mutual understanding and trust (use intervention);
   • Promotion of spaces for meaningful dialogue (use intervention), which can promote agreement, mutual understanding and trust (change mechanisms).

3 In a *context* where there is poor inter-sector communication and relations, introducing the Diagnostic Review (government piece of evidence) into use interventions in the wider policy ecosystem was an important facilitator of much-needed honest discussion about how to strengthen the country's response to VAWC and therefore the use of the evidence. Examples of

interventions included the government-led study tour to Uganda, the Violence Prevention Forum (CSO-led), the Social Lab (CSO-led) and Shelter Movement work (CSO-led), through the knowledge brokering role of government (*use intervention*).

4   In the context of well-established and vibrant CSOs with a history of community mobilisation and policy reform advocacy and a democratic government that embraces participation in political processes, pressure from grassroots CSOs pushed government to implement some of the recommendations.

Lessons around use of evidence in the VAWC sector

The case study shows how, though use interventions are critical to facilitate use of evidence, policy making and implementation is a long process that is highly contested and without a clear beginning or end. Therefore use interventions enable change in a nonlinear, and sometimes unpredictable, chain of reactions. Knowledge brokering is an important facilitator of evidence use; however, this process has to be built into the research process. This is because policy decisions are made at different stages of policy development – problem identification and analysis, options analysis, choice of intervention, implementation and M&E. It is important therefore to appreciate that the power to shape policy shifts between different stakeholders through the policy process. We have also shown how the contestation and power shifts not only happen between government and NGOs but also within government institutions, particularly in intersectoral policies addressing complex social problems. Government is not homogenous and neither are departments. Within departments, units can have different views on policy and it is possible to have contestations within departments as well as between departments.

Evidence uptake is a continuous process that happens both during and after the research process. If space is created for cross-sectoral discussions during the evaluation process, it can offer opportunity to build consensus on contentious policy issues.

We conclude with some lessons.

Research processes need to overcome the impact of strongly held values, beliefs and norms

In a sector like VAWC with strongly held values, beliefs and norms, evidence use is more than a technical endeavour. These values can be held by individual policy makers, politicians and staff in organisations, making it difficult for research that challenges these values to influence policy and transform the way policy and programmes work. Researchers and evaluators in the sector are therefore not only involved in the process of producing knowledge for policy making, but they are engaged in a process that questions societal values, beliefs and norms. Opening the research process to interrogation by people who hold different positions in spaces where they can interact with one another and with the research process can open research to take in the different perspectives, enriching the research and strengthening advocacy possibilities.

Safe spaces where meaningful conversations can be held are critical, as are the skills to facilitate such conversations. Steering committees, when managed well, can create safe spaces for different views to be debated during the research process, thus informing analysis, conclusions and recommendations from research. But these spaces for dialogue can also be provided for outside of the research process. External stakeholders such as think tanks and CSOs have key roles to play in this regard, as this case study has demonstrated.

The composition of the research team matters

Given South Africa's history, VAWC disproportionately affects black communities which are often the intended beneficiaries of programmes targeting poverty-related issues, and are also often the objects/subjects of research. Representivity in research teams can address the sense of 'othering' of communities. Representivity, however, is not just about including researchers of different races, gender or sexual orientation (or whatever social categorisation is important in a specific context). It is also about representation of different world views, ideologies and experiences that relate to the populations being studied and those that the research process aims to influence. Such an approach to setting up research teams can enrich research processes and make researchers sensitive and responsive to issues that might make it difficult for certain people to receive the messages from the research.

Wider lessons

Importance of government internal capacity for research/evaluation and knowledge brokering

Government internal evaluation and research capacity is important for effective evidence use. Evaluation/research units in departments need to have the capacity to work with policy makers and implementers as knowledge brokers to develop evidence agendas, have systems to access research carried out by institutions outside of government and have the capacity to make sense of external research and to advise policy makers. They need to create spaces for dialogue between their departments and external researchers. Where research is commissioned, these units still need to have the capacity to shape and guide the research process to ensure it remains relevant and can be used effectively. Where government has strong evaluation/research capacity, it is better placed to shape the research agenda, ask the right policy questions and guide the production of evidence to ensure that it responds to policy needs.

Complexity of internal government policy-making processes

Some of the challenges with evidence use related to how policy making unfolds in the South African government. Most policy discussions are not open to participation by non-government stakeholders. They happen between and within departments and public entities, in management fora, at clusters, Cabinet and so forth, and consultation with wider stakeholders often only happens when this process is completed. It can be difficult for a policy maker to push an idea through these different government structures simply because it is evident in research, particularly if it challenges dominant values and views. Government needs to be more open to including wider views earlier on in processes and individual policy makers need to be supported through what can be lengthy policy processes.

Evidence needs to be used for the underlying meaning, not just compliance with recommendations

This case study shows that it is possible for departments to implement recommendations and therefore tick the box of instrumental use without this affecting the wider meaning underlying the policy, and so actual policy content and implementation. Organisations may use research evidence to make minor changes to policy and programmes, but not necessarily to transform policy approaches. In the Diagnostic Review, the respondents acknowledged that the recommendations that were implemented were the least controversial and therefore easier to implement. The evidence-informed decision-making sector needs a better understanding of how to support decision makers and institutions and develop means of measuring evidence use that overcome this challenge.

And finally

This chapter has focused on an evaluation in a complex sector, with inter- and intra-organisational dependencies and rivalries, and strongly held and differing values which often differ between policy makers, and between policy makers and researchers. It highlights the mistrust and miscommunication between many researchers and policy makers and how this had to be mediated. The chapter showcases an evaluation conducted carefully and sensitively, paying a lot of attention to process and not just product which has led to significant use, both instrumentally and conceptually. The evaluation was helped by an established national evaluation system, formalising many of the elements likely to promote use. The focus on systems which can build co-ownership is critical. We also see the importance of facilitating meaningful dialogue within departments, across departments, and with wider stakeholders – facilitation skills which are rare in government. The latter is an area where more work is needed to see how to build the skills and systems which can promote such dialogue, can build trust and openness to evidence, and can help to build changes in understanding, in motivation to do things differently and in the capability to do so.

Note

1 Since its launch in July of 2016, the Global Partnership to End Violence Against Children has promoted the concept of pathfinding, which aims to raise awareness, stimulate leadership commitment, galvanise action, and establish a standard of national violence prevention throughout the world (www.end-violence.org/pathfinding-countries).

References

Ademiluka, S.O. 2018. Patriarchy and women abuse: Perspectives from Ancient Israel and Africa. *Old Testament Essays,* 31(2), 339–362.

Amisi, M.M. and Vawda, A. 2017. Strengthening democratic governance in the building of integrated human settlements through evaluations. In Podems, D. (ed.), *Democratic evaluation and democracy: Exploring the reality.* Charlotte: Information Age Publishing, pp. 127–138.

Barberton, C., Abdoll, C., Ragwala, L., Budlender, D. and Mohamed, Z. 2018. *Performance and expenditure review: Cost implications of funding for NPOs following the Nawongo court judgements.* Government Technical Advisory Centre, National Treasury, Cornerstone Economic Research. Retrieved from www.gtac.gov.za/perdetail/Cost%20implications%20of%20 funding%20NPOs%20following%20the%20NAWONGO%20court%20judgements.pdf

Chipkin, I. and Meny-Gibert, S. 2011. *Why the past matters: History of the public service in South Africa.* Retrieved from https://pari.org.za/past-matters-histories-public-service-south-africa/

DPME. 2017. *The evaluation of the non-profit regulatory system.* Department of Planning, Monitoring and Evaluation and the Department of Social Development. Unpublished report.

DPME and DSD. 2016. *Diagnostic review of the state response to violence against women and children.* Department of Planning, Monitoring and Evaluation, and the Department of Social Development. Retrieved from https://evaluations.dpme.gov.za/images/gallery/DPME%20-%20VAWC.pdf

Gender Links and The Medical Research Council. 2010. *The war@home: Findings of the GBV prevalence study in Gauteng, Western Cape, KwaZulu Natal and Limpopo Provinces of South Africa.* Retrieved from https://genderlinks.org.za/programme-web-menu/publications/the-warhome-findings-of-the-gbv-prevalence-study-in-south-africa-2012-11-25/

Gould, C., Mufamadi, D., Amisi, M.M., Dartnall, E., Moruane, S., Abdoll, C., Connors, J., Naicker, S., Shai, N., Malek, E., Rezant, B., Edelstein, I., Mabunda, A., Mayet, Y., Frost, K., Dippenaar, W., Kader, Z., Iewaks, A. and Moeketsi, J. 2019. *What will it take to prevent interpersonal violence in South Africa?* Institute for Security Studies (ISS) policy brief, Pretoria. Retrieved from https://issafrica.org/research/policy-brief/what-will-it-take-to-prevent-interpersonal-violence-in-south-africa

Gould, C., Mufamadi, D., Hsiao, C. and Amisi, M.M. 2017. *Preventing violence in South Africa: From policing to prevention.* Institute for Security Studies (ISS) policy brief, Pretoria. Retrieved from https://issafrica.org/research/policy-brief/reducing-violence-in-south-africa-from-policing-to-prevention

Hall, K. and Mokomane, Z. 2018. The shape of children's families and households: A demographic overview. In Hall, K., Richter, L., Mokomane, Z. and Lake, L. (eds.), *Children, families and the state.* South African Child Gauge, Children's Institute, University of Cape Town. Retrieved from www.ci.uct.ac.za/sites/default/files/image_tool/images/367/

Child_Gauge/South_African_Child_Gauge_2018/Chapters/the_shape_of_childrens_families_and_households.pdf

Kahan, D.M. 2007. *Culture and identity-protective cognition: Explaining the white male effect in risk perception*. Faculty Scholarship Series. 101. Retrieved from https://digitalcommons.law.yale.edu/fss_papers/101

Lamb, G. and Warton, G. 2011. *Why is crime in South Africa so violent? A rapid review*. Programme to Promote Pro Poor Policy Development, Pretoria. Retrieved from www.psppdknowledgerepository.org/search/adsearch/send/62-rapid-evidence-reviews/275-why-is-crime-in-south-africa-so-violent-a-rapid-review

Meer, F. 2016. *Women in the apartheid society*. Retrieved from www.sahistory.org.za/archive/women-apartheid-society-fatima-meer-0

Pawson, R., Greenhalgh, T., Harvey, G. and Walshe, K. 2005. Realist review: A new method of systematic review designed for complex policy interventions. *Journal of Health Services Research & Policy*, 10(1), 21–34. https://doi.org/10.1258/1355819054308530.

Rauch, J. 2000. *The national crime prevention strategy*. Retrieved from www.csvr.org.za/docs/crime/1996nationalcrime.pdf

Statistics South Africa. 2016. *Community survey 2016-in brief*. Retrieved from http://cs2016.statssa.gov.za/wp-content/uploads/2017/07/CS-in-brief-14-07-2017-with-cover_1.pdf

Ward, C.L., Artz, L., Leoschut, L., Kassanjee, R. and Burton, P. 2018. Sexual violence against children in South Africa: A nationally representative cross-sectional study of prevalence and correlates. *Lancet Global Health*, 6, e460–e468. Retrieved from www.thelancet.com/action/showPdf?pii=S2214-109X%2818%2930060-3

Weyrauch, V., Echt, L. and Suliman, S. 2016. *Knowledge into policy: Going beyond 'Context matters'*. Retrieved from www.inasp.info/sites/default/files/2018-04/Going%20beyond%20context%20matters%20%E2%80%93%20framework.pdf

World Bank. 2018. *Overcoming poverty and inequality in South Africa: Assessment of drivers, constraints and opportunities*. Retrieved from http://documents.worldbank.org/curated/en/530481521735906534/pdf/124521-REV-OUO-South-Africa-Poverty-and-Inequality-Assessment-Report-2018-FINAL-WEB.pdf

7 The influence of local ownership and politics of the use of evaluations in policy making

The case of the public procurement evaluation in Uganda

Ismael Kawooya, Timothy Lubanga, Abdul Muwanika, Edwin Muhumuza and Rhona Mijumbi-Deve

Summary

This case study sought to understand the mechanism leading to the use of evidence from an evaluation of public procurement systems in Uganda undertaken in 2012–13, led by the Office of the Prime Minister (OPM) and the Public Procurement Development Authority (PPDA). The public procurement sector had undergone major changes over the years. The impetus for the evaluation was the need to improve the effectiveness and efficiency of the system, and was agreed to by Cabinet and supported by the World Bank through its Technical Advisory Support Unit. An independent consultant undertook the evaluation, working closely with the PPDA. Various structures oversaw the evaluation, including OPM and the Evaluation Sub-committee. The consultant was responsive to government requests for advice and maintained regular communication, reporting on a monthly basis. Ultimately, this resulted in an evaluation that was owned by government and seen to be of high quality. The evaluation led to revision of procurement thresholds and flexibility for sectors that need specialised procurement. It demonstrated to the PPDA the importance of regularly reviewing and updating regulations, standards and guidelines.

Background

Uganda has established mechanisms within government to improve the quality of policies through the use of evidence. OPM has, since 2005, led efforts to strengthen the national Monitoring and Evaluation (M&E) system, including setting up a national evaluation system with an Evaluation Sub-Committee (ESC) and a Government Evaluation Facility (GEF), M&E units in each government ministry, department or agency (MDA), and building their M&E capacity. To date, over 30 evaluations have been conducted with various inputs into policies using this system. However, little is known of how these evaluations have actually been used in policy making.

This case study focuses on evidence from an evaluation carried out in 2012 to assess and learn of the impact of public procurement reforms. The evaluation was completed after the laws amending the Public Procurement and Disposal (PPD) Act had been assented to by the president but before regulations and standards were enacted. Although the process for amending this Act had begun, not enough was known about how the previous law performed and it was felt to be necessary to understand how the current law might work. This prompted a request for an evaluation into the effectiveness of public procurement reforms in Uganda. This case sought to understand how the evidence from the evaluation was used during the amendment process of the PPD Act and the factors influencing its use. The case draws out lessons on how evidence might be used in similar settings in other countries in Africa. It specifically focuses on the complex relationships and interplay between the actors, institutions and processes within public procurement and how these affected the use of evidence in this process.

The research was undertaken from October 2018 to August 2019 using qualitative data collection methods and analysis, including document review and semi-structured interviews. Documents reviewed included both published and unpublished documents. Semi-structured interviews involved key informants from (1) government institutions: OPM, Ministry of Finance, Planning and Economic Development (MoFPED), Uganda National Roads Authority and PPDA; (2) the donor community; and (3) an evaluator representative. The participants interviewed were identified from stakeholder lists included in the appendices of evaluation reports and snowball sampling. Of the 12 potential interviewees, nine responded and were interviewed.

The context

Background to Uganda

The Government of Uganda outlines key strategic priorities for development every five years in a National Development Plan (NDP). The current NDP II introduces an ambitious goal, Vision 2040, which sets out strategies to transform Uganda's economy to middle-income status by 2040 through infrastructure development in energy, oil and roads (European Commission et al., 2015; National Planning Authority & National Planning Authority, 2009).

Uganda receives significant budget support from development partners (DPs), and the World Bank is the biggest contributor, with a contribution estimated at 4.8% of GDP in 2012/13 (European Commission et al., 2015). As such, the interests of DPs have had significant influence on the public financial management reforms undertaken by the government.

Critics often point out that, despite apparently good policy frameworks, implementation is lacking. For example, the World Bank's Country Policy and Institutional Assessment showed that Uganda scored an average of 3.6 against the average score of 3.1 in sub-Saharan Africa.[1] However, on accountability, transparency and corruption in the public sector, Uganda scored a miserly 2.0 against a sub-Saharan Africa average of 2.7 (World Bank & Government of Uganda, 2004).

The institutional context to the procurement sector

An estimated 60% of the country's budget is spent on public procurement, which is comparable to a range of 40%–70% spent by developing countries (Khi V. Thai, 2009). Public procurement is organised in Uganda through the PPDA Act 2003, which defines procurement as 'acquisition by purchase, rental, lease, tenancy, franchise, or any other contractual means, of any type of works, services, or supplies or any combination' (Government of Uganda, 2003).

Public procurement is decentralised, meaning that central and local government entities are responsible for their own procurement processes from planning to implementation (Government of Uganda et al., 2003; Procurement and disposal of assets authority, 2004, 2005). Public procurement processes with government MDAs are managed through a procurement cycle at the procuring and disposing entity (PDE), which includes a user department that initiates the process to procure a service or good, and a procuring and disposal unit (PDU) that coordinates the administrative process. An accounting officer designated by the secretary to the Treasury is responsible for the accountability of funds disbursed to the PDE.

A number of different surveys have concluded that corruption in the government is an acknowledged way of 'doing' business (Procurement and disposal of assets authority, 2011). The World Bank estimated that Uganda lost about USD 500 million to corruption annually before 2011 (Procurement and disposal of assets authority, 2011). During the OPM and the Karuma dam scandals in 2009 and 2002, DPs withdrew and/or froze aid to the government (Harold, 2012; Michael, 2002; Walubiri, 2012).

Influential actors and stakeholders

State actors and stakeholders

The president of Uganda is a leading proponent of public sector reforms and has on several occasions made political proclamations that set the precedent for reforms (Nabyonga-Orem et al., 2014).

Public financial management (PFM), including procurement, falls under the MoFPED, which is responsible for policy formulation, while the PPDA has been established as an autonomous regulatory body that regulates and monitors compliance to the PPDA Act by all government ministries, departments and agencies (MDAs). The MoFPED's Procurement Policy and Management Department is responsible for managing and coordinating public procurement reforms through initiation of public procurement policy reviews.

The PPDA Authority is mandated by the PPDA Act to regulate and monitor compliance and performance and ensure the necessary capacities are in place for public procurement. The Authority recruits and supports procurement officers for all government entities, ensuring interaction between the regulator and implementing entities through capacity building (Government of Uganda, 2003). The PPDA Authority has a research unit and has been involved in a number of research activities to improve the efficiency and effectiveness of procurement reforms. Structural mechanisms are established to ensure that the reports from the research unit are discussed and decisions are made by the Procurement Performance Monitoring System.

The OPM coordinates and implements the strengthening of the national M&E system. The Evaluation Sub-Committee (ESC) is an initiative within OPM to support public sector evaluations through technical guidance and is composed of experts from development partners (DFID and the World Bank), OPM, MoFPED, Uganda Bureau of Statistics and the Economic Policy Research Centre at Makerere University. The topics for evaluation are identified by the permanent secretaries or directors of respective government entities, presented to Cabinet, and discussed in the Joint Budget Support Framework (JBSF). Engaging Cabinet ensures that there is high-level buy-in from government. The prioritised list of evaluations is then agreed on and forwarded to the ESC. The purpose, methods and finances of the evaluations are discussed within the ESC.

> I think the public sector M&E policy is also important because in that policy, we (OPM) articulate requirements, for example, that evaluations should be independent; therefore, we procure evaluators for the public sector; therefore, we are required to follow the necessary laws and regulations concerning procurement.
> (Respondent 7 – Government)

As the system is decentralised, all government entities have discretion over their own procurement. Sectors with unique practices (such as engineering, roads and health) have separate procurement standards and regulations. These institutions are able to instigate reforms, in consultation with PPDA, to ensure that the necessary procurement regulations and guidelines are in place.

Non-state actors and stakeholders

Services and goods are provided to MDAs by the private sector under the guidance of the PPDA. These providers can influence the procurement process through lobbying the MDAs or the PPDA for more flexible policies and standards in accountability, corruption and fraud.

Civil society organisations such as non-governmental organisations, faith-based and community groups are instrumental in presenting community opinions on corruption and malpractices in public procurement. They do so under the umbrella of the Anti-Corruption Coalition Unit as well as other laws, such as the Access to Information Act, 2005, that provide for the right to access of information.

Communities also have an influence through community *barazas*, which were started by OPM in 2009. These are open events, organised by local governments, at which district service providers report on progress and the public is able to discuss issues related to implementation of services and infrastructure in their area. The PPDA also uses them to provide and receive information on specific procurement processes.

> Those Barazas ... are holding the accounting officers accountable. PPDA is presenting those findings to civil society organisations that are making noise when those contracts are not made.
> (Respondent 6 – Government)

Development partners

DPs providing substantial budget support through the Poverty Eradication Action Plan and Poverty Action Fund include the World Bank, DFID, African Development Bank (ADB), United Nations Development Programme (UNDP), United States Agency for International Development (USAID), and Deutsche Gesselleschaft für internationale Zusammenarbeit (GIZ). DPs are particularly interested in how their funds are spent, as they have to report to their respective country's taxpayers. Consequently, they have a high interest in financial accountability and transparency of funds, which led to sustained pressure to institute public financial management reforms, including those on procurement. DPs also support evaluation through providing funding to evaluations, now formalised through pooled funds under the GEF.

> They (DP) have their own rules and guidelines . . . they have the financing agreements – they can make certain policy decisions. So, they (DP) have had a huge influence on public procurement in this country – ADB, World Bank and the like.
> (Respondent 5 – Government)

The policy timeline

The public finance (Tender Board) regulations of 1977 were passed under the 1964 Public Finance Act, which replaced the colonial system where public procurement for most government entities was conducted through a central tender board (Dza et al., 2013; Khi V. Thai, 2009; Sabiiti and Muhumuza, 2012). However, the promulgation of a new constitution in 1995 expanded the size of government:

> The first thing that happened was the decentralisation policy, the many constitutional bodies got created, then acts of parliament created many agencies, privatisation, so many regulators. . . . So it was not feasible to continue with . . . sending requests to a certain unit in the Ministry of Finance to procure a phone, a car, building. It was just not possible anymore.
> (Respondent 5 – Government)

In 1997, a national task force set up by the MoFPED affirmed that the centralised procurement model had outdated regulations and procedures and was fraught with inefficient and fragmented processes, corruption and fraud. The National Task Force made four recommendations for public procurement: drafting and enacting a legal and regulatory framework for public procurement, decentralising public procurement to the procuring entities, establishing a statutory autonomous body to set rules, monitoring procurement and review complaints, and harmonising procurement policies and practices at both central and local levels of government.

In 2001 the public (procurement) finance regulation was enacted, dissolving the Central Tender Board (Khi V. Thai, 2009; Sabiiti and Muhumuza, 2012). In the same year, the World Bank supported the first Country Procurement Assessment Review 2001 (CPAR) to benchmark key performance criteria and the organisation of a public procurement system, which formed the basis of establishing indicators for M&E within the sector. This culminated in the passing and enactment of the Public Procurement and Disposal of Public Assets Act, 2003, regulations, guidelines and policies (Act 1 of 2003) (Government of Uganda et al., 2003), which provided for the establishment of an autonomous body known as Public Procurement and Disposal of Public Assets Authority (PPDA). The Act prescribed the objectives, functions and powers of the Authority, but without provisions for local governments. Therefore, in 2006, the Local Government Act was amended to include these.

In 2009, the government initiated the amendment of the PPDA Act 2003 to include the Local Government Act amendments which was passed by Parliament in 2011. The regulations, standards, guidelines and circulars were completed in 2014 and the Act finally enacted.

The evidence journey

In 2010, priority topics for evaluation had already been decided on between the government and DPs, and the amendments to the PPDA Act of 2003 were underway. Concerns were raised that the amendments did not address the challenges that had previously existed in procurement. The World Bank, in particular, argued that there was a need for an evaluation of the procurement sector to better understand these challenges. The evaluation was commissioned in 2011 by the Government of Uganda through the OPM, with technical assistance from the Technical Administration Support Unit (TASU) of the World Bank and funding from the World Bank and DFID. In October 2012, an Indian consulting firm was contracted by TASU through open tender to carry out the evaluation.

The purpose of the evaluation was to assess the effectiveness of the PPDA Authority on procurement practices in the public sector, with particular focus on the roads and energy sectors. The evaluation had three specific objectives:

- To assess the effectiveness, efficiency and sustainability of procurement reforms/interventions undertaken in Uganda since 2003
- To identify lessons learnt and provide recommendations for informing future PFM interventions in public procurement
- To draw lessons learnt from both intended and unintended results and propose solutions/measures to provide sustainability of successes realised so far.

A three-level management system was set up to provide support and oversight to the consultants during the evaluation – a management committee, a reference group and an evaluation sub-committee to provide support and guidance. These included technical experts in procurement and evaluation from PPDA and OPM. The steering committee played the oversight role, together with TASU.

The use of evaluations in policy making 121

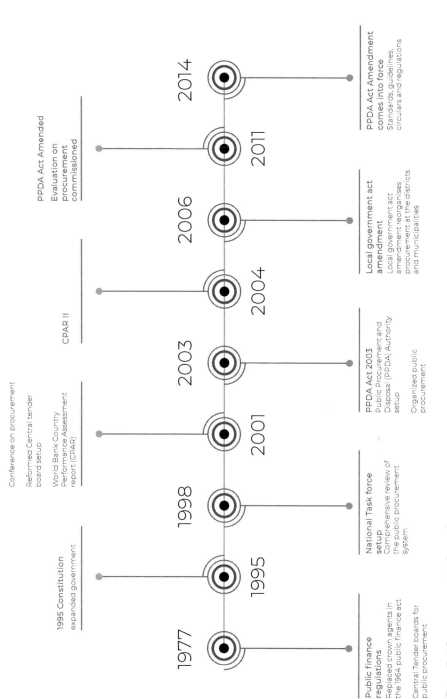

Figure 7.1 Procurement timeline reform
Source: Author generated.

The evaluation was initiated with a scoping mission, during which the consultants met with key stakeholders. Of significance was ensuring buy-in from the PPDA Authority as the lead government agency in the implementation of the evaluation. This was done through meetings and personal contact between the consultant and officials from OPM and the PPDA Authority. The Authority identified and delegated a contact person to act as liaison for the consultant, and office space was provided.

At the beginning, the consultants were invited to comment on the amendment to the PPDA 2003 before it was passed (such as on definitions and clarifications where confusion might ensue), as the amendment process was already underway.

> Now if PPDA Authority did not agree or was not on board in terms of the purpose/ usefulness of this evaluation ... then whatever came out would not be taken on board that easily. That is ... the consultants were presenting their findings every week and these players were picking out what mattered to them.
>
> (Respondent 3 – Government)

The consultants conducted an initial assessment to understand the context of public procurement in Uganda, from which an inception report was drafted and commented on by the steering committee and the PPDA Authority. They then proceeded to implement the evaluation, keeping the steering committee and TASU appraised of the field findings on a monthly basis. The final report was drafted and approved in 2013, commented on, discussed and revised with guidance from the steering committee and the PPDA Authority.[2]

Overall, the evaluation was received positively. The OPM's M&E department considered the evaluation to have had a rigorous methodology and findings were robust.

> We rate this as one of the very good evaluations undertaken – done properly – satisfied with the quality of results. It was international competitive bidding-firm from India became the best. The evaluation sub-committee approved the evaluation report with many comments but were satisfied with the final product.
>
> (Respondent 8 – Government)

Using the findings of the evaluation

In this research, use has been categorised as conceptual, instrumental, process or symbolic (see Chapter 2). Instrumental use of evidence involves responding to specific findings or recommendations, while conceptual use is generally when the evaluation is used to enlighten, influence, inform or clarify a policy issue indirectly (Amara et al., 2004). Negative symbolic use involves applying research results to legitimise or support an already determined decision or policy (Amara et al., 2004), while positive symbolic use increases the profile of the sector or topic.

In terms of instrumental use, the evaluation report had specific recommendations that were adopted in the guidelines, standards and circulars passed by Parliament in 2014, including:

- Revision of procurement thresholds for different bidding methods and implementing a system to update these;
- Flexibility for sectors that need specialised procurement, for example, roads, electricity and health;
- The solicitor general's approval was required for all procurement above UGX 50 million but this created unnecessary delays, especially in sectors that deal with huge budgets (e.g. construction). This was revised to above UGX 200 million but there is still contestation that this is too low for some sectors.

The PPDA Authority was in the middle of revising the Act and the regulations – this evaluation enriched the argument for the revision of the Act and regulations (Key informant 8).

In terms of *conceptual use*, the evaluation demonstrated to PPDA the importance of regularly reviewing and updating regulations, standards and guidelines. Government had undertaken the amendment of the PPDA Act without reviewing its effectiveness and efficiency. Indeed, it can be argued that the evaluation also influenced the use of evidence in the revision of the law in the public procurement sector. This can be shown with the current amendments for the procurement law that are considering using the evaluation as a blueprint for the next evaluation. The evaluation was also reported to have had a significant effect on the conduct of evaluations in Uganda and has been incorporated into the curriculum of students learning about evaluation.

Understanding factors influencing use of evaluation

Demand for evaluation

The evaluation priorities had already been identified and did not include procurement, while the amendment process of PPDA 2003 was already underway (Respondent 8 – Government). It is unlikely that the evaluation would have taken place without pressure from the World Bank and the influence DPs had on government because of the budget support they provided. In addition, there was broad agreement among key players about the complexity of the challenges that the sector had experienced in the past and the need to gather evidence and insights into the underlying reasons behind these.

It is also important to note that while pressure from the DPs was the key driver behind demand, the existence of an evaluation culture with well-developed frameworks and mechanisms provided a mechanism for demand to be implemented, including:

- The existence of a National Evaluation Policy and Board with requirements for and guidance on evaluation;
- Process of identification and prioritisation of evaluation topics involving and driven by leadership within government (permanent secretaries or directors of respective government entities and Cabinet);
- The JBSF, comprising key government institutes and development partners and providing a platform for discussion and influence on prioritisation of evaluation topics.

Interventions that promoted and ensured use

This section hypothesises mechanisms between the approaches and interventions used prior, during and after the evaluation and how this affected the use of evaluation findings and recommendations. These are summarised in Table 7.1 and used to inform lessons and reflections in the final section.

Table 7.1 Use interventions and their effect

Use intervention	Effects and change mechanisms activated enabling use of evaluation
National M&E Policy and National Evaluation Board	Provided requirements for and guidance on evaluation to ensure credibility of evaluations
Independence of implementing agency from beneficiary agency	On setting up evaluation, it was decided that an independent agency oversee it to minimise bias in the event of conflicts of interest. The OPM was the implementing agency and the beneficiary agency, PPDA, provided guidance throughout the evaluation. This was pivotal to the eventual *agreement* with evaluation results, and so likely to be used.
ESC, which selected evaluations and JBSF	Provided clearly defined mechanisms for collaborative identification and prioritisation of evaluation topics involving leadership within government across multiple sectors, arms of government and DPs. This enabled *agreement* between key actors such as OPM and PPDA Authority in particular on the need for evidence to better understand and address policy challenges within the public procurement sector.
Structures and processes for commissioning and managing the evaluation	These ensured credibility (independence, engagement of highly experienced consultants and use of rigorous and robust methods etc.), thereby ensuring *trust* in evidence generated from the evaluation
Regular meetings and consultations between evaluation team and PPDA	This created a platform for building *trust* and *agreement* on evaluation objectives, methodology and approach and the way forward at every stage of the evaluation, enabling a sense of *ownership* and *acceptance* of findings
Regular meetings with stakeholders of the evaluation	Increased *awareness*, *confidence* and *ability* of stakeholders to engage with evaluation process and findings

A key factor identified as influencing use was the extent to which there was a sense of ownership of the process and findings. Ownership can be affected by multiple things: drivers behind demand; ensuring a shared agreement and understanding around the purpose, objectives and methods; the entity commissioning the evaluation (particularly if different from end users), the extent to which political and technical leadership is involved, the way in which consultations and discussions are carried out and so forth.

> One of the challenges was that ownership question. Once these evaluations are decided by somebody outside and that person manages the funds and procures and just sends the person, you rarely find the kind of ownership needed to implement some of these things. Yes, I might have been involved at my level, but we tended to sense that you are briefing the owner (really) like a second party. If an evaluation is being done on impact of procurement reforms, the Executive Director and the highest level should really be at the centre of it all. But if they are being briefed – it is like me coming to you stuff about your house. You are listening to it like I should be knowing better. That ownership question still has to be answered.
> (Key informant 5)

Table 7.1 shows the use interventions that played a role with this evaluation. Many of these arise from the emerging national evaluation system and reflected the need for credibility and ownership.

Barriers and enablers to evidence use

This section identifies and reflects on some of the factors in the wider context which influence use of evidence.

Abilities to understand and navigate the realities of the wider political and social environment

Policy making is a political process that considers the interests of diverse groups. These interests have to be weighed with the greater good by policy makers, taking into consideration factors such as ethics, culture, costs and politics. Whereas Uganda has had a multiparty political system for 13 years, the ruling party has been in power for 30 years. Policies for politically sensitive sectors are often made in favour of the party in power, regardless of the available evidence. Some respondents indicated that politically sensitive sectors are cautious of how they use evidence, as their decisions may be overridden by political decisions.

> Of course, you can't do away with political interference/workmanship because these are political decisions. Evidence is only used to inform these decisions. You need to be aware of the political situation in the country and if it is considered politically sensitive – for example, the agriculture

> evaluation was so politically sensitive. This means that the evidence would still get disregarded.
>
> (Respondent 2 – Non-government)

Political events such as elections, strikes or protests often create environments in which individuals are sensitive to sharing information that may be used against them. Another factor influencing willingness of individuals to provide information is perceived risks associated with confidentiality. In the case of a sector such as procurement that has multiple players, it is easier to trace information back to individuals at the district level than at the national level. This, in turn, created challenges for ensuring that evidence gathered was comprehensive and accurate, which is necessary to ensure credibility and therefore use.

Familiarity with the context is key for findings to be relevant and recommendations feasible.

> It was done by foreigners from India. . . . They did very well in terms of their competencies but . . . all recommendations should have context. You must . . . understand all the different social, political and technological context you are dealing with.
>
> (Respondent 5 – Government)

The *timing* as well as time taken to undertake and finalise an evaluation are important in this regard. This evaluation took two years to complete which may have possibly affected the quality of the discussions during the policy process.

> If, for example, you do an evaluation on energy towards a general election, you will not get a lot of evidence. They will even say why are you doing it at this time when we are going for general elections. So, the timing becomes critical. For example, in this case the PPDA had been in place for some number of years and maybe the findings of the evaluation would trigger the need for a mini or comprehensive review of the Act because much as it was focusing on the two sectors, the principle would cut across.
>
> (Respondent 3 – Government)

National systems and processes guiding evidence

At the national level, there are well-established systems for M&E in the public sector, such as the GEF at the OPM, discussions of performance monitoring reports from the OPM, M&E unit by the Cabinet Secretariat and so forth. Another is the regulatory impact assessment guidelines used by policy makers when considering a policy review (Ministry of Finance Planning and Economic Development, 2004).

Influence of DPs

DPs were influential in evidence use, both positively and negatively. On the one hand, their interest in an environment with proper fiduciary mechanisms and level of influence was instrumental in ensuring that the evaluation was commissioned and used. On the other hand, some respondents spoke about donors pushing their own agendas that might not necessarily be in the best interest of the host country (such as the structural adjustment reforms). In addition, in a situation with limited trust between the host and the donors, the host country might simply agree to an evaluation supported by the donor to appease the donor. However, this often leads to a lack of ownership with the report being shelved and findings not even discussed.

> The World Bank was interested in procurement and paid for the evaluation. There was a lot of push from the World Bank during the process. This could have introduced bias.... But I do not think it should matter because procurement is very important.
> (Respondent 2 – Non-government)

Cultures, systems and capacities

Decision-making structures within the PPDA Authority established a culture in which evidence is reflected on. These structures consider evidence generated through reports from PDEs, audit reports or the government procurement portal and use evidence at different managerial levels. The PPDA has a research unit responsible for gathering evidence about public procurement through monthly reports to the Authority, investigations and audits, in addition to coordinating with research institutions to conduct relevant policy research (e.g. integrity surveys). The reports from the evidence-gathering activities are discussed through structural mechanisms established within PPDA, such as meetings and presentations at each hierarchical administrative level up to the board, so that decisions can be made.

It has been argued that organisations with mechanisms for generating evidence are more likely to build a culture that values the use of evidence within policy making (Goldman, 2018). This was the case with PPDA, which established the PPMS in 2009 as a mechanism for regular gathering of quantitative data. The data collected is summarised and reported on a monthly basis and these reports are shared with the MoFPED, which initiated procurement policies.

The capacity of policy makers to use evidence was raised, and that policy makers' background influences their ability to interpret evidence. Policymakers should understand the value of evidence in policy decisions and how to interpret it to motivate them to use the evidence.

Leaders and champions

In this evaluation, for example, individuals in leadership positions pushed for a stronger M&E function in all government programmes, such as the former permanent secretary in the OPM and the prime minister, championing the use of M&E evidence.

> The PS at the time had just started and thought this was a difficult job. He then looked at what he could use as leverage and discovered that the OPM was responsible for coordination of government business. He empowered

OPM. He looked at the mandate and wondered how you do that. So, there he looked at evaluations.

(Respondent 2 – Non-government)

The experience of the procurement sector showed that adequate and comprehensive stakeholder consultations positively influence the use of evidence in policy-making processes. Engaging enough stakeholders increases the opportunities for evidence to be used in the decision-making processes. During the engagement processes, some of these stakeholders might champion the use of evidence or at times use the evidence directly for policy decisions.

Interview respondents also identified risks associated with the use of evidence by influential individuals. For example, policy makers interested in pushing their own agenda may use the evidence to support an already predetermined position (an example of negative symbolic use).

The nature of the evidence itself

Interview respondents also noted that the reliability of data (actual or perceived) affects how the evidence is used in the policy-making process. Government data is often incomplete or inaccurate leading to lack of trust by policy makers in the data or the sources (Respondent 5 – Government).

Equally important is how evidence is communicated. Researchers need to ensure that it is packaged in an accessible format and easily obtainable and understood. This includes considerations around language, accessibility or media. Evidence and recommendations also need to be specific, providing clarity in findings and guidance. The more generic, the less likely they will be used.

Reflecting and learning from experience

How the context and intervention influence the use of evidence

Context is key, and in that particular context, which mechanisms have led to what outcomes, which we summarise as the Context-Mechanism-Opportunity configuration. We take the *mechanisms* to include the actual evidence generation, interventions applied to promote use and change mechanisms (such as building agreement or awareness) that these use interventions sought to achieve. The *immediate outcomes* were changes in capability, opportunity or motivation to use evidence, while the *wider outcomes* were actual changes in policy or practice.

Key elements in the wider context in this case study were a fairly well-established national evaluation system which provided a framework for evaluations required and informed decision-making processes. There was also a recognised need for reforms within the procurement sector and pressure from the World Bank to undertake the evaluation to support the reform process. The evidence generation process was felt to be robust and credible, carried out by a well-qualified independent consultant guided by evaluation clients and the beneficiary agency, PPDA.

Mechanisms critical to ensuring use of the evaluation findings included processes and structures that enabled ownership and trust in the process. These included the use of committees for oversight and technical guidance, involvement of stakeholders and credible consultants at all stages. In addition, regular meetings with the client, beneficiaries and wider stakeholders strengthened awareness, confidence and the ability of stakeholders to engage with the evaluation process and findings. The quality of the evaluation and trust in the process ensured the motivation to utilise findings, and the sector reform process created the opportunity to do so.

Ultimately, this resulted in revision of the Act and regulations (i.e. instrumental use of the evaluation findings). In addition, the evaluation demonstrated the value and importance of evidence in decision making and is informing the conduct of evaluation in the country.

Lessons for the country and beyond

Ensuring independence

For a sector such as procurement, with significant levels of funding and affecting multiple other sectors and stakeholders, the level of independence, real or perceived, is critical to maintaining a sense of credibility and trust, and therefore ensuring use of evaluation findings.

In this case, independence was maintained by a separation of roles between the agencies commissioning, implementing, and the ultimate users of the evaluation. The organisational structure of the evaluation provided the process with independence from political interference, which also enabled the evaluation team to engage with respondents at ease. Some of the key features of this structure included agreement on purpose and relevance of the evaluation by key decision makers in Cabinet and the JBSF, while PPDA's role was primarily to provide technical guidance, ensuring that evaluation was aligned with the sector policy needs, providing feedback, commenting on reports and so forth.

Ownership

Across many countries in Africa, the role and influence of DPs is significant as a result of budget and other support. In situations where DPs are involved in evidence generation and use, attention needs to be paid to ensuring local ownership of the process and findings.

This case study demonstrated the importance of an evaluation process that the PPDA considered its own. The stakeholders had preparatory meetings with GPCL consultants, chaired by the executive director of the PPDA. A liaison officer was selected as the PPDA contact person to work with the consultants and office space was provided for them by the PPDA. In initial meetings, stakeholders agreed on the purpose of the evaluation and way forward. There was constant interaction between consultants and the PPDA. The positive nature of the relationship was reflected by the invitation extended to the consultants to comment on the amendment before it was passed by Parliament. However, there was also a feeling that since the initiation of the evaluation came from the OPM and not the PPDA, the evaluation was imposed on the PPDA without significantly involving senior management. Overall, there was a positive effect on the openness of the Authority to the evaluation and willingness to utilise findings in the regulations, guidelines and standards in the amendment process.

Credibility and trust

Evidence that is not trusted and perceived as credible is unlikely to be used. Efforts to ensure credibility of the evaluation included using an independent agency to provide oversight (OPM), procuring a competent consultant for the task and ensuring rigorous and robust methods. The consultants undertook a scoping mission to understand the context, and baseline surveys on public procurement. During the evaluation, the consultant had monthly progress meetings with the evaluation sub-committee to update on progress and agree on a way forward. These meetings kept the stakeholders appraised of and provided valuable feedback to the evaluation process. In addition to the meetings, the consultant provided reports – inception, activity, scoping and final – that were commented on by the PPDA and evaluation sub-committee before being adopted as final reports. These efforts allowed the stakeholders to trust the findings from the evaluation and consider them during the amendment of the regulations, guidelines and standards.

> Continuous feedback in the process is critical because it brings out the challenges that one is encountering during the evaluation process and that helps with coming up with strategies to address them before the final thing. But also, weekly feedback helps the stakeholder, the beneficiary, to know whether the evaluation is on track and likely to meet the purpose why it was initiated.
> (Respondent 3 – Government)

Capability

Irrespective of how credible or robust an evaluation may be, it needs to be received within an environment that is capable of utilising the evidence. This capability is determined by culture, structures and processes, skills and technical experience.

The PPDA put in place structures and processes such as public procurement management system (PPMS) to continuously gather data and statistics on the state of public procurement and processes and to discuss these results at different managerial levels. The authority had also previously commissioned surveys, especially on corruption within the public procurement system, and had in place structures to discuss and consider the findings from all evidence-gathering activities. The evaluation was jointly conducted by consultants and members of the PPDA, thereby increasing the PPDA's skills in conducting evaluations, as well as interpreting and communicating the evidence to policy makers.

A final thought

The Ugandan government has taken steps in institutionalising the use of evidence with structures and policies to support evidence generation, translation to policies, and implementation. The OPM has been at the forefront of driving the evidence agenda in government through the GEF and Evaluation Subcommittee and through chairing the JBSF. There is also a M&E framework and regulatory impact assessment guide among policies that guide government entities in the implementation of evidence-informed policy making in their departments. However, in practice, evidence-informed policy making in Uganda is always going to be a challenge because many decisions are political and made without consideration of the evidence. This case study presents an opportunity to understand some of the reasons behind this and hopefully the insights generated may contribute to addressing the persistent challenges and barriers to use.

Notes

1 A weighted score that assesses a country's sustainable growth and reduction of poverty across 16 criteria. It has a minimum score of 1 and maximum of 6.
2 Examples of bottlenecks and issues identified by evaluation include:

- Procurement thresholds have not been revised since 2003;
- The procurement plan is not systematically used as a monitoring tool;
- Absence of specialised standard bidding documents for infrastructure sector such as design and build, performance-based contracting;
- Delays in approval from contracts committee at almost all stages of procurement cycle;
- Delays in obtaining approval from the Solicitor General for contracts above UGX 50 million.

References

Amara, N., Ouimet, M. and Landry, R. 2004. New evidence on instrumental, conceptual, and symbolic utilization of university research in government agencies. *Science Communication*, 26(1), 75–106. https://doi.org/10.1177/1075547004267491

Dza, M., Fisher, R. and Gapp, R. 2013. Procurement reforms in Africa: The strides, challenges, and improvement opportunities. *Public Administration Research*, 2(2). https://doi.org/10.5539/par.v2n2p49

European Commission, Independent Evaluation Group, & Government of Uganda. 2015. *Joint evaluation of budget support to Uganda final report*. Kampala: European Commission, Independent Evaluation group, Government of Uganda.

Goldman, I. 2018. *Baseline on performance M&E culture in the public sector in Uganda, Benin and South Africa*. Wits.

Government of Uganda, Ministry of Health, & Ministry of Agriculture, F. and A.I. 2003. *Uganda food and nutrition policy*.

Harold, E.A. 2012. What lies beneath the corruption in the office of the Prime Minister? *Daily Monitor*.

Khi, V.T. 2009. *International handbook of public procurement*. 6000 Broken Sound Parkway NW, Suite 300 Boca Raton, FL 33487–2742: Taylor and Francis.

Michael, P. 2002. AES uncovers bribery in Bujagali Dam Project. *New Vision*.

Ministry of Finance Planning and Economic Development 2004. A guide to good regulation. In: PROGRAMME, R. B. P. (ed.). Kampala: Government of Uganda.

Nabyonga-Orem, J., Ssengooba, F., Mijumbi, R., Kirunga Tashobya, C., Marchal, B. and Criel, B. 2014. Uptake of evidence in policy development: The case of user fees for health care in public health facilities in Uganda. *BMC Health Services Research*, 14(1), 639. https://doi.org/10.1186/s12913-014-0639-5

National Planning Authority, & National Planning Authority. 2009. *National development plan 2010/11–2014/15*.

Procurement and disposal of assets authority. 2004. *Annual report (Year Ended 2004)*. Procurement and Disposal of Assets Authority.

Procurement and disposal of assets authority. 2005. *Report of the fifth procurement sector review*. Workshop held on 29 June 2005 at Speke Report Munyonyo.

Procurement and disposal of assets authority. 2011. *Annual report for financial year 2010/11*. Kampala: Procurement and Disposal of Assets Authority.

Sabiiti, C.K. and Muhumuza, E. 2012. *Second generation procurement. Moving from compliance to results in public procurement. Trends, challenges and opportunities from the Uganda experience*. Presented at the International Public procurement conference, Seattle, USA.

Walubiri, M. 2012. Nsibambi regrets OPM scandal. *New Vision*.

World Bank & Government of Uganda. 2004. *Country procurement assessment report (CPAR)*. Kampala: The World Bank.

8 Rapidly responding to policy queries with evidence

Learning from Rapid Response Services in Uganda

Ismael Kawooya, Isaac Ddumba, Edward Kayongo and Rhona Mijumbi-Deve

Summary

The Rapid Response Service (RRS) is a knowledge translation service in Uganda that responds to a decision maker's needs for evidence with synthesised relevant evidence, contextualised and summarised in an accessible package. The RRS was set up in 2010 at the Regional East African Health Policy Initiative, Uganda node, at Makerere University, and has supported over 65 policy processes at the national and district levels. This chapter follows three cases where this evidence was used to inform policy or practice, one involving the RRS at national level, the mandatory food fortification policy, and two at district level, focusing on community distribution of misoprostol to women and reducing the turnaround time for Gene Xpert results, both in Mukono District. The evidence from the RRS was used in different ways, leading to the mandatory food fortification policy after a voluntary food fortification programme, sensitising stakeholders to implement a controversial misoprostol distribution programme to reduce postpartum haemorrhage, and to reduce the turnaround time for diagnosis of tuberculosis.

Introduction

The Rapid Response Service (RRS) is a promising knowledge translation innovation established to respond to urgent, targeted and tailored individual policy makers and institutional needs for evidence, initially in the health field. The evidence requested is synthesised, summarised and contextualised to a particular policy problem and local setting within the time needed for a policy decision to be made. The RRS at Makerere University in Uganda defines 'urgent' as a policy decision that must be taken within 28 days (Mijumbi et al., 2014). The RRS was piloted and set up in 2010 at the Regional East African Community Health Policy Initiative (REACH-PI), Uganda node, at Makerere University, College of Health Sciences, the largest and oldest academic university in Uganda. Since 2010, the service has supported over 65 health care policy processes (Mijumbi-Deve et al., 2017).

This case study uses three separate but related mini-cases to share experiences and lessons on the use of RRS and factors that enable or hinder its use. The first case relates to use at the national level, where RRS responded to policy questions on the national voluntary food fortification programme. The setting for the second and third cases is at the sub-national level, examining how RRS was used to support decisions by the district health team (DHT) in Mukono District.

Qualitative data collection methods, including document review and semi-structured interviews, were employed for this case study. The document review included both published and unpublished documents related to the RRS food fortification programme and health services delivery at the district level. Nine key informants were purposively identified and interviewed using semi-structured interviews based on their involvement in the three case studies.

Understanding the context

The health sector

The population of Uganda is estimated at 42 million as of 2018 (World Bank, 2019), with the majority residing in rural areas. Uganda is a low-income country with an estimated GDP growth of 5.3% in 2018 (African Development Bank, 2019). Health care funding is inadequate, with total health expenditure estimated at 7.2% of GDP. The sector is characterised by a household out-of-pocket health care expenditure estimated at 41% (WHO, 2017).

The Ugandan health care system is largely decentralised, with most primary services provided by local governments at the district or lower sub-county level, covering health care service delivery and implementation of primary health care (Bossert and Beauvais, 2002). Health care financing, planning, decision making, mobilisation of resources and coordination of services are part of the central function of the Ministry of Health (MOH) (Ministry of Environment, Water and Natural Resources, 2015).

Health care service delivery is organised through a hierarchy of administrative/referral levels from the village health team (VHT), followed by Health Centres, which refer patients on to HC IV or district hospital level, responsible for the implementation of primary health care and supervision of the lower health facilities. The district is the next administrative level responsible for coordination, supervision and implementation of health services at the district (Ministry of Health, 2013). The regional and national referral hospitals are the higher points of health care service delivery, to which the lower health facilities eventually refer patients.

The lower level decision-making structural processes include the district health teams (DHTs) and the Health Sub-district (HSD) management team at the sub-county level, responsible for planning, organising and coordination of health services within the district and HSD, respectively. These form the extended DHT that meets once every quarter at the district and the HSD, respectively, to discuss challenges in the implementation and coordination of health programmes within the district.

Policy making can be influenced by a number of actors, such as Cabinet; other government entities, such as the Office of the Prime Minister and Ministry of Finance, Planning and Economic Development; other ministries, departments or agencies; Parliament; civil society or non-governmental organisations (e.g. Uganda National Health Consumers Organisation); the private sector;

development partners (DPs), and public and private tertiary academic institutions involved in research.

The Rapid Response Service

The story of the RRS in Uganda begins with REACH-PI, established 15 years ago to replicate the success of the Tanzania Essential Health Interventions project (TEHIP). TEHIP, which was conducted in two districts in Tanzania in 1999, showed that the use of research evidence had significant positive effects on the implementation of policies in the communities (Kammen et al., 2006; Kasale et al., 2004). REACH-PI was therefore set up to bridge the gap between researchers and decision makers in an iterative, dynamic and interactive fashion using cutting-edge mechanisms and designs such as the piloting of the RRS in 2010 (Kammen et al., 2006). From 2010–2012, the RRS supported decision makers at the MOH, civil society organisations, private institutions and DPs through a pilot phase, by the end of which the RRS had supported over 65 policies in two years (Mijumbi-Deve et al., 2017). Following this success, the International Development Research Council, Canada, provided funding to REACH-PI from 2015 to scale up the RRS at the national and sub-national level. There was specific interest for including the sub-national level because they were not represented in the pilot phase, despite having shown early enthusiasm for the service, and it was important to understand the factors that would enable or hinder the use of the RRS at the sub-national level (Mijumbi et al., 2014; Mijumbi-Deve et al., 2017).

RRS is demand driven and the commitment is to respond to the need for evidence to inform decisions in crisis situations (real or perceived) within 28 days. The service was set up to benefit a wide range of users in the health sector at senior to mid-levels including policy makers in government at all levels, civil society, academia, multi- and bilateral DPs and the private sector. The scope of the services is defined to include governance, delivery arrangements, health financing and health technology assessment (Mijumbi et al., 2014). Researchers hired by the RRS support policy making through searching, appraising, summarising and contextualising research evidence, and they maintain regular contact with decision makers and other stakeholders while doing so.

The service model was designed in 2010 specifically to meet the needs of the country. The need for evidence in relation to a specific policy concern or challenge is identified by a decision maker. This may include clarification of a policy problem, identifying policy options and/or implementing strategies for a policy option (Mijumbi et al., 2014). The decision maker then contacts RRS, which triggers a cascade of steps starting with clarifying the question and expressing it in an answerable format, organisational arrangements, health financing, governance, implementation strategies and health technology. Policy queries that are out of scope for the service are rejected and where possible, redirected.

After the question clarification step, the researchers search for relevant systematic reviews and appraise, contextualise and summarise the evidence in a maximum of four pages, in a jargon-free language understood by the policy maker (Mijumbi et al., 2014; Mijumbi-Deve and Sewankambo, 2017). The summary brief is then reviewed by local and external experts, often from within the RRS network or identified as authors in the literature cited (Mijumbi et al., 2014). Once the corrections and inputs from the review process have been responded to, the brief is submitted to the decision maker within the time agreed on between the policy maker and user. After this, the brief is used to present evidence in policy discussions, including stakeholder dialogue and debates. Recommendations emerging from stakeholder dialogue or other forums are a secondary product in the RRS.

The cases

The mandatory food fortification regulation

TRANSITIONING FROM DEVELOPMENT FUNDED INITIATIVES

Food fortification is aimed at increasing the coverage of micronutrients in the most prevalent local foods or supplements (Harvey et al., 2010; WHO Regional Office for Africa, 2013). Today, this is a priority of the Ugandan MOH Health Sector Strategic Plan (Government of Uganda, 2005; Ministry of Health, 2019) and required by law. Fortification is done for selected food products; oil, salt, maize and wheat, with micro-nutrients such as vitamins, iron, zinc and folic acid.

In 1996 at the United Nations, Uganda signed onto the global commitments to end micronutrient deficiencies. This prompted a series of initiatives, including projects financed by DPs, particularly USAID. In 2002, a National Working Group (NWG) on Food Fortification was established at the MOH to provide leadership in the food fortification programme. In 2004, voluntary regulations and standards for food fortification, the Food and Drugs Act (Food Fortification) Regulations were passed by Parliament and a national food fortification campaign programme was started. Only one large private industry participated in the programme, adding fortificants to oil and flour (Fiedler and Afidra, 2010).

The East Central and Southern Africa food fortification guidelines were developed in 2007, prompting all member states of East Africa to ensure standardised food fortification. Soon after, the Global Alliance for Improved Nutrition (GAIN)[1] provided the Ministry of Health with a grant to strengthen the voluntary food fortification programme. A multi-sectoral NWG[2] was set up at the Ministry of Health with support from the director general of Health Services. In 2008 a food consumption survey supported by USAID assessed the dietary intake in the different regions in Uganda. This survey formed the benchmark for assessing the different food vehicles that could be used to deliver fortificants. The programme involved testing and purchasing of the machines and fortificants including vitamin A, zinc and iron for the private sector. This encouraged private industries to fortify oil, flour and wheat, and over 80% of industries participated and complied with food fortification regulations and standards. As such the programme was considered a success (WHO Regional Office for Africa, 2013).

> The industries were ready to do it and that made it possible. This was a very expensive venture and that is where the development partner came in. We

had to ship in most of the equipment that was used. The fortificants were very expensive.

(Respondent 7 – Non-government)

SEEKING EVIDENCE TO INFORM DIALOGUE AND THE DEVELOPMENT OF STRATEGIES FOR SUSTAINABILITY

In 2011, the grant was coming to an end and concerns emerged around the sustainability of the programme as industrial food fortification was still voluntary and the cost heavily subsidised by a grant. Since these costs would be assumed by the private industries, it was feared that they would drop out. Consequently, a representative of the DP for GAIN approached a researcher from the RRS to request evidence for the steps to ensure that the programme continued after the funding ended.

The RRS provided the following two relevant rapid response briefs:

- The first affirmed that food fortification was a proven and preferred strategy for alleviating micronutrient deficiencies because it was shown to be effective, cost effective, and achieved a wider population coverage in high quality studies.
- The second summarised evidence on how a public health (food fortification) programme can be sustained. A key message was that successful implementation and careful consideration of sustainability at the inception of the programme are essential components for sustainability.

These briefs enabled the DP to request REACH-PI to coordinate a national policy dialogue with the MOH and all stakeholders around the sustainability of the programme. Stakeholders from the NWG were first consulted on the sustainability of the programme. Their inputs were incorporated into a draft report that was tabled for discussion during the dialogue. With much input from the DP who met the costs for fortification, consensus was reached on the need for mandatory regulations because the food fortification programme had been voluntary.

The DP noted that there was a danger of reversing these successes if the costs for fortification are incurred by some willing private industries. They would be forced to pass on these costs to the final consumer, making their products more expensive and less competitive. A mandatory policy was therefore necessary to ensure all industry players were obliged to fortify the included foods.

Community distribution of misoprostol to women in Mukono district

PILOTING A CONTROVERSIAL HEALTH STRATEGY

In 2009, the reported maternal mortality rate in Uganda was high, averaging 438 per 100,000 live births (Uganda Bureau of Statistics (UBOS) and ICF International Inc, 2012). It was estimated that almost one in four maternal deaths was due to postpartum haemorrhage (PPH). Pregnant women were delivering at home without medical support because of the inadequacies at health facilities such as shortage of health workers, no refrigerators and stock outs of uterotonics such as oxytocin.

During this period, the WHO issued a recommendation that misoprostol be used in the third stage of labour where superior uterotonics such as oxytocin were not readily available (WHO, 2009). An opinion piece in *Lancet* 2011, advocated for community distribution of misoprostol as a way of ending morbidity and mortality due to PPH (Potts et al., 2010). A number of DPs including the Maverick Collective's Population Service Initiative (PSI) supported this recommendation and several low-income countries began providing misoprostol in peripheral health facilities.

The Programme for Accessible Health Communication and Education (PACE) Uganda, a local non-governmental organisation, conducted an initial pilot in Mubende District in 2012 that proved the feasibility of distributing misoprostol to pregnant mothers during the last trimester. With funding from the PSI, PACE Uganda advocated for community distribution of misoprostol to the MOH and requested to test its feasibility in five selected districts. An implementation strategy was designed by PACE, experts at the MOH and an independent expert from Makerere University. A key focus was to ensure restricted supply, and a robust communication strategy to ensure the proper use of misoprostol. Once approved by the MOH, PACE Uganda engaged the DHTs in the selected districts.

SEEKING EVIDENCE TO MINIMISE RISK

In rolling out this strategy, PACE Uganda approached the DHT at Mukono district for their input and approval for a pilot programmatic study involving distributing misoprostol using the existing emergency kits for pregnant mothers, known as a 'mama kit'. Interviewees noted a number of problems, however.

The most common indication for misoprostol is abortion, which made it controversial in the community. Its misuse for abortions would create a perceived conflict of interest of the Implementation Partner (IP), PACE Uganda, whose projects focused on sexual reproductive health, particularly family planning. In addition, misoprostol is only available with a doctor's prescription and through a pharmacist. Instead, the pilot study was proposing distribution through VHTs, who had minimal academic qualifications.

> Misoprostol had conflicting issues. We have a partner who has been working in family planning, that is PACE then comes out with a different project which was using VHTs to distribute 'mama-kit' which contained misoprostol and that was not a policy. So we thought it prudent that it not being a policy, there would be issues which Mukono District might answer.
> (Respondent 1 – Government)

Before accepting the pilot programme, the district needed surety against misuse of the drug and evidence of due diligence on the effects of community distribution of misoprostol. The DHT requested the RRS for support to gather evidence around the optimal distribution mechanisms of misoprostol to inform a meeting between the DHT and PACE Uganda about the way forward.

> My District Health Officer (DHO) is proactive and he fears (being) incriminated. So he said, [mentions name], you better ask [RRS] and see what they tell us because if they give misoprostol and they get issues it will be me who gets to answer which means that the DHO is fully answerable to whatever they [IP] do [sic].
> (Respondent 2 – Government)

The research question was clarified thus: 'How can distribution of misoprostol to pregnant women for the prevention of PPH be optimised?' The brief described three models for the distribution of misoprostol, depending on who administers it. They also emphasised that evidence from the studies showed that providing misoprostol to pregnant women did not reduce health facility deliveries.

Reducing the turnaround time for Gene Xpert results for TB in Mukono district

In 2012, Uganda started using the Gene Xpert MTB/RIF[3] in selected health facilities to improve the diagnosis and burden of tuberculosis by improving the case detection rate (Hanrahan et al., 2016). However, because of the prohibitive costs of purchasing and maintaining the machines and cartridges, a few selected facilities with high patient volume centres were made central referral facilities for more than one peripheral facility for Gene Xpert MTB/RIF. Motorcycle riders followed predetermined schedules and routes to transport sputum specimens to and from central facilities.

Respondents noted that this system caused delays in returning results to patients and led to dropouts.

> Because we have hub riders the problem by then was that the hub riders were not delivering the results in time. We had cases where patients were waiting for results for close to two months and with the rapid response team we were guided. We increased the number of hub riders.
> (Respondent 8 – Government)

DHT had quality improvement meetings in 2015 to identify and improve efficiencies, for example, increasing the number of riders and trips to facilities. However, this was not successful in addressing challenges.

> They were trying to increase hub riders then too, they wanted to get someone who can sit down and sort the results. The results were being mistakenly taken to other facilities and yet there were still issues. Even though you get someone to sort results still the[re] would be errors because they are

human. And also they had improvised that as we wait for the Gene Xpert MTB/RIF to do ZN.[4]

(Respondent 1 – Government)

The Mukono DHT approached the RRS for relevant evidence for a brainstorming meeting with the IP about improving the turnaround time for Gene Xpert MTB/Rif. The question was: 'How can the sputum specimen referral system be strengthened to reduce the turnaround time in Mukono district?' The brief to the policy maker summarised relevant evidence, which was scarce at the time. However, based on the experiences of the early infant diagnosis specimen referral system in HIV, three options were suggested: considering adopting innovative technologies such as SMS/GPRS printers, using VHTs to link patients to the sputum specimen referral, and conducting a systems diagnosis for a local cause.

Using the evidence

It is not always possible to isolate a linear relationship between the generation and use of evidence obtained from the RRS, including its conceptual, symbolic or instrumental use. Conceptual use refers to using evidence to elucidate a policy during discussions; symbolic use refers to using evidence to legitimise or support a predetermined position; and instrumental use refers to direct and specific use in the decision-making process (Amara et al., 2004).

Conceptual use

Evidence from the RRS is often used by the decision maker to stimulate debate and clarify issues and evidence in policy-making forums. Evidence relating to the national food fortification programme focused on ensuring sustainability of the programme and was taken up in the national policy dialogue. The stakeholders from the NWG on Food Fortification discussed the challenges of ensuring sustainability with little or no ownership from the MOH, and the importance of having adequate resources. At first, it was feared that the mandatory programme would be unsustainable for participating private industries because the costs of fortification would make their products more expensive and less competitive than those of industries not fortifying. Some industries who had been left out of earlier discussions but who were necessary for the success of the programme were brought into the National Policy dialogue discussions. These included the Ministries of Justice and Trade.

> This had to be done properly to get the industry on board. It was important for them to be part of the process from the start. I have to acknowledge the efforts of private sector import in the fortification.
> (Respondent 7 – Non-government)

An example of conceptual use at district level was that the evidence provided to the district clarified initial perspectives about the possible abuse of misoprostol and a mistrust in how distribution was to be achieved. The evidence confirmed that there were no reported cases of abortions among pregnant women provided with misoprostol at over 12 weeks of gestation, and that the distribution actually increased the number of health facility deliveries. The district also used evidence of the successful distribution of misoprostol to sensitise the community and health care workers.

> I was surprised actually it had worked. In your evidence, they had done a trial in Mubende. I did not know that. We did it in our own context. We modified it to suit our contexts.
> (Respondent 1 – Government)

Symbolic use

Evidence from RRS can be used to support a pre-determined position of the policy maker. For example, the district leadership articulated concerns about the distribution of misoprostol in the community, anticipating possible repercussions if it affected any woman adversely. The synthesised evidence clarified a number of perceptions about any possible adverse effects.

Instrumental use

Evidence can be used directly in the formulation of policy options and/or implementation strategies. For example, the brief provided by the RRS to the district health leadership identified strategies for increasing the efficiencies and turnaround time for Gene Xpert MTB/RIF. Some of the suggestions were implemented, for example, the use of GPRS printers for all hub points and mobile phones.

> The issue was delay. Then when that was done, they had to connect CPHL servers to Mukono servers. So as soon as they are done, they are relayed as they are done. The other thing was they would send text messages to those facilities which were far that these were results for patients a, b, c and d. Then others they would print. Then in a space of three days, the patient would get treatment there and then.
> (Respondent 1 – Government)

Understanding the factors that enabled and hindered use of evidence

Demand for evidence from RRS

Important drivers for the demand for evidence from the RRS included the presence of champions and need. RRS is demand driven and responds to needs identified by the decision makers. All three examples cited earlier were difficult or controversial and therefore unlikely to have been resolved without evidence to inform and bridge the different views.

Another driver of demand is the need to justify funding to, for example, DPs. The users often want use evidence to improve their justification for funding.

> There was credible information that had to be trusted and this also motivated the DPs to continue funding. Actually, the food fortification programme is still going on.
> (Respondent 7 – Non-government)

Use interventions that triggered change to enable use

The briefs provided by the RRS do not in themselves trigger use of the evidence they contain. A number of interventions are often used concurrently to strengthen uptake and eventual use. These are illustrated in the examples in the following subsections.

Visibility

The team at Makerere University invests in ensuring that decision makers are informed of the existence, value added and importance of RRS. They do so through regular formal and informal interaction with networks at the districts and the MOH in trainings, meetings, etc. For example, in the food fortification programme, the policy maker heard about the RRS from an acquaintance who had received an RRS brief. She then requested evidence on the sustainability of the food fortification programme. In another example, in Mukono the RRS sensitised leaders about the RRS in 2016 as it piloted its sub-national phase.

The team also engages in advocacy for the research product using social marketing and so forth. Research is also carried out to understand the target group and how best to communicate and package messages, ensuring that communication, awareness raising, and advocacy are effective.

These efforts created *awareness* about and positive attitudes towards RRS, enabling use of evidence in decision making.

Decision-making cultures

The interviewees noted more demand for evidence in units where decisions are taken through comprehensive and inclusive consultations, which then enables evidence use. At district level the review meetings spurred a demand for evidence.

> Evidence was existing in the district but in a rudimentary way. We have got a district quality assurance committee, so they used to do analysis . . . and

they come up with strategies, but those strategies were not informed by evidence but still it was there. So, when evidence comes in it just bridges.

(Respondent 1 – Government)

Accessibility

RRS provides evidence contextualised to the policy maker's setting, appraised and summarised in simple language and an accessible format to facilitate decision making. Relevance and accessibility ensure *understanding* of the evidence and how it relates to policy questions and needs.

Dialogue and interaction

The RRS process includes dialogue and interaction between researchers, decision makers and members of the public with a stake in the particular policy question. Respondents also noted that evidence use is increased when those who generate and use the information are involved in the evidence-informed decision-making process. For example, in the cases at the district level in this chapter, the assistant DHO attended training on the RRS for district officials and maintained contact with the team about different policy concerns he needed support with before the evidence request was put forward to RRS.

Regular dialogue and interaction allow for the building of *relationships* and *trust* between decision makers, stakeholders and researchers as well as an *understanding* of one another's realities and perspectives, all of which can be central to enabling evidence use.

Demand-driven approaches

RRS responds to queries and requests raised by decision makers. The specific evidence is requested to address a specific policy concern and through an iterative engagement process between the decision maker and researcher, the questions are clarified and defined. This ensures *ownership* of the evidence generated and increases the probability of use.

Credible processes

The generation of evidence by known and trusted experts in a particular area enables *trust* in the evidence, increasing the likelihood of use. The decision makers view the systematic and transparent processes and neutrality of the RRS as important for the use of evidence.

> The game changer was when we engaged [mentions name] who had done his studies around that. He is an authority in Uganda about maternal and child health. So, he gave a lot of input on how we would manage the mothers and how we would exclude, for example, those with complicated

pregnancies. We would exclude them because that would increase their risk for PPH.

(Respondent 5 – Non-government)

Another strategy to ensure credibility was submitting the briefs to trusted, knowledgeable leadership in the particular area, who then present it to stakeholders.

Changes in capability, motivation and opportunity

The RRS provides training to decision makers to sensitise them about the value for evidence-informed decision making, and how to find and appraise the evidence. Through working with researchers, the decision makers develop the ability to articulate their needs for evidence as they become more aware of the question clarification process and are able to define their policy queries.

The RRS promotes evidence use by responding promptly to decision makers' needs. This motivates them to seek evidence and increases their confidence during discussions.

Barriers and enablers to use

Evidence is generated and use interventions employed in a wider context that can influence actual use of evidence positively or negatively. Factors identified in the three cases enabling and hindering use of evidence generated from RRS are discussed in further detail in the following subsections.

Macro-context

LEVELS OF PRIORITY

The profile of a particular policy matter can be raised by external influences, within the region or more globally. For example, the East, Central and Southern Africa Community was influential in ensuring that Uganda undertake a food fortification programme according to the set standards, making it relevant to consider evidence for the sustainability of the food fortification programme. The pilot of the community distribution of misoprostol followed a recommendation from the WHO in 2009 to justify its implementation.

It emerged that evidence for the policy of a specific programme is easier to use if it has been identified as a priority within the country. For example, the food fortification programme was mentioned both in the Health Sector Strategic Plan and the National Development Plan, making the evidence for the sustainability of the programme relevant to the ministry's objectives, thus giving the RRS the ability to convene a national policy dialogue (MOH, 2019).

AUTONOMY TO MAKE DECISIONS

Respondents noted that decentralisation enables officials at the lower level of the health system to seek evidence for a policy concern by giving them autonomy to make decisions. A stakeholder noted that being able to make an impactful decision allows these officials to consider evidence that can affect a public health programme within their jurisdiction.

(Respondent 1 – Government)

POLITICAL INFLUENCE

Respondents noted that politicians at any level can influence a community's opinion, thus thwarting a course of action. In such situations, the technical leadership seeks evidence as an insurance policy. This was highlighted in the case for the distribution of misoprostol where any adverse event would make it hard to argue for misoprostol with the politicians if there was no evidence.

> We work with politicians. If you make an issue and the mother dies, even though you have a Ministry of Health letter, the DHO will call on 'kanzindalo (megaphone)' to explain why the mother died and the DHO sent people to kill. They were like I would rather have evidence to back me up if it goes beyond my limit of control.
>
> (Respondent 2 – Government)

Where there is political support and/or demand for evidence from politicians a respondent noted that:

> Then also you can [also] think about the political support was also key, because Mukono has most of the time been working with our political leaders [sic] and they have helped us a lot especially in mobilisation, supporting some of the things that are supposed to be approved by the local council.
>
> (Respondent 2 – Government)

Institutional context

RELATIONSHIPS AND TRUST

Interview respondents discussed the impact of relationships and levels of trust between the knowledge broker and the district leadership on positive perspectives and responses to the evidence. 'Having good working relationship on social grounds can make you really make a positive decision. . . . but if you are not on good terms, a positive decision becomes a problem' (Respondent 8 – Government).

Organisational cultures and capabilities

DECISION-MAKING RESPONSIBILITIES

Interviewees noted that how individuals at different levels perceive their responsibilities can affect their demand for evidence and its eventual use. For example, where district officials saw themselves as implementers rather than decision makers, they did not engage with the evidence (Respondent 1 – Government). They indicated that once a department or institution is empowered to take policy decisions, it is more likely to consider evidence in making them. At local government level, the district health office is empowered to take decisions related to health and only has to inform the Chief Administrative Officer, who is the overall accounting officer for the district.

In addition, stakeholders also noted the importance of empowering individuals, especially at junior levels, to undertake policy decisions and therefore seek evidence for those decisions.

STRUCTURES AND PROCESSES

Stakeholders noted that evidence is more likely to be considered in a department that demands accountability. Respondents noted that health District League Tables, which are published and presented at annual gatherings at the Joint Review Missions, are an accountability tool that encourages policy makers to consider evidence to improve their performance.

Stakeholders also reported that the way the system is structured to report its findings affects how evidence is used. Health care policy makers are required by the system to report on the performance of specific indicators, particularly quantitative ones. They therefore consider evidence to improve quantitative measurements but not the quality of processes in implementation.

Feedback mechanisms were also identified as being important. Respondents gave the example of Mukono District that uses feedback as a form of quality assurance for the RRS brief once submitted to the district. This feedback mechanism encourages discussion on the evidence provided.

Interviewees noted that having mechanisms for generating data facilitates the demand for evidence and subsequently a culture where evidence is sought for a number of policy concerns. For example, at the district level, the Health Management Information System is used by biostatisticians to inform decisions at the specific level. In situations like Mukono District, where policy makers have been actively using this system to understand their performance and seek strategies, they are often eager to seek evidence for better strategies to improve their performance.

INCENTIVES AND DISINCENTIVES

Policy makers interviewed noted that they might consider the use of evidence if there were personal incentives, such as recognition of personal achievement of positive outputs from the use of evidence, and where policy makers are open-minded towards new initiatives. For example, a policy maker at Mukono District reported the uptake of evidence from the RRS was possible because the leadership was open-minded.

On the other hand, stakeholders interviewed noted that certain policy makers view the use of evidence as an extra task and therefore do not seek it. They would rather repeat plans from previous years because this is less demanding.

> Actually, most of the districts use evidence, if you are to ask districts for the last five years. Give us your annual work plan. They are all the same. But do you think things change? No, because the [official] only does it because he has to. He does not put an extra effort to see what does not work in the previous year, what can we change?
>
> (Respondent 1 – Government)

Respondents noted that previous results from using evidence affect future demand or use. Once the evidence has been shown to solve prior challenges, the policy makers are more inclined to evidence to solve challenges.

CHAMPIONS AND LEADERS

Stakeholders noted that champions are important for the consideration and uptake of evidence. Evidence champions are individuals in positions of influence who favour evidence use in policy and implement calculated approaches to increase the use of evidence in decisions. Their influence has been shown in studies on the factors affecting uptake of evidence-informed decision making (Basaza et al., 2018). For example, in the national food fortification programme, a stakeholder noted the importance of having top management as champions at the MOH (Respondent 7 – Non-government).

Champions can also be politicians. Instances were reported where politicians demanded accountability from technocrats. This, in turn, pushed the demand for evidence to improve the performance of government programmes. As one interviewee noted:

> And [also] having political heads who are also demanding. If you have political heads who are making noise in the community, then they ask you what new thing you are doing, and you do not show anything – man, it is better you just leave.
>
> (Respondent 1 – Government)

Capacities

SKILLS AND KNOWLEDGE FOR EVIDENCE USE

Respondents noted that certain skills are important for the consideration and use of evidence. For example, a stakeholder pointed out that leaders need the skills to search for evidence using a computer, the lack of which might limit their access and use of evidence 'someone who can sit on the internet, navigate the options and look for knowledge' (Respondent 1 – Government).

Interviewees also said that knowing how to generate and analyse data and search for evidence is important for evidence-informed decision making because it stimulates demand for evidence. A policy maker noted that many policy makers do not use evidence because they do not know where to find it, and therefore sensitising them about RRS has been very important.

RESOURCES

Stakeholders reported that a department needs internet and computer services to access evidence and services from the RRS, and that it enables them to search for evidence after training (Respondent 1 – Government).

Reflecting and learning from the use of evidence

How context and intervention influenced the use of evidence

The use of evidence described in this study takes place within the wider context where (1) services are largely decentralised to local governments; (2) decision making takes place at different levels; and (3) DPs play a significant role in influencing policy and driving the use of evidence. Mechanisms used to ensure the use of the service provided by RRS (i.e. evidence) include building understanding and trust in RRS through capacity-building and awareness-raising interventions. Importance is also given to building trusted relationships between decision makers, stakeholders and researchers through regular dialogue and intervention. Credibility and ownership are ensured by engaging with individuals known and trusted, the use of a tried and tested methodology, responding directly to demands, and working closely with the decision makers to ensure that demand is clearly articulated. The evidence itself is then presented in a manner that is relevant and accessible to the decision maker and is often accompanied by dialogue and discussion to allow all stakeholders to engage with it.

In the three cases described in this chapter, these interventions have successfully led to direct instrumental use of evidence. Other cases have elements of symbolic use, where evidence simply validates a decision maker's existing position.

Lessons for the health sector

The health sector in Uganda has had a number of initiatives supporting the use of evidence at MOH. However, challenges to evidence-informed decision making becoming part of the policy processes in the health system include access to evidence, interest of stakeholders and availability of resources. Knowledge brokers such as RRS increase policy makers' access to evidence. However, it is important that the knowledge brokers have sufficient understanding of context to present evidence and recommendations that are socially and culturally appropriate, and thereby increase the acceptance of evidence use in the decision-making processes.

Its adoption is at a nascent stage in districts, with the RRS being one of the few initiatives attempting to support the work of decision makers at the district level. It is clear that increasing access to and availability of evidence serves the district health officers' overwhelming demand for evidence and therefore increases the possibility of evidence-informed decision making at the districts. These efforts are hampered by the limited visibility and awareness of the services RRS provides. There is a need to ensure the visibility and relevance of the service, thereby raising the awareness of the intended users and promoting its continued application, especially at the national level.

Lessons for the country

The experiences of RRS demonstrate that research evidence can promote the efficient and effective use of resources and minimise wastage. However, the use of evidence in health policy making in Uganda and beyond is still suboptimal despite efforts to bridge the research-to-action gap. It is important to reflect and learn from experience, as small but significant changes can make a huge difference. For example, at the district level, the quarterly review meetings could add a requirement that the evidence needs to be referred to prior to the adoption of an implementation strategy.

A final thought

An important lesson from the three case studies is that evidence needs an advocate to attract the attention of the decision maker. Investments are required upfront by the evidence advocates to strengthen the readiness of evidence users to demand and use the evidence, for example, by creating awareness of the existence and value of the evidence and building skills necessary to interrogate and apply evidence. Throughout the process, parallel actions can make a significant difference. These can include advocacy around the topic and the research process, building of relations and, perhaps most importantly, establishing trust in the process and the outcomes.

Notes

1 Global Alliance for Improved Nutrition is a UN Swiss-based foundation set up to tackle malnutrition globally.
2 Comprising MOH, Department of Food Science and Technology, Makerere University, Ministry of Agriculture, Animal Industries and Fisheries, National Agriculture Research Organization, Uganda Bureau of Statistics (UBOS), the Uganda National Bureau of Standards (UNBS), Ministry of Trade, the National Drug Authority (NDA), Ministry of Justice, and the Food Biosciences Research Centre (WHO Regional Office for Africa,

2013). Food fortification is a multisectoral response to micronutrient deficiency in women and children in Uganda. Brazzavile, Republic of Congo: Regional Office for Africa.
3 TB/RIF refers to *Mycobacterium tuberculosis* complex/Resistance to rifampicin.
4 ZN is a test for tuberculosis, also known as the Ziehl-Neelsen stain.

References

African Development Bank. 2019. Uganda economic outlook [WWW Document]. *African Development Bank – Build. Today Better African Tomorrow.* Retrieved 15 August 2019, from www.afdb.org/en/countries/east-africa/uganda/uganda-economic-outlook.

Amara, N., Ouimet, M. and Landry, Ré. 2004. New evidence on instrumental, conceptual, and symbolic utilization of university research in government agencies. *Science Communication*, 26, 75–106. https://doi.org/10.1177/1075547004267491

Basaza, R., Kinegyere, A., Mutatina, B. and Sewankambo, N. 2018. National framework for the sustainability of health knowledge translation initiatives in Uganda. *International Journal of Technology Assessment in Health Care*, 34, 120–128. https://doi.org/10.1017/s0266462317004482

Bossert, T.J. and Beauvais, J.C. 2002. Decentralization of health systems in Ghana, Zambia, Uganda and the Philippines: A comparative analysis of decision space. *Health Policy Plan*, 17, 14–31. https://doi.org/10.1093/heapol/17.1.14

Fiedler, J.L. and Afidra, R. 2010. Vitamin A fortification in Uganda: Comparing the feasibility, coverage, costs, and cost-effectiveness of fortifying vegetable oil and sugar. *Food and Nutrition Bulletin*, 31, 193–205. https://doi.org/10.1177/156482651003100202

Government of Uganda. 2005. *Food and drugs (Food Fortification) regulations, 2005*. Government of Uganda, Kampala, Uganda.

Hanrahan, C.F., Haguma, P., Ochom, E., Kinera, I., Cobelens, F., Cattamanchi, A., Davis, L., Katamba, A. and Dowdy, D. 2016. Implementation of Xpert MTB/RIF in Uganda: Missed opportunities to improve diagnosis of tuberculosis. *Open Forum Infectious Diseases*, 3, ofw068–ofw068. https://doi.org/10.1093/ofid/ofw068

Harvey, P., Rambeloson, Z. and Dary, O. 2010. *The 2008 Uganda food consumption survey: Determining the dietary patterns of Ugandan women and children*. Kampala: USAID.

Kammen, J. van, Savigny, D. de and Sewankambo, N. 2006. Using knowledge brokering to promote evidence-based-policy making: The need for support structures. *Bulletin of the World Health Organization*, 84, 608–612.

Kasale, H., Mbuya, C. and Lobulu, W. 2004. Case study confirms TEHIP's lead role in better health. *TEHIP News*.

Mijumbi, R.M., Oxman, A.D., Panisset, U. and Sewankambo, N.K. 2014. Feasibility of a rapid response mechanism to meet policymakers' urgent needs for research evidence about health systems in a low income country: A case study. *Implementation Science*, 9, 114. https://doi.org/10.1186/s13012-014-0114-z

Mijumbi-Deve, R., Rosenbaum, S.E., Oxman, A.D., Lavis, J.N. and Sewankambo, N.K. 2017. Policymaker experiences with rapid response briefs to address health-system and technology questions in Uganda. *Health Research Policy and Systems*, 15, 37. https://doi.org/10.1186/s12961-017-0200-1

Mijumbi-Deve, R. and Sewankambo, N.K. 2017. A process evaluation to assess contextual factors associated with the uptake of a rapid response service to support health systems' decision-making in Uganda. *International Journal of Health Policy Management*, 6, 561–571. https://doi.org/10.15171/ijhpm.2017.04

Ministry of Health. 2013. *Guidelines for governance and management structures*. Kampala: Government of Uganda.

Ministry of Health. 2019. Nutrition [WWW Document]. Retrieved 28 March 2019, from https://health.go.ug/departments/nutrition.

Potts, M., Prata, N. and Sahin-Hodoglugil, N.N. 2010. Maternal mortality: One death every 7 min. *Lancet*, 375, 1762–1763. https://doi.org/10.1016/s0140-6736(10)60750-7

Uganda Bureau of Statistics (UBOS), ICF International Inc. 2012. *Uganda demographic and health survey 2011*. Kampala, Uganda: UBOS, Calverton, MD: ICF International Inc.

WHO. 2009. *WHO guidelines for the management of postpartum haemorrhage and retained placenta (No. 978 92 4 159851 4)*. Geneva, Switzerland: WHO.

WHO. 2017. *Primary health care systems (PRIMASYS): Case study from Uganda, abridged version*. Geneva, Switzerland: WHO.

WHO Regional Office for Africa. 2013. *Food fortification: A multisectoral response to micronutrient deficiency in women and children in Uganda*. Regional office for Africa, Brazzavile, Republic of Congo.

World Bank. 2019. The World Bank in Uganda [WWW Document].

9 The potential and the challenges of evaluations to positively influence reforms

Working with producers in the Benin agricultural sector

Bonaventure Kouakanou, Dossa Aguemon, Marius S. Aina, Abdoulaye Gounou and Emmanuel M. David-Gnahoui

Summary

In 2006, a new President of Benin was elected with a particular interest in good governance. He considered public policy evaluation as key to good governance and established an Office for Evaluation of Public Policies and a national evaluation system (NES). This chapter focuses on an evaluation of the agricultural sector development policy in Benin that was carried out in 2009 at an early stage of the NES, and how the evidence was used to inform later policies. The research for this case study used qualitative and participatory methods, including a document review, 20 interviews and three mini-workshops. The 2009 evaluation was not used instrumentally, but it made a significant conceptual contribution in terms of understanding the needs of the sector. In 2008 to 2009, the role of civil society and agricultural producer organisations in policy development was transformed, and they began to play a key role in management of the sector. This case illustrates the potential for evaluations to inform policy making and implementation in Benin, and the challenges of doing so. The role of producer organisations was key to the uptake of evidence into policy, based on a more inclusive and effective process of evidence generation and use.

Background

In 2006 a new President of Benin was elected. President Boni Yayi considered public policy evaluation as key to good governance and established an Office for Evaluation of Public Policies (*Bureau d'Évaluation des Politiques Publiques* (BEPP, later BEPPAAG)) and a national evaluation system (NES). Benin is now one of three African countries with a formal national system for the evaluation of public policies and programmes, along with Uganda and South Africa.

This chapter focuses on an evaluation of the agricultural sector development policy which was carried out in 2009. The research for the chapter involved qualitative and participatory methods that included document review, 20 interviews and three mini-workshops. Participants in the workshops and interviews included the minister, senior officials and monitoring and evaluation (M&E) managers of the Ministry of Agriculture and other ministries, development partners (DPs), representatives of civil society organisations (CSOs) and members of producer unions and agricultural professional organisations. The co-authors include the deputy minister and senior officials from the ministry.

The use of evidence in agricultural policy in Benin

Background to the case

The main stakeholders in the agricultural sector include the presidency, the Ministry of Agriculture, Livestock, and Fisheries (MAEP) and ministries involved in related activities (finance, development, environment, decentralisation, water and sanitation, health, education, etc.). Decentralisation to communes (local governments) means local governments have a role in projects in their area (MDGLAAT, 2010, p. 25).

In terms of non-government actors, the Platform of Civil Society Organisations in Benin (PASCiB) is a national organisation which is influential in decision making in the agricultural sector. The National Platform of Agricultural Farmer and Producer Organisations (PNOPPA) also plays a strong role. Producer unions are federated to PNOPPA, which organises services to members such as procurement, market research, marketing support and facilitation of access to finance.

DPs have been catalysts and facilitators in the development and even implementation of agricultural policies in Benin. DPs support evaluations and research and most evaluations are funded by DPs. In several cases DPs have supported professional or civil society organisations, which has strengthened their influence in decision making. At present DPs are very influential in shaping public-sector policy.

The journey of the agricultural sector development policy

From 1990 to 2019 Benin's agricultural sector underwent various policy changes. In this section we follow this evolution and highlight the mechanisms that influenced their development.[1] Figure 9.1 provides an overview.

In July 1990 the Marxist military government was replaced by a democratically elected government. The Letter of Declaration of Rural Development Policy (LDPDR) of May 1991 was the first policy document of the so-called democratic renewal era in Benin and it initiated the state's withdrawal from the activities of production, marketing and processing, and the transfer of those roles to other stakeholders including producer organisations and the private sector (MDR, 2000, p. 4).

The second policy document, the Declaration of Rural Development Policy (DPDR), came into force in July 2000.

In March 2006, a new government was elected under President Boni Yayi, who expressed concern about the lack of capacity in the agricultural sector and the desire to rapidly strengthen the sector. The Ministry of Agriculture developed a strategic plan for the revival of the agricultural sector, the *Plan Stratégique*

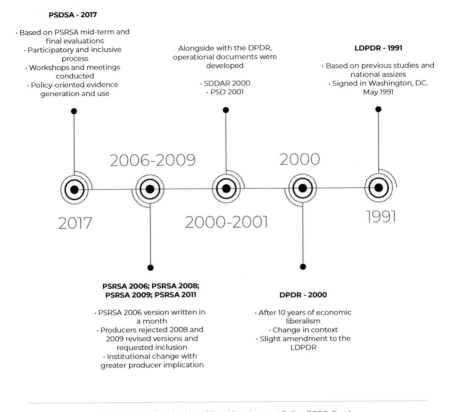

Figure 9.1 The journey of the agricultural sector policy

Source: Author generated.

pour la Relance du Secteur Agricole (PSRSA) 2006–2015. The ministry developed the plan internally and in only one month.

The PSRSA was a great improvement compared to former policy documents. However, it was rejected by producer unions and DPs, because of their exclusion from its formulation. After intense and lengthy discussions, a more inclusive revision process was initiated. The second version of the PSRSA was the subject of a government seminar on 12 June 2008. The recommendations of this seminar were followed up by a group of technical staff from the Ministry of Planning and from the Ministry of Agriculture. The validation of the 'new' PSRSA took place on 30 July 2008 after a stakeholder validation workshop. DPs expressed reservations about the content (Mongbo and Aguemon, 2015, p. 8), which were endorsed by PNOPPA, which criticised the ministry staff for 'treating other actors in the agricultural sector as their subjects' (Ibid., p. 8).

For some public servants, revising the PSRSA questioned the skills of the technical group that drafted it. However, the dependence of the agricultural sector on DPs for funding and the DPs' financial support to the revision process (Ibid.) led to the relaunch of the PSRSA review process in April 2009. Several workshops were held which were inclusive and participatory and led to a critical reduction of the influence of the ministry. PNOPPA's role in the workshops was significant, through the quality of its proposals and the contribution of its representatives within the extended workgroup and the technical subcommittees (Ibid., p. 13).

Despite this move to wider inclusion, a ministerial decree in February 2010 established a steering committee to work on the finalisation of the policy without any prior consultation and with only a single representative of non-state actors on one subcommittee (Mongbo and Aguemon, 2015, p. 10). After consulting with representatives of civil society, PNOPPA made a counter-proposal recognising the increasing importance given to producer organisations in the agricultural policy of ECOWAS. As a result, non-government players took on more prominent roles and the technical subcommittee was chaired by a senior technical official from the Ministry of Agriculture rather than a politician (Mongbo and Aguemon, 2015)

The 2009 evaluation happens in parallel

Meanwhile, BEPP was starting the new evaluation system and an evaluation of policies in the agricultural sector was scheduled for 2008 as one of the first evaluations of the new system. The aim of the evaluation was to carry out a diagnosis and propose approaches for the revival of the sector. The evaluation was managed by a steering committee which validated the methodological framework and ensured that the assessment was conducted independently. Members of the steering committee were drawn from the President's Office and from the ministries of planning, finance and agriculture, and included professionals from the Benin M&E Association.

The evaluation was conducted by an independent service provider and was of good quality. Evaluation professionals, other ministry agents, the President's Office and DPs contributed extensively to discussions based on the solid evidence provided by the evaluators. This brought a range of stakeholders into the learning from the evaluation. A three-day stakeholder validation workshop involving a wide range of stakeholders was held in December 2009, during which the final evaluation report was endorsed.

Meanwhile, over 2008–2009, institutional reshuffling was taking place within the agricultural sector. The evaluation report came out in December 2009, at a time when changes in the institutional framework made it easier for producers to be involved in policy-making processes and utilisation of evaluation results.

The results and recommendations of the evaluation (Table 9.1), many of which were focused on the PSRSA, brought forward evidence needed at the right moment, and the recommendations helped design effective policies for the sector that are still in force to date.

156 Bonaventure Kouakanou et al.

Thus, after the 2009 evaluation and as part of the revision of the PSRSA, the institutional framework for policy orientation and monitoring included the following guiding principles for governing the agriculture sector:

- Participation of all actors;
- Clear division of roles and responsibilities among key stakeholders;
- Public-private partnerships for agricultural development;
- Refocusing and strengthening of the state in its regulatory functions;
- Empowerment of all actors according to their mandates;
- Accountability

(MAEP, 2017a, p. 3).

The adoption of these principles strengthened stakeholder participation in agricultural policy development, making broad ownership and implementation more likely.

The revisions to the PSRSA

The revision of the PSRSA not only introduced non-government actors into policy making for the first time, but also initiated a process of improving data production and use. Evidence that came out of the 2009 evaluation became a significant input in developing subsequent sector policies (MPD, 2016, p. 6). This raised the profile of evaluation as a method for evidence generation and stimulated the demand for evidence. Thus, with the PSRSA, the demand for evidence became less for compliance, at the request of DPs or the ministry, and more use-oriented based on the actual needs of producers in the field.

The final version of the PSRSA (2011–2016) was adopted in September 2011 (MAEP, 2011). Mid-term and final evaluations of the PSRSA were carried out internally by MAEP in 2014 and 2016, reflecting that the ministry was committed to the process (MAEP, 2016). The evaluations were strongly supported by DPs, served as a baseline for the development of the PSDSA (Strategic Plan for the Development of the Agriculture Sector) and a solid foundation for writing the current PSDSA 2017–2025 and the PNIASAN, the National Plan for Agricultural Investment, Food Security and Nutrition, for 2017–2021.

The strategic plan for the development of the agricultural sector – PSDSA 2017[2]

In 2016 a new head of state was elected. Given that the head of state wanted to stamp his vision on the sector, the agricultural sector was asked to develop a new strategic plan for the development of the agricultural sector (PSDSA). The PNOPPA chairman noted how the ministry officials had been influenced by the PSRSA: 'As soon as this new vision was announced, ministry officials would take a recycled version of the old documents out of their laboratories and put it into effect. It's no longer the case now'. The establishment of an inclusive institutional framework had created an environment where the development of public policy is no longer just the responsibility of the ministry. As noted by a respondent from Belgian Cooperation, 'the empowerment of producer organisations had a huge impact. Whether it is the National Chamber of Agriculture,

PASCiB or PNOPPA, these organisations have become indispensable and even take the lead on several issues'.

The PSDSA 2017 had the advantage of being developed using evidence from the independent 2009 evaluation and internal 2014 and 2016 evaluations of the PSRSA by the ministry. According to the director of planning, the incorporation of evidence into PSDSA development has systematised the approach and strengthened relevance and stakeholder ownership. The first PSRSA of 2006 was produced in only one month. It took 18 months to finalise the PSDSA 2017 through a much more effective and inclusive process. However, the predominant role of non-state actors holds the potential for greater ownership and more effective implementation.

Why evaluations were required and the role that evidence generation played

From evidence generation to utilisation

The evaluation of the agricultural sector, which was completed in 2009, was good quality and very credible. At first MAEP staff rejected the evaluation results because of sensitivity that the evaluation was too critical. Then, the Ministry of Planning and Development took over the management of the evaluation and chairing of the steering committee. The final validation occurred after a laborious process. The report remains one of the best evaluations to date and has been referred to extensively.

Table 9.1 shows the recommendations of the evaluation report (2009), and the degree to which the recommendations have been implemented.

The results of the 2009 evaluation were shared at a three-day stakeholder validation workshop, which enabled stakeholders to engage with the findings. Benin's NES did not specify a formal process to take forward the recommendations, such as an improvement plan. However, because stakeholders had participated in the validation workshop they internalised the findings and were able to use these when the opportunity emerged. Note that there is now a follow-up mechanism to see where recommendations have been implemented and by whom.

Towards mid-2010, agricultural sector stakeholders had the urgent task to complete the revision of the PSRSA. The most available and reliable evidence at that moment was the freshly validated results of the 2009 sector evaluation. Meetings were held where the methodology for development of the PSRSA was reviewed in light of the evaluation results and recommendations. These meetings included formal meetings, workshops and thematic group work, lobbying, and advocacy by different categories of actors involved in the agricultural sector. A roadmap was defined and agreed, and a list of themes on which different groups should work. Leaders were designated for each theme on the basis of their skills rather than their position in the public administration (Mongbo and Aguemon, 2015, p. 10). Thus, non-state actors including producer unions, CSOs and chambers of commerce fully entered public policy-making processes in the agricultural sector, with the support of DPs.

Table 9.1 Recommendations from the 2009 evaluation and what has been implemented

	Recommendations	Subsequent policies and implementation
Sector strategic vision of development	1. MAEP develops a new agriculture sector policy in line with Benin's new development orientation	The existing PSRSA policy was revised and adopted by government in October 2011. At the end of the 2011–15 PSRSA, the mid-term and final evaluations were used for drafting the PSDSA 2017–2025 and its operational plan. They were both adopted by the government in November 2017.
	2. Government prepares and Parliament adopts a law on agriculture adapted to the vision of the emerging economy and Benin's strategic development approach	• The draft law is being finalised, pushed by producer unions and civil society actors and supported by DPs. • Parliament required an ex-ante evaluation prior to the introduction of the law. • Approval of the law is a conditionality for key EU funding. The adoption of the law is expected to be completed by September 2019. The EU will monitor progress.
Strategic programming of Interventions	3. Government considers the 2006 version of the PSRSA as an interim strategic plan pending drafting of a new agricultural sector policy and adoption of a law on agriculture	See recommendation 2. In addition to the drafting of the new agricultural sector policy, other documents were produced, including: the promotion of 13 agricultural sectors; the establishment of an efficient financing system for the agricultural sector; implementation of the institutional and organisational reform of the ministry; the establishment of the Benin Agency for the Promotion of Agricultural Value Chains (ABePROFA).
Operational programming and management of the interventions in the sector	4. Government provides sufficient funding for the agricultural sector (as per Maputo and Malabo commitments)	Not implemented. On average, over the 2011–2017 period, 7% of total state expenditure was invested in the agriculture sector, without reaching the 10% recommended (MAEP, 2017e).
	5. MAEP develops synergy between educational and agricultural policy reforms	This did not happen. There is still institutional fragmentation. (DPP MAEP, 2015).
	6. The ministry implements strategies to facilitate access to inputs specific to agriculture sectors other than cotton	Several initiatives on the implementation of specific inputs have been carried out without leading to an appropriate mechanism for distribution of specific inputs.
	7. The ministry sets up a consultation framework for synergistic implementation of projects and programmes	In 2013 the National Guidance and Monitoring Council (CNOS) was created for implementation of the PSRSA, but only established in December 2015, one month prior to the end of the PSRSA. Thus, coordination and monitoring of the PSRSA at the strategic level was not effective during this period. However, the CNOS reform has been well implemented and today it has 12 regional and 77 local branches, one for each region and local government (commune).

Recommendations	Subsequent policies and implementation
8. The ministry adopts results-based management tools with a well-functioning M&E system with performance and impact indicators for each program and project	A number of executives have been trained but most have retired. The capacity-building process for new managers at both central and decentralised levels was continued with donor support. Currently EU funding and capacity building are being used on the Programming, Planning, Budgeting and Monitoring chain for different stakeholders in the agriculture sector including non-government actors. This will assist with real-time production of implementation data of flagship projects.

Source: The recommendations are taken from the report on the evaluation of agricultural sector development policy (December 2009) and the subsequent policies are drawn from key-informant interviews.

Since 2011, PNOPPA has initiated a significant number of studies, the most important being the ones that generated the Farmer Memorandum, a consensus document produced after more than 40 meetings at local, regional and national levels that summarised the expectations of stakeholders on the content and orientation of the law on the agricultural sector (PNOPPA, 2016, p. 4). According to the former president of the platform, 'transparency and evidence use have become systematic in their operating mode; for their own reputation, every decision has to be evidence-based'.

A *Conseil National d'Orientation et de Suivi* (CNOS) – National Guidance and Monitoring Council – was established in February 2013 to guide and regulate the national agricultural sector development policy. It is a public-private partnership formalised through a framework agreement, specially established to encourage the private sector to invest in the agricultural sector. It is chaired by the president and has 25 members, including ten ministries, the Benin Chamber of Agriculture, the Benin Chamber of Commerce and Industry, PNOPPA, PAS-CiB, and the National Association of Local Governments of Benin (ANCB). It has structures at regional and commune level with decision-making autonomy and they provide reasoned opinions on all issues related to agricultural sector policies and strategies (Government of Benin, 2013). CNOS has been critical in developing and maintaining a culture of planning, monitoring and evaluation in the whole agricultural sector. Its local branches involve grassroots actors in monitoring agricultural information. They produce data on areas to be planted, input requirements and yield per hectare, and propose corrective measures to improve production. In doing so, the CNOS, especially at the local level, has increased producers' capacity, and their participation in the collection of basic data for evidence generation. Such information is the centrepiece of the collection of statistics that is treated and consolidated at the level of the Directorate of Agricultural Statistics.

The quality of evidence from the 2009 evaluation helped stimulate demand for further studies. Since 2011, PNOPPA has initiated a significant number of studies, ranging from A Document Review on the Maize Sector and Its Added

160 Bonaventure Kouakanou et al.

Value Chains in Benin (June 2011) to A Study on the Cash Purchase of Fertiliser by Producers in Benin (October 2011). Those studies responded to the needs in the field and led to development of a policy for the maize sector, as well as for sectors such as cassava, rice, cashew, pineapple, aquaculture, milk, table eggs, meat and market gardening, and so policy making has become more evidence-based.

Unintended consequences

The 2009 evaluation was carried out at the same time as a major transformation of the institutional framework, with the strengthened role of PNOPPA. With this strengthened collaboration among stakeholders, the evidence produced by the 2009 evaluation was used as the basis of new policies including the introduction of sector legislation and the inclusive and evidence-based development of the PSDSA. Moreover, from there on, evidence was used more extensively in decision making. Table 9.1, summarises how far the evaluation recommendations have been acted on. As can be seen, the evidence informed several noteworthy changes including changes to the law, development of subsequent studies such as on maize (which resulted in a new maize policy), establishment of CNOS, capacity development programmes and so forth. Thus the 2009 evaluation has had a significant influence on the progress of the agricultural sector.

The PSRSA review was a historic trigger that profoundly changed the status quo in the agricultural sector. The institutional framework in force today is based on a proposal by the PNOPPA which, until 2008, had never played a significant role in informing policy but is today leading in introducing legislation for the agricultural sector. This change is the most important unintended consequence arising from the implementation of the agricultural sector policy and related processes.

What promoted or inhibited use of the evaluation?

This section explores the way use of the evaluation results and other evidence was promoted, using the analytical framework from Chapter 2. We analyse the type of use that happened, what interventions promoted use, and the factors that helped or hindered use.

How do we understand the use that happened?

In the analytical framework we refer to instrumental, conceptual, process and symbolic use. In terms of *instrumental use*, recommendations 1 and 2 from the 2009 evaluation (see Table 9.1) were directly implemented and the revision of the PSRSA was completed as advised in 2011. The process leading to the adoption of the agriculture sector orientation law is underway. Recommendations to become inclusive of producers were taken on board.

However, the biggest impact has been *conceptual use*. The evaluation report stands as a major landmark for the quality and quantity of the information it brought which helped to bring clarity to the sector. It informed subsequent discussions developing the PSRSA. In the introduction of the Farmer Memorandum, almost all the background information utilised came from the evaluation report. The cross analysis of previous policy documents showed their limitations and facilitated the use of the evaluation to inform the revision of the PSRSA.

In terms of *negative symbolic use*, the previous history was of public policies in the agriculture sector in Benin being developed by the ministry for compliance purposes, without involving stakeholders. In terms of *positive symbolic use*, as one of the first evaluations commissioned by the BEPP, the 2009 agricultural sector evaluation enhanced the importance of evaluations in providing evidence for policy making and implementation.

Process use can also be seen, that is use not from the findings but from the learning process which the evaluation supported, and the ownership assumed by producers in policy design processes. The experience of the revision of the PSRSA created awareness of the importance of a more inclusive and collaborative platform of stakeholders. That context fostered the use of evidence and therefore more demand for generation of user-oriented evidence. Many studies, especially the ones on the 13 targeted agricultural sectors, were commissioned by producer associations for their own use, based on the evaluation recommendations.

What interventions promoted use?

Table 9.2 summarises some of the interventions which we see operating in this case.

A key factor in the use of the evaluation was the *quality and impartiality* of the evidence from the 2009 evaluation that showed the value of sound evaluations as promoted by the NES.[3] When the urgent task came to complete the revision of the PSRSA, the most readily available credible evidence at that moment was the freshly validated results of the 2009 evaluation, and the same stakeholders who had validated the results of the 2009 evaluation were able to use that understanding to inform the development of the subsequent policy.

What enabled and what hindered the use of evidence?

Factors enabling use

The establishment of a national evaluation system: The presence of BEPP (Bureau for Evaluation of Public Policies) resulted in an evaluation being conducted that might otherwise not have happened, and ensured its quality and independence. The NES has progressively become established and a theory of change is now a mandatory criterion for the eligibility of projects or programmes for the Public Investment Programme (BEPPAAG, 2017).

The commitment of non-state actors and their pressure on government: The opening of the policy space to include non-state actors like PNOPPA, PASCiB and chambers of agriculture and commerce created a revolution in policy making in agriculture in Benin.

Table 9.2 Interventions that influenced use

Intervention	Effect
Elements of the emerging NES	
Focus on making the evaluation credible	The approach in the NES was to outsource evaluations and commission a consultant using an external recruitment process. This resulted in a good quality, impartial evaluation.
Evaluation Steering Committee comprising key stakeholders	The fact that the steering committee brought together key stakeholders facilitated the subsequent *ownership* of the results of the evaluation. The recommendations of the evaluation were then used as the basic material for the revision of the PSRSA.
Stakeholder validation workshop	A three-day workshop was held in December 2009 during which the final evaluation report was approved. This helped to build *awareness* of the importance of good evidence, promoted *interaction* and involvement of stakeholders and *agreement* on the emerging findings.
Role of MAEP M&E unit	The MAEP M&E unit organised the validation workshop which played a key role in building *interaction, awareness* and *agreement* amongst stakeholders.
The report was made public	The report is available and *accessible* online. As one of the first evaluation reports of the newly established NES, it served as a reference for users.
Other elements contributing to use	
Communication of results	After the stakeholder workshop, there was an immediate *opportunity* for use in the revision of the PSRSA. The same stakeholders were also the ones working on the PSRSA revision. This helped a lot in the *ownership* of the results and their consequent use.
Steering committees for policy development	After the contention on development of the PSRSA, non-state actors played key roles in steering committees for policy development, promoting *ownership* and *motivation* from these actors to champion the new policies.
Dialogue processes	Different types of meetings were held with stakeholders in the agricultural sector where the PSRSA development methodology was reviewed in light of the evaluation results and recommendations, a roadmap drawn up and themes taken forward.
Advocacy by DPs	The unhappiness of DPs with the emerging content of the early PSRSA led to other stakeholders having the *confidence* to raise concerns, notably in relation to the dominant role of MAEP.
Capacity building of producers by DPs	Strengthening of PNOPPA, in particular, gave producers the *ability* to play a strong role in the policy process.
Study tour to Mali	A study tour to Mali generated *awareness* and *commitment* amongst stakeholders.

Active role played by DPs: The involvement of non-state actors was sustained by DPs. DPs provided financial and technical assistance and capacity-building to ministries, civil society, producers' unions, chambers of agriculture, NGOs and so forth.

Donor conditionalities: The World Bank and the EU's conditionalities in budget support mean that the realisation of certain indicators triggers financial bonuses. In 2017, an allocation of EUR 11 million from the EU was dependent on achieving the indicator: 'The Government has adopted the sector policy documents over the period 2017–2021 (PSDSA/PNIASAN)'.

The need for more relevant evidence: Many interview respondents highlighted the need for evidence to be relevant. The production of evidence is not a weak link in policy development in Benin; it is rather the relevance of the evidence. In this case, evidence generation has gained impetus because (1) demand for evidence has increased and (2) since the policies are more relevant, they need a more diversified base of more reliable evidence.

Establishing rules in favour of evidence generation and evaluation: It has become mandatory to use reliable data to inform policies and programmes. From the 2014 fiscal year parliamentary budget discussions, the Parliament of Benin made it obligatory for the government to conduct ex-ante evaluations prior to the submission of any project or programme for which ratification is required.[4] This provision promotes the production of evidence and will boost future demand.

Factors inhibiting evidence use

Repeated structural reforms on paper without time to implement and learn: After every election, governments change and so policies change. In agriculture there have been ten ministers in ten years, seriously undermining institution building. Many ministers reinvent programmes and policies and ignore well-founded public policies initiated by a predecessor. Frequent reforms mean that emergent programmes do not have time to bear fruit. These then restart from zero.[5]

Fear of the unknown and reluctance to abandon routine practices: 'That is the way we do things' expresses experience and know-how but it can also hinder adjustment to the current situation. The fear of losing power and control over interventions in the sector explains how a PSRSA steering committee was appointed made up almost exclusively of civil servants, despite a prior decision to involve producers.

Lack of communication among stakeholders: The ability to work together to drive a policy process assumes skills in collaboration that the sometimes-opposing positions of the actors do not always allow. Government actors have a tendency to claim official legitimacy and consider themselves superior to other actors.

Administrative red tape: Public administration at all levels is ponderous and slow-moving. A promising study may be abandoned because no one has championed it. After the 2009 evaluation, there were multiple unproductive meetings of high-level officials which did not result in action.

Inadequate resources: The PSRSA needed to be revised in 2009, but it could not be done as there was no budget. Inadequate resources affect the ability of actors to plan or to set up reliable M&E mechanisms. The reverse also happens, that is planning is not realistic for the resources likely to be available.

Conclusions and emerging lessons

From ticking the box to actual evidence-based policy and practice

In the past, although the process of revising agricultural policies did include stakeholder consultations, the policy documents were written by departmental staff. The actual clients were not able to contribute their lived experience. Historically, the writing of policies was more concerned with fulfilling the requirement of producing a document than developing a well-thought-out and implementable policy to be taken forward systematically. Few actors, including ministry officials, actually read the policy documents. None of these documents succeeded in transforming the sector until the involvement of producers, CSOs and chambers of agriculture in sector decision making. Stakeholders claimed their right to participate. 'It is about us the producers; you do not do us a favour by involving us!' (President of PNOPPA, Feb 2019.).

How did the context and intervention influence the use of evidence

What can we learn about evidence use arising from the Benin case? In the *context* of the 2009 evaluation, the policy space was dominated by government, with policies being revised frequently on paper, without effective diagnoses, and without the opportunity to really implement them.

A credible evaluation was undertaken (*evidence generation*) with relevant findings and recommendations, and having a NES helped ensure evaluation quality (*use intervention*). Most of the stakeholders that validated the evaluation final report were then involved in the restructuring of the sector's institutional framework. They seized the opportunity of the available evidence to complete the revision of the PSRSA, and the PSRSA of 2011 bears a strong imprint from the 2009 evaluation.

The *context* changed after 2010 with the involvement of producers. The context was now much more integrated, with government working closely with non-state actors, and there was much more drive from the producers to ensure that policies were relevant, and that appropriate strategies were implemented. In this context we see more examples of *evidence generation*, for example studies for the development of 13 sector value chains. A wider range of *use interventions* was applied, including involvement of all stakeholders through a series of dialogues, study tours, systematisation of data collecting and use for cotton campaigns, value chain development to increase production of food crops, enhancement of evidence management through the establishment of a directorate for agricultural statistics and so forth. We see higher levels of *capability* and *motivation* at individual and organisational levels. In terms of *outcomes* we see the policies agreed with stakeholders, a law on the agriculture sector, the creation of the CNOS, capacity development programs for ministry staff and producers with agreement between stakeholders on ways forward, much wider awareness of the results of evidence generation, and ultimately use. As a result of implementing many of these recommendations, Benin is now the biggest producer of cotton in Africa.

Emerging lessons

The process of researching and writing this chapter has itself been a learning opportunity for the agricultural sector, both for the MAEP and other stakeholders, and for the NES. It shows:

- The importance of conducting *high quality evaluations*. The rigour and quality of the evidence generated by the 2009 evaluation motivated stakeholders to trigger structural change in the sector's institutional framework.
- The importance of *timing*. Having evidence available at a time of change motivates use. This points to the need to anticipate and develop an evidence base prior to when it is actually needed, so that policy and decisions can be undertaken relatively quickly.
- The importance of a *national evaluation system* to promote use. A NES can ensure the involvement of stakeholders, develop systems like improvement plans, promote effective dialogue in the sector, and ensure that there is a knowledge broker in the ministry and/or in BEPP who will make sure that the results get used.
- The importance of involvement and *commitment from key stakeholders* including the clients of the system, which can stimulate the effective use of evidence. This helps build the momentum for change.
- The importance of *development partners*. DPs provide critical support to stakeholders and in taking processes forward. The technical assistance and the financial resources for non-state actors are extremely important. There are limitations because of DPs' project orientation, as projects have a limited life, and overreliance on DPs can cause a sustainability challenge. Also DPs have their own agendas which have to be managed.

Concluding remarks

What answers will the coalition with producers bring to the sector's questions related to planning, M&E, financing, human resources, access to quality inputs, standardisation, revitalisation of production, processing, marketing and so forth? The role of the MAEP has become more complex and it struggles with how best to operationalise the complementarity between central government and producers. Producer unions and CSOs are not yet sufficiently established to fulfil the roles potentially assigned to them.

The evaluation system in Benin is becoming more institutionalised, with the decision in 2019 to have an ex-ante evaluation prior to any projects, programmes or action plans being submitted for approval.[6] The decision to have theories of change for new programmes and policies should help implementation planning and suggests a focus on programme implementation.

Ten years after the 2009 evaluation of the agricultural sector development policy, the sector bears the imprint of the changes that occurred. The evaluation recommendations are a landmark in evidence around the changes occurring in the sector. A noteworthy lesson is the necessity to provide an institutional framework which involves producers. Without this, evidence generation is unlikely to result in use.

Annex 9.1 Summary of the main landmarks in Benin's agriculture sector 1990–2009

Year	Main landmark
1991	The Letter of Declaration of Rural Development Policy (LDPDR)
1993	Development of the National System of Agricultural Extension
1994	Strategy Document and Action Plans for the Livestock Sub-sector
1995	Programme for the Restructuring of the Agriculture Sector
1995	Round Table on the Rural Sector (September)
2000	The Declaration of Rural Development Policy (DPDR)
2000	The Master Plan for Agricultural and Rural Development
2001	The Strategic Operational Plan
2001	Sub-sectoral and Transversal Action Plans
2001	Creation of the Network of Benin Chambers of Agriculture
2001	National Strategy Document for the Cotton Sector
2001	National Policy for the Promotion of Women in the Rural and Agricultural Sector
2001	Adoption and Implementation of Programme – Budget Approach
2001	Agricultural Millennium Development Goals
2004	Reform of Local Centres for Agricultural Development
2006	The Strategic Plan for the Revival of the Agricultural Sector (PSRSA)
2006	Growth and Poverty Reduction Strategy Document
2007	Recruitment of 2,000 trainers for Local Centres for Agricultural Development
2007	Signature of Economic Partnership Agreements with the European Union
2007	Advisory Policy for Family Farming
2007	Implementation of the System of Representation of Agricultural Professional Associations
2007	Adoption of the Law on Rural Land Reform in Benin
2007	Adoption of the National Strategy for Agricultural and Rural Training
2008	Revision of the Strategic Plan for the Revival of the Agricultural Sector (PSRSA)

Source: MPDEPP-CAG. 2009, Benin Agriculture Sector Evaluation Report, p. 28.

Notes

1 The 2009 evaluation report has a whole section devoted to the analysis of the different policies from a historical point of view (pp. 24–46). Much of the information presented in the journey of the policy comes from this report.
2 The Strategic Plan for the Development of the Agriculture Sector; in French, *Plan Stratégique de Développement du Secteur Agriculture* (PSDSA), was adopted by the government in November 2017.
3 Many other public policies have been evaluated since and are made available on the Presidency of the Republic site (www.presidence.bj/evaluation-politiques-publiques).
4 The decision was made after the minister in charge of the evaluation of public policies made his budget presentation highlighting the importance of evaluation.
5 A typical example of this is the reforms of regional centres responsible for agricultural promotion for which the research did not identify any studies or evidence that indicated their soundness.
6 This came after the Minister for Evaluation of Public Policies made a presentation to support his departmental budget in {arliament.

References

BEPPAAG. 2017. *Guide méthodologique national d'évaluation*. UNICEF. 124 pages. Bureau d'Evaluation des Politiques Publiques et de l'Analyse de l'Action Gouvernementale, Bénin.
Government of Benin. 2013. *Request from the Government of Benin for financing of the food production support project in Alibori, Borgou and Collines Departments (PAPVI-ABC)*. Retrieved 23 August 2019, from www.gafspfund.org/sites/default/files/inline-files/4.%20Benin_GAFSP%20proposal%20EN.pdf.
MAEP. 2011. *Plan stratégique de relance du secteur agricole (PSRSA)*. 107 pages. Ministère de l'Agriculture, de l'Élevage et de la Pêche, Bénin.
MAEP. 2015. *Document actualisé de politique nationale des semences végétales – Benin*. 20 pages. Ministère de l'Agriculture, de l'Élevage et de la Pêche, Bénin.
MAEP. 2016. *Rapport d'évaluation du plan stratégique de relance du secteur agricole 2011–2015*. 88 pages. Ministère de l'Agriculture, de l'Élevage et de la Pêche, Bénin.
MAEP. 2017a. *Cadre institutionnel d'orientation et de suivi du secteur agricole*. 24 pages. Ministère de l'Agriculture, de l'Élevage et de la Pêche, Bénin.
MAEP. 2017b. *Cadre programmatique du secteur agricole*. 148 pages. Ministère de l'Agriculture, de l'Élevage et de la Pêche, Bénin.
MAEP. 2017c. *Plan Stratégique de Développement du Secteur Agricole (PSDSA) 2025 et Plan National d'Investissements Agricoles et de Sécurité Alimentaire et Nutritionnelle PNIASAN 2017–2021*. 131 pages. Ministère de l'Agriculture, de l'Élevage et de la Pêche, Bénin.
MAEP. 2017d. *Stratégie nationale de promotion des filières agricoles intégrant l'outil clusters agricoles*. UFAI. 73 pages. Ministère de l'Agriculture, de l'Élevage et de la Pêche, Bénin.
MAEP. 2017e. *Rapport de performance du secteur agricole, Gestion 2016*. 54 pages. Ministère de l'Agriculture, de l'Élevage et de la Pêche, Bénin.
MDGLAAT. 2010. *Recueil de lois sur la décentralisation*. 107 pages. Ministère de la Décentralisation, de la Gouvernance Locale, de l'Administration et de l'Aménagement du Territoire, Bénin.
MDR. 2000. *Déclaration de Politique de Développement Rural*. 27 pages. Ministère du Développement Rural, Benin.
Mongbo, R. and Aguemon, D. 2015. *Action publique, acteurs, ressources et pouvoir: cas de la relecture du Plan Stratégique de Relance du Secteur Agricole au Bénin*. Communication au Colloque 2015 de l'APAD.

MPD. 2016. *Synthèse de l'étude sur l'utilisation des résultats des évaluations réalisées au cours de la période 2010–2013*. Direction Générale de l'Évaluation. 8 pages. Ministère du Plan et du Développement, Bénin.

MPDEPP-CAG. 2009. *Évaluation de la Politique de Développement du Secteur Agricole au Bénin*. Rapport Final. 137 pages. Ministère du Plan, du Développement, de l'Évaluation des Politiques Publiques et du Contrôle de l'Action Gouvernementale, Bénin.

PNOPPA. 2016. *Imaginons et construisons ensemble le devenir de notre agriculture: Plaquette de mobilisation pour la collecte de fonds pour la réalisation du Mémorandum Paysan*. 6 pages. Plateforme Nationale des Organisations de Paysans et de Producteurs Agricoles, Bénin.

10 Parliament and public participation in Kenya

The case of the Wildlife Conservation and Management Act 2013

Mine Pabari, Yemeserach Tessema, Amina Abdalla, Judi Wakhungu, Ahmed Hassan Odhowa and Ali Kaka

Summary

This chapter explores the role of Parliament in policy making through citizen engagement and public participation, drawing on experiences from the review and enactment of Kenya's Wildlife Conservation and Management Act 2013. The chapter identifies and discusses the particular contextual factors that enabled and/or hindered the use of evidence generated through the public participatory processes. It concludes by providing lessons and reflections for strengthening the involvement of the wider public in policy making in Kenya and beyond.

Introduction

In 2013, problems in managing the wildlife sector in Kenya came to a head. The levels of poaching had been steadily escalating over the years and Kenya, together with Tanzania and Uganda, was being heavily criticised by the international community for not having stringent enough laws to curb the crimes. At the same time, the legislation, developed in 1976 and amended in 1989, was not aligned with the country's new constitution which came into effect in 2010. There was therefore a sense of urgency across the country about putting in place legislation appropriate to the situation and needs of the country's wildlife sector.

The Wildlife Conservation and Management Act 2013 (WCMA 2013) has, as its long title, An Act of Parliament to Provide for the Protection, Conservation, Sustainable Use and Management of Wildlife in Kenya and for Connected Purposes (Republic of Kenya (RoK), 2014). Approved by Parliament in December 2013, the Act came into force on 10 January 2014, replacing the Wildlife Act, Cap 396 of 1976. WCMA 2013 was realised through an intense process of citizen engagement and public participation.

This chapter examines the role of a parliamentary body leading public participation in policy making in Kenya, using the case of WCMA 2013. The chapter explores the rationale behind citizen engagement as the source of evidence used and identifies critical factors that influenced the process and outcomes of this engagement within the political and social context.

The methodology for this chapter is a case study using data drawn from a literature review and interviews. The literature reviewed covered published and unpublished documents such as correspondence, published articles, Hansard reports from the Kenyan Parliament and thematic reports, among others. Semi-structured interviews were conducted in November 2018 with 22 key informants, drawn from government institutions, non-governmental organisations (NGOs), community-based organisations (CBOs) and private individuals directly and indirectly involved in the WCMA 2013 process. The interviewee list was informed by a review of the literature and drew from interviews with policy makers involved in driving the review process. Referrals, or the snowball sampling method, were also used.

The context

A turbulent history

Wildlife management in Kenya is a highly charged and emotional topic, with tensions that can be traced as far back as Kenya's independence in 1963.

Formal legislation around wildlife in Kenya began under colonial rule, with the first hunting regulations dating back to 1898. During the colonial period, a number of protected areas were established on lands formerly used and inhabited by communities. Many communities, especially pastoralists, were dispossessed of livestock dispersal areas, seasonal migration routes and, perhaps most importantly, watering points. This caused deep resentment and ambivalence towards protected areas (E. Barrow and Fabricius, 2002). These systems have been described as state-driven, top-down management of protected areas (E. G. C. Barrow et al., 2000; Kabiri, 2010a; Western, 2000). Following independence in 1963, Kenya maintained many of the systems created by the colonial regime.

The post-colonial Sessional Paper No. 3, Statement on the Future of Wildlife Policy in Kenya (Kenya, 1975), remains the guiding policy document for wildlife management to date, and was put into force by the Wildlife Conservation and Management Act (1976), Cap 376 (Kabiri, 2010). The Wildlife Conservation Act of 1976 allowed landowners to manage and receive payments from commercial hunting. However, this was quickly overturned with a ban on consumptive utilisation in 1977, said to have been driven by animal rights groups and the tourism industry (Nelson, 2010). This policy decision has been a central stumbling block in the various attempts that have taken place over the years to devolve authority over wildlife (Ibid.). Since then there have been multiple debates, often with highly polarised views stemming from very different conservation ideologies. A major criticism of the natural resources legislation in Kenya has revolved around exclusion of local communities, which has had a negative impact on the conservation of Kenya's environmental resources, including its wildlife.

The 1989 Wildlife (Management and Conservation) Amendment Bill established a parastatal organisation under the Ministry of Tourism and Wildlife, the

Kenya Wildlife Service (KWS), to conserve and manage Kenya's wildlife. Prior to the formation of KWS, the government exercised centralised authority and a top-down approach to wildlife protection and management, with minimal involvement of non-state actors. With the introduction of KWS, a number of alternative management models were introduced aimed at enabling greater involvement of communities in wildlife management (Anyonge-Bashir and Udoto, 2012; Western et al., 2015) Like many government institutions, however, KWS has struggled with inadequate funding and instability in leadership and vision and has undergone multiple changes over the years.

Limitations in government's capacity to manage wildlife gave room for other stakeholders to engage in conservation of wildlife resources around the country. NGOs, with the support of development partners, have made an important contribution to promoting different types of wildlife management regimes that cater for wildlife outside of protected areas. They have also been engines in Kenya's wildlife policy processes at all stages, either individually or through formal and informal alliances and networks.

The involvement of local communities and the private sector in wildlife management has historically been localised around communally or privately owned areas, which later came to be known as 'conservancies'.[1] These were areas set aside by individuals or communities to conserve endangered species or increase benefits from wildlife through tourism, often with the support of NGOs and/or privately owned companies (Kenya Wildlife Conservancies Association, 2016). In April 2013, the Kenya Wildlife Conservancies Association (KWCA) was established to leverage and strengthen the voices of community groups around the country. Since its establishment, KWCA has been a key player in legislative review processes affecting the sector and was an active participant in the WCMA 2013 review process.

Previous attempts to revise legislation of the wildlife sector

In 2006 a technical steering committee comprising representatives of different stakeholder groups reviewed both the government's policy towards wildlife described in Sessional Paper No. 3 of 1975, Statement on Future Wildlife Management Policy, and the Wildlife Conservation and Management Act, Cap 376. Funding for this was provided by the United States Agency for International Development (USAID) through the World Wildlife Fund (WWF). The technical steering committee conducted widespread stakeholder consultations and reviewed available literature and research, particularly from southern African countries, the US and Australia. There was a perception that local studies were not good enough at the time. Despite this limitation, the committee felt that the two documents that resulted from the extended consultative process were a fair representation of people's aspirations for the wildlife sector. In 2007, the draft Wildlife Policy and Act were finalised and submitted to the Ministry of Wildlife, Environment, Water and Natural Resources (MEWNR). Unfortunately, the timing coincided with a fraught general election year, and the document was shelved for future action.

172 *Mine Pabari et al.*

In 2010, another NGO, the East Africa Wildlife Society (EAWLS), also secured funding from USAID through the NGO, Pact Kenya, to revise the draft Policy and Act in collaboration with the ministry and KWS. This process was carried out by a technical task force comprising experts in the sector, and primarily involved expert review and input with a final stakeholder review and validation meeting. In January 2012, the team submitted the revised document to the MEWNR. The ministry approved the draft bill submitted by the technical committee and published it in the Kenya Gazette in July 2013 for public input. The draft bill drew many responses, and individuals interviewed for this case study said that the version that eventually reached Parliament in 2013 was missing critical sections. Multiple interviewees reported that alterations were made driven by individual ulterior motives. Concerns raised around the lack of clear and transparent mechanisms and processes between technical drafting and presentation to Parliament led to both documents being shelved.

Catalysts of change

In 2010, Kenya adopted a new constitution which was a critical turning point for the country on multiple fronts. Of particular relevance to this case are (1) the emphasis placed on sustainable development (Article 10) and the environment (Article 69); (2) the changes the constitution brought about in the roles of Parliament (Article 94) (3) and the involvement of the public in policy making.

The strengthened role of the legislature in policy making is aptly described by one of the interview respondents:

> One of the things that the 2010 Constitution did was move to a presidential system of government. In a presidential system of government, the executive proposes, and the legislature takes the lead in a very hands-on manner to midwife the policy process without somebody breathing on it. We used to have a different system of government which was a hybrid where some members of the executive were in parliament. So, this was a parliamentary-driven process once the document had been tabled in the house.
>
> (Respondent 14 – Government)

Public participation is a key pillar of the 2010 Kenya Constitution. The National Assembly defines it as 'the process of interaction between an organisation and the public with the aim of making an acceptable and better decision' (The Clerk of the National Assembly, 2017). Various articles of the 2010 Kenya Constitution guarantee public participation. Article 118(1)b, for example, requires Parliament to 'facilitate public participation and involvement in the legislative and other business of Parliament and its committees'. Article 118(1)(a) further provides that Parliament 'conducts its business in an open manner and its sittings and those of its committees shall be open to the public'. Relevant committees of Parliament facilitate public participation through mechanisms which include, but are not limited to, petitions, submissions of memoranda, public hearings, consultations with relevant stakeholders and consultations with experts on technical subjects. The 2010 constitution specifically guarantees public participation in the environment sector through Article 69(1) which reads as follows: 'The State shall – (d) encourage public participation in the management, protection, and conservation of the environment'.

The years leading up to 2013 were marked by a spike in wildlife poaching, with elephant and rhino populations being decimated in many parts of Africa. In March 2013 the Convention on International Trade in Endangered Species (CITES) identified Kenya, Tanzania and Uganda as members of the 'Gang of 8' countries fuelling the illegal trade in ivory. The three countries were heavily criticised for not having stringent enough laws to curb the escalating wildlife crime.[2] In Kenya, the law at the time treated poaching as a 'petty crime' and in the words of one of the interview respondents, 'almost offered incentives to poach' (Respondent 12 – Government). The government was therefore under significant pressure from within and outside the country to do its part to stop the global illegal trade.

Revising the Act

The journey

The first elections held under the new constitution took place in March 2013. As one of the first Acts of the new Parliament, the journey of the WCMA 2013 pioneered the provisions for public participation in the legislative process.

In 2013, the MEWNR submitted a bill to Parliament for review and debate. The Act was then charged to the Departmental Committee on Environment and Natural Resources (DCENR), which led the citizen engagement process. The DCENR is a parliamentary committee, comprising 29 members of Parliament, which is mandated to review all legislation relating to climate change, environment and natural resources.

The DCENR was supported by Parliamentary Research Services (PRS). PRS, as of 2019, comprised of 30 researchers. The unit supports Parliament by providing background information, briefings, policy analysis and reports, among others, to support evidence-based legislation and decision making by members of Parliament. PRS also provides support to house committees, such as the DCENR, which includes receiving, collating and analysing input from the public (Respondent 1 – Government).

In September 2013, responses from the public to the draft bill submitted in 2012 were discussed in a retreat convened by the DCENR together with the ministry, led by the Cabinet Secretary.

As required under Article 118 of the constitution, the DCENR invited members of the public, through the national newspapers, to submit any representations they may have on the Act. Responses from the public were received through written proposals and telephone calls to PRS. Proposals came from several organisations including community coalitions and associations such as the KWCA, NGOs and members of the public. Written submissions referred to published research, grey literature and individual experiences. The PRS received, collated, and analysed written and oral proposals from stakeholders and provided the interface between the DCENR and stakeholders (Republic of Kenya (RoK), n.d.). Submissions made to DCENR ranged from proposals aimed at strengthening the institutional frameworks (such as including community representatives on the KWS Board of Trustees) to creating provisions (such as the provision of incentives for wildlife management as a land use).

The DCENR met seven times to discuss the draft bill, including two meetings where stakeholders were given the opportunity to present their proposals and arguments in person. In addition, the DCENR also invited individuals representing opposing sides of the wildlife consumptive utilisation debate to attend a closed-door session with committee members.

At a second reading in Parliament, the committee normally simply presents a report on the process to date. In this case, the committee presented both the report as well as proposed amendments to the Act. This then allowed for discussion and debate within Parliament and resulted in additional amendments which were incorporated by the chairperson. A decision on all amendments was taken at the third reading of the bill, presented to the Committee of the Whole comprising all the Members of Parliament. The Act was approved by Parliament in December 2013 and came into force on 10 January 2014, replacing the Wildlife Act, Cap 396 of 1976.

Amendments to the Act

There was a broad consensus among interview respondents that, given the poaching crisis, the Act needed to be passed urgently and that it was sufficiently adequate to do so. However, it was also recognised that there were flaws in the legislation and, to the credit of the DCENR, the Committee monitored the performance of the Act with periodic input from PRS. Matters flagged by PRS were transmitted to the ministry to give their official response to the committee.

PRS used information available in mainstream and social media, as well as information provided directly by stakeholders engaged in the earlier consultation processes. PRS compiled a brief on poaching trends, which triggered an investigation by the committee on the unrelenting poaching menace in the country. Also, as part of the WCMA 2016 amendment process, the DCENR convened breakfast meetings with stakeholders and other relevant government bodies, including the judiciary, to discuss specific amendment proposals. In addition, shortly after the passage of WCMA 2013, the NGO, Africa Network for Animal Welfare (ANAW), the Judiciary Training Institute and Kenyans United Against Poaching (KUAPO) initiated the formation of a task force to amend the bill. The task force worked on proposed amendments to the bill and presented the revised document to DCENR at a meeting in December 2014.

The DCENR chairperson followed up with due process of a first reading at Parliament, releasing the call for public input and participation. In response to its call for public participation, the DCENR received proposals from a number of civil society organisations. Unfortunately, after the first reading, the process stalled as the country underwent a general election and Parliament was dissolved. This reset the approval process and the amendment bill had to undergo the entire development procedure from the beginning. Initially there was reluctance to restart the process until the new wildlife policy was in place. However, the process was restarted, and certain sections of the WCMA 2013 were amended through the Miscellaneous Amendment Bill in December 2018. The long road to the enactment and amendment of the WCMA 2013 is summarised in Figure 10.1.

Outcomes

Case study respondents unanimously recognised that simply bringing the Act into being after 16 years was an accomplishment. Perhaps one of the greatest achievements of the process was the strong sense of ownership across the diverse group of stakeholders – from the different arms of government to NGOs and CBOs and individual members of communities living with wildlife. This notwithstanding, the shortcomings of the Act are also heavily criticised, and the country continues to grapple with developing legislation that balances conserving wildlife with ensuring that the sector contributes positively to livelihoods and the economy in what is, today, a highly dynamic and complex macro environment.

Some of the most significant outcomes of the review process, as identified by interview respondents, are discussed in the next subsection.

Instrumental use

The Act comes into force and reflects citizen views on new directions for the sector. Interview respondents were unanimous that the engagement of a wide range of citizens played a critical role in ensuring that the Act was passed this time around, and that the Act reflected many of the submissions and inputs made by contributing stakeholders. Fundamental changes in the Act that emerged from the review process are as follows:

- *Kenya Wildlife Service*: In addition to enhancing KWS's role and mandate, the Act called for a significant restructuring of KWS's powerful board of trustees. The Act requires the board to be more representative of the sector by including representatives of wildlife, finance and county governments as well as NGOs, community-managed areas and privately managed wildlife areas. In addition, for the first time, the board is required to ensure that community representative include both men and women. The composition of the board at the time of writing this case study met these requirements.
- *Compensation*: Compensation for destruction of property, injury, and loss of life due to human-wildlife conflict was always contentious and was inadequate to non-existent prior to the Act. For example, the Act designates monetary compensation for the loss of human life at KES 5 million (~USD 50,000), whereas it was previously pegged at KES 200,000 (~USD 2,000). The Act also seeks to streamline the bureaucratic process for accessing

176 Mine Pabari et al.

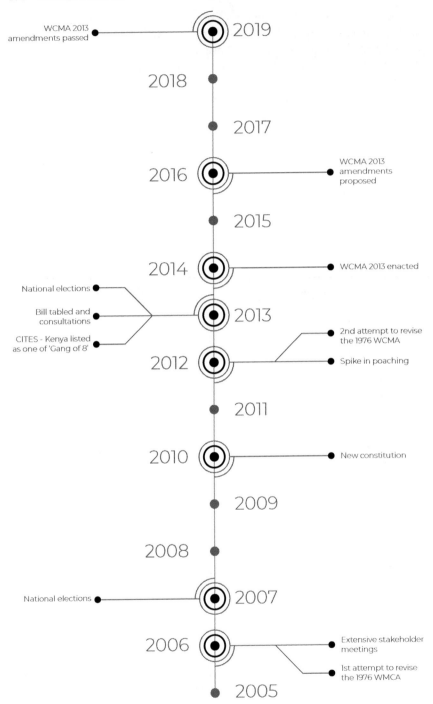

Figure 10.1 The WCMA 2013 journey
Source: Author generated.

compensation and for the disbursing of funds. However, the operationalisation of monetary compensation has met challenges, including inadequate funds to meet demand (also discussed under Barriers to Effective Public Participation).

- *Offences and penalties*: Prior to the Act, penalties for wildlife crime were minimal and provided little deterrent to offenders. The Act introduced more stringent penalties, particularly for killing wildlife categorised as endangered by CITES, including hefty fines and significant time behind bars. An example penalty is KES 20 million (~USD 200,000) or life imprisonment for killing a Category A species (e.g. elephant and rhino). According to a study carried out by the NGO, Wildlife Direct, following the enactment of the Act 'substantial improvement in the processes and outcomes of wildlife crime cases' was realised (Dr. Paula Kahumbu et al., 2017, p. 8).
- *Incentives and benefit sharing*: The perceived lack of tangible benefits from wildlife to landowners and communities has been counterproductive to long-term conservation objectives. As a significant percentage of wildlife resides outside of protected areas, communities that bear the costs of wildlife on their lands have been pushing for enhanced benefits derived from consumptive and non-consumptive use of wildlife. Thanks to the Act, wildlife conservation is now a recognised option for land-use management.[3] Landowners can apply for licences to derive benefits ranging from wildlife tourism to game farming. At the time of writing this case study, the ministry was looking to carry out further research into practical and feasible ways to improve benefit sharing and community engagement.

Process use

Experiences used to strengthen tools and skills for public participation in government: The lessons from the WCMA 2013 review were used to develop and strengthen national processes for public participation. A format for stakeholder participation was developed, drawing on the WCMA 2013 experience, which was adopted by DCENR, and later by the National Assembly. The former chair of the DCENR worked with Parliament and other bodies to incorporate the developed tools to inform future committees. This included input to the development of a 'Committee Management Manual' for the National Assembly and for county assemblies. Guidelines and check lists for good practices developed are being used in training sessions on public participation held regularly at national and local levels.

Rebuilding of trust and relationships between government and civil society: Policy development processes for the wildlife sector had suffered from a lack of legitimacy. Citizen engagement in policy-making processes built relationships between the different actors and stakeholders involved. These relationships were important for credibility, helped the government understand the root causes of the diverse perspectives in the sector and opened up spaces for the creation of mutual agendas.

Understanding the successes and the challenges

The constitution made public participation a requirement, but it was not the only driving force. Previous attempts to review the Policy and the Act made it clear that *meaningful* citizen engagement was critical to the successful revision of the Act by creating greater transparency and therefore minimising the risks of 'political sabotage' (as experienced in the 2010–2013 review process). Perhaps more importantly, there was a strong conviction that the very nature of the sector, with its diversity of stakeholders, interests and ideological positions, demanded public participation. These characteristics, as well as the history of the sector, also made effective participatory processes extremely challenging. It is therefore important to unpack, understand and learn from (1) factors that facilitated and hindered the public participatory processes led by a parliamentary committee; and (2) outcomes that emerged as a consequence.

> Wildlife is a resource that belongs to all Kenyans; for us to conserve it, the diversity of all Kenyans must be involved.
> (Respondent 12 – Government)

Interventions used to trigger changes necessary for effective public participation

For the review process to have successfully resulted in the enactment of the Act, with the buy-in and endorsement of stakeholders, a number of changes needed to take place. These included rebuilding trust, increasing levels of support for, and willingness to engage in, public participatory processes. In addition, this involved ensuring that opportunities were created for stakeholders to engage and that they were sufficiently aware of how to utilise these opportunities. Because of the subtle and invisible nature of these elements, understanding how they are realised (and under what circumstances) can be extremely challenging. The interventions used by the DCENR, by other arms of government and by members of civil society that ultimately resulted in these changes, are summarised in Table 10.1 and discussed in further detail after the table.

> The timing was ripe for action. Poaching and other crises have always come and gone and hence the pressure from the poaching crisis does not present the totality of the picture. Also, the poaching crisis is a global phenomenon and not uniquely Kenyan.
> (Respondent 4 – Non-government)

Factors enabling and hindering participation

Enabling factors

Fortuitous circumstances and timing: Two factors, the sense of urgency created by the poaching crises and the constitutional requirement to update the legislation,

Table 10.1 Use interventions and change mechanisms

Intervention/strategy employed	Effect and change triggered which enabled use
Dialogue and debates convened by the DCENR enabled engagement between sectoral experts (national and international) and policy makers using strategic for a, such as breakfast meetings	Over a period of three months, the DCENR conducted an intense process of consultation involving seven meetings, including two stakeholder forums, one-to-one discussions and a review of several submissions from the public (Annex 1). Some of the changes that this process triggered that ensured the use of evidence in the review of the Act included: • Development of *relationships and understanding* of one another's perspectives and realities • Deepened insights and *understanding of sectoral realities* and challenges • Packaging of information in a manageable manner which helped policy makers *understand* and *relate the evidence* to the specific policy challenges • Increased spaces to ensure that citizens have equal voice, thereby increasing a sense of *ownership* of the process
Both the DCENR and civil society independently convened and facilitated dialogue, debate and conflict towards consensus positions	
The DCENR created templates and processes for stakeholder inputs to be submitted in an organised manner and in direct response to the Act	
Civil society organisations collaborated with each other to develop joint submissions	
Knowledge brokering roles were played by PRS and civil society. Examples are: • Proactive identification, outreach and guidance to civil society and other organisations to encourage submissions and share existing data and research • Consolidation and synthesis of submissions and evidence acquired and making these available to the DCENR in a digestible format. This included generation of draft reports around specific areas requiring further debate	
DCENR created spaces specifically to generate additional insights around highly conflictual areas by bringing together individuals with directly opposing views to debate them in the presence of committee members	
Proactive outreach and engagement (particularly with local communities living in remote wildlife-rich areas)	
Closed-door meetings with influential actors to further enable consensus building as well as pre-empt the risks of political sabotage and influence	

were significant in creating an environment where stakeholders were willing to come to the table and work together to move the legislation forward. It is also important to note that the review process took place well after the elections, which provided a less politically charged environment for decision makers to engage with the evidence presented to them.

A well-organised civil society with established relationships: The multiple attempts to revise the policy in previous years were far from unproductive. In each of the review processes, members of civil society gathered, or conducted, research around policy matters of specific interest to them. The lobbying, advocacy and debates that took place enabled them to develop their positions and strengthen their arguments over time, as well as to form relationships with like-minded entities and influential actors and institutions. These preparatory actions were all critical in enabling them to respond quickly to the calls for public participation in a collective and organised manner. This was carried out through the preparation of joint submissions and sharing key pieces of research and other forms of evidence with the DCENR. A good example in this regard is the working relationships forged between the judiciary, NGOs (ANAW, KUAPO), KWS (under the ministry), DCENR, and PRS, which led to the proposals that resulted in the WCMA 2016 amendment document.

Representation of key stakeholders in the wider community: While it is recognised that local communities are significant players in the sector, engaging them in policy-making processes is challenging. Many reside in remote areas with limited access to telephones, newspapers and so forth. Additionally, not all communities are organised under well-governed structures. One of the advantages of the legislature leading the process was that having members of Parliament in the DCENR ensured that the views of the communities they represented were included during the review process. The existence of platforms and networks such as KWCA was also instrumental in this regard, as were the relationships NGOs had established through their field-based projects and other initiatives.

Skills, experience and expertise to take advantage of enablers and facilitators: A number of the governmental and non-governmental entities involved were individuals in leadership and management positions that had extensive experience in the sector and in facilitating multi-stakeholder processes and influencing policy. As such, they were able to take advantage of the enabling situation to mobilise and influence.

Effective knowledge brokers: A number of the stakeholders involved had the capabilities and experience to be knowledge brokers. PRS was able to play an important role as 'transmitters, interpreters and synthesisers of information' (Draman et al., 2017, p. 27). NGOs were also well positioned to play knowledge-brokering roles, carrying out studies to gather evidence around particular issues or drawing on existing research and presenting this evidence in a concise format to the committee.

Barriers to effective public participation

Lack of guidance and regulations for effective participation: Prior to the new constitution, spaces for public participation were limited, and government enjoyed unfettered power. When the WCMA 2013 was being revised, there were no regulations or guidelines in place, and capacity for participation and participatory processes was limited. This, coupled with the fact that the process was under immense time pressure, resulted in a number of shortcomings. For example, there was no scoping or analysis to identify stakeholders that needed to be involved, and outreach was only through an English-language newspaper. Calls for participation were only released for a short period with hearings convened only in the capital city. Therefore, it is very likely that representation, and therefore citizen knowledge and views gathered, were incomplete and/or insufficiently balanced. A number of interviewees also felt that the process was rushed with calls for engagement released at the last minute, which did not allow them sufficient time to prepare.

> Public participation is good, but it has to be determined what exactly is being sought – quality or quantity of participation. To a certain extent the WCMA process had quantity, but not quality participation. This is partly evident in the scramble to revise parts of the Act beyond its enactment. Lawmakers need to determine the quality of the stakeholders that they engage in policy-making process. Social science can help us determine this. The question of quality does not mean that people have to be formally educated, but they need to be connected to the issues they represent
>
> (Respondent 3 – Non-government)

Resource limitations and consequences for equitable participation and evidence quality: Budgetary resources and the time available to the DCENR was far from adequate. Therefore, the committee relied on individuals and organisations with resources available to them to access and gather evidence and to mobilise and gather views from their networks (particularly local communities). This resulted in questions and concerns around elite capture and the robustness of the evidence that ultimately influenced the contents of the Act.

NGOs in Kenya are driven by a variety of ideological positions in their approach to wildlife management, and the well-funded and organised NGOs often have sway over the type of decisions made by government institutions as these institutions are often weak and lack resources (Kabiri, 2010b; Norton-Griffiths, 2010). According to a number of respondents, wrangling for public opinion and legislative backing on either side of the debates (particularly with regards to consumptive utilisation) seems to be mainly driven by NGOs, with both sides claiming to represent the views of communities. Individuals interviewed expressed concern that community groups in wildlife areas adopted the views and ideologies of the dominant NGO in their specific area.

Others felt that the debates were being driven silently by the development partners who were providing financial support to different groups. Government representatives interviewed expressed frustration at being pulled in many directions by powerful NGOs. It was also expressed that, in the absence of a strong government with a clear vision for the wildlife sector and the capacity and wherewithal to implement its priorities, influential local and international interest groups would continue to hijack the public participation process. A few respondents suggested that a more strategic approach would be to first build the capacity of government and then engage the public.

> There is a continuous focus on working with the big conservation organisations, side-lining smaller ones . . . a monopoly within conservation bodies that have direct links to senior government officials. What does this mean for the grassroots organisations?
> (Respondent 22 – Non-government)

> Public participation has changed due to social media. Many issues are led by urban people who have no idea about the cost of hosting wildlife on land. The loudest voices in consumptive use discussions come from urban centres.
> (Respondent 11 – Non-government)

Poor knowledge management and learning culture: Previous processes generated a wealth of citizen views and evidence to inform policy challenges that the sector was grappling with. However, without a mandatory repository and mechanisms for tracking both the decisions and the evidence and rationale behind the decisions, each process started anew. Amongst those interviewed, this was recognised as an important lost opportunity.

Knowledge and understanding of the legislature as a whole: Ultimately, policies are finalised and endorsed by the legislature as a whole through the National Assembly. Therefore, final policy decisions are vulnerable to the politics that is inherent to parliaments. According to interview respondents, the level of understanding of the realities of the sector by members of Parliament had significant bearing on the final document. An example frequently cited by interviewees was that of compensation. In 2013, despite the dialogue and debate that had already taken place, changes were made in Parliament to the clauses on compensation to raise the levels to be paid out. A number of interviewees felt that this was a political decision pushed forward by members of Parliament in response to pressures from their constituencies. Interviewees also pointed out that because this was unrealistic and unimplementable, it has significantly hindered the performance of the Act and affected the level of public support that the Act originally had.[4]

Reflecting on, and learning from, the experience of the review of Kenya's WCMA 2013

How context and intervention influenced use of evidence

The changes that occurred as a result of the WCMA 2013 review process occurred within a particular context and because a set of deliberate interventions were applied which triggered change mechanisms (such as building trust, commitment, confidence, etc.). These changes were changes in capability, opportunity or motivation (immediate outcomes) which ultimately brought about changes in policy and practice (wider outcomes).

The context included a constitution that had recently been revised and a requirement that all legislation in the country be aligned to it. Furthermore, a poaching crisis had led to high levels of international and national attention on the sector, adding to the sense of urgency. Finally, the timing was right. Elections had been held and a new government was in place with the space to engage in debate and discussion.

Evidence came in multiple forms and from multiple sources. The evidence included verbal and written submissions providing arguments and recommendations for changes to the Act, drawing on experience, published research, and grey literature. This was consolidated by the PRS who also gathered additional evidence and prepared briefs on specific topics, such as experiences from other countries. Multiple interventions were used to ensure that citizens were willing and able to actively engage and that the evidence provided and gathered was reflected upon and utilised by the Committee.

Interventions used by the Committee as well as different stakeholders and actors included convening of dialogue and debates involving policy makers, experts and practitioners (such as breakfast meetings); negotiated submission of joint statements by CSOs; one-to-one meetings to manage influence and conflict; the use of templates and structured processes to ensure that evidence was submitted in an organised manner and in direct response to the Act; and proactive outreach and engagement with stakeholders outside of the city, particularly local communities living in remote, wildlife-rich areas.

As a consequence, the spaces to ensure that the voices of all citizens were heard equally were strengthened, allowing for building and strengthening of trust and relationships. This enabled the participating stakeholders to better understand the perspectives, challenges and realities of one another as well as the wildlife sector. Policy makers received information in a manageable manner which enabled them to understand and relate the evidence to specific policy changes.

The outcomes that emerged included an *increased motivation* by civil society to engage in policy-making processes and by government to continue to gather evidence to address continued policy challenges. The experiences and relationships developed also increased *opportunities* for stakeholders to engage in policy-making processes in the country, providing research evidence and views. Furthermore, it led to *increased capabilities* including skills and tools for government to manage participatory processes, and an improved understanding of the realities and challenges of the sector and different stakeholder groups.

The Act itself was revised and many felt that it reflected their submissions and inputs. This ultimately led to changes in practice and policy in the sector, which continue to unfold today with the development of the policy and regulations.

Practical considerations around public participation and the role of Parliament

Important ingredients for effective engagement and participation

The will from all parties to engage in a constructive manner and an enabling environment (such as appropriate timing and supportive legislation) are absolutely essential but are, in themselves, unlikely to result in effective public participation for policy making.

From the experiences of the WCMA 2013 review process, building blocks for an effective process include the following:

1. Guidelines and regulations to ensure best practice for all stages of the process;
2. Shared understanding of policy-making processes within the country;
3. Positive relationships and trust amongst stakeholders and actors involved;
4. Appropriate communication strategies and tools to convey and receive information with and amongst different types of stakeholders and actors;
5. Knowledge management processes and mechanisms to gather, organise and share information in a manner that can be accessed and utilised by the stakeholders involved.

A number of these building blocks take time to establish (for example, positive relationships and trust). As such, participatory and engagement processes should ideally be normalised as part of institutional culture (government and non-governmental).

> We need to talk about wildlife ownership, rights and benefits and make these dialogues routine occurrences, and have them led by the government.
> (Respondent 5 – Government)

Roles and responsibilities–Remembering the principles of form and function

Ensuring that public participation contributes to a robust policy-making process is highly dependent on multiple functions and roles being carried out successfully. Examples of functions and roles include acquiring and supplying evidence, demanding and using evidence for decision making, and brokering and facilitation between suppliers and users. Ensuring that the right skills and knowledge are in place is as important as is being cognisant of shortcomings and mitigating for associated risks.

> Politicians like evidence – but people need to understand that it is their [the politicians'] purview to interpret the facts!
> (Respondent 12 – Government)

The impact of leadership

The right leadership was absolutely critical in the complex context in which the WCMA 2013 review process took place, with its turbulent history and multiplicity of values, beliefs and needs. In this case, the leadership comprised two champions (the Cabinet secretary of the MEWNR and the chair of the DCENR) who worked together to navigate the review through to its conclusion. Leadership characteristics identified as being instrumental in enabling them to do so included the following:

- Trusted and respected individuals
- Positive track records in policy making and in the sector
- Knowledge of the realities of the sector
- Established relationships and networks
- Political savvy with abilities to understand and navigate politics and power.

Some final thoughts on public participation in policy making

The value of citizen engagement and public participation in the revision of the Act in 2013 was unquestioned during this study. It was said to have resulted in ownership of the Act that was vital to its progression through to Parliament and final enactment. However, it was also recognised that reliance on contributions from citizens and the wider public alone carries significant risk. Individuals involved in this study pointed out that all actors and groups have agendas and biases. In the case of the wildlife sector in Kenya, these biases are often deeply entrenched and difficult to shift. It was noted by respondents that there were tendencies to selectively utilise research and other forms of evidence to argue for their positions. At the same time, issues falling outside of these interests tended to be ignored. This was said to be partially attributable to the limited bandwidth available to effectively engage in all debates. In addition, individuals pointed out that there are tangible risks associated with lobbying and advocacy, particularly when in opposition to influential actors (such as donors and government). These risks are only likely to be taken in relation to issues of utmost importance and where the stakes are high. The wildlife sector in Kenya is driven by strong ideological values which resulted in *lot of noise coming through from social media and fake news* with multiple *emotional as well as science-based arguments* (Respondent 12 – Government).

Ultimately, therefore, there was consensus amongst those contributing to the study that public participation was invaluable and essential, yet insufficient. It was felt that there should have been better use of multiple sources and types of evidence, including independent research.

These experiences, including the successes and challenges, generated a wealth of lessons and insights which have continued to strengthen participation in policy and decision making in Kenya. It is hoped that these lessons will be of value to other countries across Africa seeking to strengthen their own development processes by better involving citizens.

Notes

1 The term 'conservancy' was first used in 1995 with the establishment of the Lewa Wildlife Conservancy (a private conservancy) and Namunyak Community Conservancy.
2 www.theguardian.com/environment/2013/mar/06/ivory-poaching-sanctions-cites, accessed December 21, 2018.
3 The highest number of conservancies were established in 2013, at the time that WCMAA 2013 was being reviewed and KWCA was established (Kenya Wildlife Conservancies Association, 2016).
4 In the financial year 2013/14, a total of KES 214 million (~USD 2 million) was released to 3,215 claimants, with 363 being death cases and 2,888 injury cases. In the financial year 2014/2015, no compensation funds were released, although a total of 140 death cases were recorded by KWS as the Service was awaiting the launch of the County Wildlife Conservation and Compensation Committees (Ministry of Environment, Water and Natural Resources, 2015).

References

Anyonge-Bashir, M. and Udoto, P. 2012. Beyond philanthropy: Community nature-based enterprises as a basis for wildlife conservation. *The George Wright Forum*, 29(1), 67–73. Retrieved from JSTOR.

Barrow, E.G.C. and Fabricius, C. 2002. Do rural people really benefit from protected areas – Rhetoric or reality? *Parks*, 12(2), 67–79.

Barrow, E.G.C., Gichohi, H. and Infield, M. 2000. *Rhetoric or reality? A review of community conservation policy and practice in East Africa*. London: International Institute for Environment and Development and International Union for Conservation of Nature.

The Clerk of the National Assembly. 2017. *Public participation in the legislative process. Fact sheet No. 27*. The National Assembly of Kenya.

Draman, R., Titriku, A., Lampo, I., Hayter, E. and Holden, K. 2017. *Evidence in African parliaments*. Oxford: INASP.

Kabiri, N. 2010a. Historic and contemporary struggles for a local wildlife governance regime in Kenya. In *Community rights, conservation and contested land: The politics of natural resource governance in Africa*. https://doi.org/10.4324/9781849775052

Kabiri, N. 2010b. The political economy of wildlife conservation and decline in Kenya. *Journal of Environment and Development*. https://doi.org/10.1177/1070496510384463

Kahumbu, P., Karani, J. and Muriu, E. 2017. *On the right path? An analysis of Kenya's law enforcement response to wildlife crime* (No. 2016 & 2017). WildlifeDirect.

Kenya. 1975. *Statement on future wildlife management policy in Kenya*. Retrieved from https://books.google.co.ke/books?id=NmBJGwAACAAJ

Kenya Wildlife Conservancies Association. 2016. *State of wildlife conservancies in Kenya report 2016*. Nairobi: Kenya Wildlife Conservancies Association (KWCA).

Ministry of Environment, Water and Natural Resources. 2015. *Status Report on the compensation of victims of human-wildlife conflict, and alleged irregularity in the recruitment of Kenya Wildlife Service Rangers and efforts by KWS in the fight against poaching of elephants and rhinos*.

Nelson, F. (ed.). 2010. *Community rights, conservation and contested land: The politics of natural resource governance in Africa*. London: Earthscan.

Norton-Griffiths, M. 2010. The growing involvement of foreign NGOs in setting policy agendas and political decision-making in Africa. *Economic Affairs*, 30(3), 29–34. https://doi.org/10.1111/j.1468-0270.2010.02018.x

Republic of Kenya (RoK). 2014. *The wildlife conservation and management act*. kenyalaw.org/lex//index.xql.

Republic of Kenya (RoK), K.N.A. n.d. *Report on the consideration of the wildlife conservation and management bill, 2013*. The fourth report of the first session.

Western, D. 2000. Conservation in a human-dominated world. *Issues in Science and Technology*, 16(3). https://doi.org/10.1017/CBO9781139047791.010

Western, D., Waithaka, J. and Kamanga, J. 2015. Finding space for wildlife beyond national parks and reducing conflict through community-based conservation: The Kenya experience. *Parks*, 21(1), 51–62. https://doi.org/10.2305/IUCN.CH.2014.PARKS-21-1DW.en

11 The contribution of civil society generated evidence to the improvement of sanitation services in Ghana

Laila Smith, Dede Bedu-Addo, Mohammed Awal and Anthony Mensah

Summary

In Ghana in the wake of government shortfalls, civil society has played a strong role in financing, researching and designing processes and projects for service delivery, unlike many of its African peers. This case study explores the role of civil society tools in showcasing sanitation services at district level, including the I Am Aware initiative (IAA) and the more synthesised District League Table (DLT), promoted through an NGO, the Ghana Centre for Democratic Development (CDD-Ghana). The latter is a tool that provides an overall assessment of social development, ranking all districts across the country. The chapter examines how different stakeholders have used the DLT as evidence for enhancing performance in the sanitation sector. It highlights strengthened evidence use in assessing sanitation performance at the local level: citizens putting pressure on district assemblies for improving performance in sanitation; strengthening avenues for citizen-level engagement, creating a source of pressure at district level; civil society using the evidence for their own project planning; and motivating district assemblies to improve performance.

Background

This case study explores the role of civil society in the generation and use of evidence in influencing performance in the sanitation sector in Ghana, with a particular focus on the contribution of the I Am Aware (IAA) initiative, drawing on the District League Table (DLT) as the evidence base. Both were promoted through an NGO, CDD-Ghana. While both these tools look at basic services in general, the chapter looks at their role in relation to the sanitation sector in particular. While the IAA and DLT play a valuable role in helping to refine and improve the quality of indicators used to monitor district level performance in sanitation, it is important to recognise they are only a small part of civil society's contribution to move the sanitation sector forward over the past two decades. The concluding part of this chapter will briefly touch on some public engagement tactics used by civil society and how they have cumulatively contributed to positive reforms in the sanitation sector more broadly.

Data collection for this case study took place in late 2018 using qualitative methods involving primary and secondary research, a desk review of published documentation on the sector in general, and research and evaluation more specific to Ghana. Thirteen interviews were conducted with selected stakeholders. Two focus group meetings were conducted, including 14 civil society representatives and private sector faecal sludge service providers active in the urban sanitation sector. Further interviews were carried out in January 2019 with district-level government officials at Amasaman in the Ga West Municipal Area of the Greater Accra Region and in April and May 2019 with the Ministry of Sanitation and Water Resource Management and CDD-Ghana.

Limitations of the study included the difficulty in tracking the work of the large number of NGOs contributing to the sector. Their work and achievements are rarely documented (with the exception of reports directly to the donors funding them) and there is no clear mechanism for gathering and disseminating their substantial contributions to sanitation service delivery. This made it difficult to trace how their efforts were contributing to overall progress in the sector performance. However, it was clear that their efforts had brought about significant change in the sector.

Context

National context

Ghana was the first African country to gain independence in 1957. The country is largely decentralised with 16 regions that coordinate the bulk of public services. As at February 2019 Ghana had 260 metropolitan, municipal and district assemblies (MMDAs) that implemented government policies and provided social services at the local level.

Ghana is one of the fastest growing economies in Africa, recently recognised by the IMF as a middle-income country. Ghana's urban population doubled from 1984 to 2013 with growth averaging 3.5%. Today, the country is one of the most rapidly urbanising countries in Africa with an estimated 54.8% of the population living in towns and cities (WorldoMeters, 2019). However, many of these people still do not have adequate access to basic services.

The sanitation sector

Sanitation the world over is a major challenge because of limited political prioritisation and low fiscal commitments, and there is a weak understanding of the factors influencing high-level decision makers to commit to improved sanitation.

In Ghana sanitation provision is fraught with inequities, with the largest gap in access to improved sanitation (WHO/ UNICEF, 2017). The brunt of poor levels of sanitation is borne by the poorest in Ghana, where as recent as 2015, only 1% had access to basic sanitation and about 19 % practised open defecation (OD) (WHO/UNICEF, 2017, Ntow, 2019). Almost 57% of the population use shared latrines – a standard that is below the UN's acceptable levels for promoting safe and effective sanitation

The Joint Monitoring Programme (JMP) established by UNICEF to track country progress towards achieving MDG targets is a universally recognised source of evidence for tracking country coverage in water and sanitation. In 2015, the JMP ranked Ghana as the second lowest in the world with 15% of the population covered by basic sanitation, following South Sudan (Ibid.). This became a point of international embarrassment for Ghana's political leadership and an important catalyst for change, together with the evidence-based advocacy campaigns driven by large INGOs active in Ghana, such as WaterAid, Trend and SNV as well as Coalition of NGOs in Water and Sanitation (CONIWAS), the sector's coalition of civil society organisations. According to the latest available domestic statistics, there has been an improvement of basic provision for sanitation moving from 15% in 2015 to an estimated 21% in 2018 (Ghana Statistical Services, 2018).

Institutions and stakeholders influencing the sector

STATE ACTORS

Following sustained lobbying from civil society in the lead up to the 2016 elections, President Nana Addo Danquah Akuffo-Addo provided crucial leadership and commitment to driving efforts in addressing the country's challenges in the sector. In January 2017, the Ministry of Sanitation and Water (MSWR) was established, absorbing the functions of the Directorate of the Environmental Health and Sanitation Division (EHSD), which had previously been in the Ministry of Local Government and Rural Development (MLGRD). The MSWR is responsible for policy formulation, harmonisation and coordination of water, sanitation and hygiene (WASH) activities, through its Water Director and Environmental Health and Sanitation Directorate (Appiah-Effah et al., 2019, p. 404). The Ministry also determines key indicators that are tracked by the Ministry of Monitoring and Evaluation.

At district level, Metropolitan, Municipal and District Assemblies (MMDAs) are the basic unit of government and the statutory deliberative and legislative body for the determination of broad policy objectives of the development processes within their jurisdictions (Government of Ghana (GoG), Ministry of Water Resources Works and Housing, 2010). They are responsible for rural, small-town and urban water and sanitation delivery using the private sector for infrastructure planning and delivery, and communities or private operators for management (Respondent 6 – Government). They also play the role of regulator, for example, approving tariffs. District assemblies (DAs) are responsible for the planning, implementation, operation and maintenance of water and sanitation facilities and the legal owners of communal infrastructures in rural communities and small towns (Water and Sanitation Monitoring Platform, 2009). Under this authority, District Environmental Health Officers educate communities on sanitation and hygiene and enforce regulations regarding the construction, use, and management of public as well as institutional and household facilities (Respondent 8 – Government).

The EHSD is responsible for sanitation policy-based oversight (Ibid). The ability to provide effective oversight is hampered by inadequate evidence from performance monitoring and annual reports from the National Development Planning

Commission (NDPC), which are usually published late. The overall responsibility for district performance rests with MLGRD as it carries the human resource responsibilities for the civil service at district level. Embedding similar roles in different ministries at different levels makes coordination a challenge. As indicated by one of the district assembly staff, their dual responsibility to MLGRD and MSWR is difficult as they feel as if their 'head is with MLGRD and legs are with MSWR' (Respondent 1 – Government). Sanitation issues are underreported because most agencies at district level do different WASH activities for which they are not responsible to MSWR. Coordination is particularly problematic with regards to the regulation, monitoring and supervision of private sector service providers.

The Sanitation Ministry is developing its own reporting system to address these coordination gaps (Respondent 8 – Government), but this has been in the making for over a decade. Although most service delivery in the sector at district level has been outsourced to the private sector, government provides little support for their work and consequently has little oversight of their activities (TREND, 2003, Focus group 1). Moreover, where activities are regulated by other agencies, the MSWR has little control over them and may not even receive reports of their activities. For instance, the Environmental Protection Agency, which regulates sanitation provision, is not under the Ministry of Sanitation. This makes coordination of the private sector's work in this area even more difficult (Respondent 3 – Private sector).

Part of the limited performance of sanitation coordination and regulation at the district level is that it has historically been an unfunded mandate. As such, the limited resource allocation for liquid waste in particular at the district level has negatively affected the effectiveness of decentralisation of sanitation service delivery.

NON-STATE ACTORS

Ghana, unlike many of its African counterparts, is a relatively inclusive society[1] with a favourable environment for civil society participation in service provision. One underlying reason is the historical leadership that civil society has provided in financing, researching and designing processes and projects for service delivery in the wake of government shortfalls. This was made possible through international donors'[2] funding of sanitation, predominantly in rural areas, over several decades. The bulk of these resources have been channelled through international non-government organisations (INGOs) and civil society organisations (CSOs).

The state's openness to consultation, debate and engagement has created an opportunity for civil society to play a leading role in moving the sanitation sector forward. This has given civil society legitimacy in the eyes of the state, which has been leveraged to ensure regular and systematised engagement with government in service delivery and polity reform in the sanitation sector.

INGOs and CSOs support government and other agencies in implementation of sanitation programmes through participation in policy dialogue; facilitation of innovation and sharing of best practices; provision of capacity support to community structures; and participation in thematic studies and/or action research. They also support collaboration and coordination within the sanitation sub-sector. These international organisations tend to work in partnership with local CSOs at the district level or in collaboration with other national CSOs.

The coordination of these international and local alliances for advocacy purposes is steered through the Coalition of NGOs in Water and Sanitation (CONIWAS), which has been vital in uniting the voice of civil society in the water and sanitation sector. This has been applied in advocacy, lobbying and engagement with the state on policy reform, and mobilising sector actors for actions that are non-confrontational but capable of resolving sector concerns.

A key protagonist for this story is the CDD-Ghana, which is not sector-focused but rather advocacy-oriented in promoting inclusive participation aimed at strengthening democratic governance and the demand for public accountability in Ghana and Africa. CDD-Ghana was established in 1998 as an independent, non-partisan, not-for-profit research and advocacy think tank. The centre uses research, ideas and partnerships to encourage dialogue to inform and influence public policy and to mobilise citizen engagement at district level on local development issues. A mentioned earlier, this case pays particular attention to two linked interventions by CDD-Ghana for evidence production at district level that have influenced a reform agenda for sanitation and social service provision: the I Am Aware (IAA) campaign leading to the District League Table (DLT) as a source of evidence for this advocacy.

Evidence gaps in the sanitation sector and the need for citizen engagement

Within Ghana, a key constraint to citizen participation, governmental accountability and responsiveness of public services is limited access to user-friendly, government-produced information on the state, provision and quality of public goods and services (CDD-Ghana, 2017; Respondent 10 – Non-government). The state needs more robust and uniform sources of evidence to continually assess the sector's key policy objectives and improve accountability and investment outcomes at both national and local levels. Meanwhile, from a citizens' perspective, the public needs greater evidence to address weak accountability at the district level and improve district assembly responsiveness to service delivery challenges.

This situation is compounded by weak incentives at all levels of government around the use of evidence. Decision making is often not evidence-based and driven by emotional or political considerations (Twende Mbele, 2019). In addition, availability of data within government entities is constrained due to limited resources and capacities for evidence generation, coordination and use at the district level and upwards. There is weak regulation by the Ministry of Sanitation and Water Resources due to the reliance on evidence from the districts, which themselves have limited capacity to assess performance in sanitation (Respondent 6 – Non-government). Where evidence is being generated by non-state actors, its use by the state is hindered by bureaucratic rigidities. For example, many civil society actors do not formally register their presence at the district level. Without this registration, the evidence from non-state actors cannot be used by district authorities when collating service delivery data.

In response to these challenges, over the years various partnerships have emerged between key national, policy and management institutions as well as CSOs to produce and manage data. These partnerships undertake analysis to inform the development of evidence-based human development policy, strategic planning, monitoring and evaluation, and management capacity, and to build the capacity of the citizenry to participate in the development process and take advantage of emerging economic activities (UNDP Ghana, 2019).

Increasing access to evidence in the sanitation sector

Many state and non-state agencies in Ghana have worked together to use evidence to move the sanitation sector forward. The key champions include UNICEF Ghana, CDD-Ghana, WaterAid, SNV and IRC working with government departments such as MLGRD, Office of the Head of Civil Service, MSWR, the Ministry of Monitoring and Evaluation (MoME), NDPC and MMDAs. Civil society, through its various engagements in generating evidence within the sanitation sector, is an important source of data and engaging in an evidence-informed way through their own respective advocacy efforts and through CONIWAS, as well as through their direct district to national level partnerships.

Bridging the gaps – the IAA and DLT tools

In 2011, CDD-Ghana began the IAA initiative, a 'non-partisan citizen empowerment tool' established to empower citizens and improve their awareness and engagement with duty bearers by providing free, user-friendly, accessible information on the provision of public goods and services in order to strengthen the demand for public accountability. Working with various partners and government agencies at both national and sub-national level, the project disseminates district-level information focused on service delivery performance through radio, town hall meetings, and the use of SMS text messages (Jones et al., 2019, p. 4). IAA has a data facility centre that helps assemble, archive, and disseminate information related to citizen feedback on service delivery performance through the channels outlined earlier. IAA conducts further analysis of the institutional, accountability and governance context of different services. These are prepared by CDD-Ghana staff and shared locally through fact sheets and briefing reports in local languages with citizens and used for discussions with government officials in live interaction sessions.

CDD-Ghana works with CSO partners who have been trained to work in the regions: each region is covered by one CSO for two districts per region. These IAA district partners organise Citizens' Social Action Groups (comprising 13 to 15 members each) within each Local Area Council/community group and these citizen accountability-demanding groups are trained on how to analyse data and use it to demand accountability and better services. Other groups include parent/teacher associations (PTAs), farmer-based organisations (FBOs), and women's and youth groups that are representative and inclusive of all zones of the project's districts. They also receive governance and accountability literacy training at the local level. The groups then go back to work with their communities to raise awareness on public service delivery issues.

In 2014, CDD-Ghana, through the IAA project, partnered with UNICEF Ghana to design and launch a new social accountability tool dubbed the Ghana District League Table (DLT), previously tested in Latin America, which summarises performance against a set of service indicators at the outcome level. It seeks to improve citizens' access to information about the state, provision and quality of basic public services in order to increase their demand for accountability and to improve responsiveness in service delivery. The DLT also seeks to support government to track development levels across the country and use peer pressure to motivate district assemblies to improve services.

The DLT is an extension of the IAA project concept. While the IAA focuses on sector-based input and output indicators, the DLT focuses on outcome indicators in six sectors: education, health, water, sanitation, security and governance. The information from these six sectors is aggregated into a single index that is used to rank all the districts in Ghana to identify those doing well and those performing poorly. All DLT data is sourced from administrative data provided through the ministries, departments and agencies (MDAs) responsible for the six DLT sectors.[3] These ministries depend on District Assembly reporting on the state of provision and quality of services generated annually. The data is collected annually and cleaned and processed by CDD-Ghana.

The IAA disseminates the DLT evidence through a website that enables users to compare quality in selected districts. This district level data is presented as graphs. Furthermore, the IAA prepares bulletins that provide infographics that compare the quality of service in particular districts to national averages. A free SMS platform is also set up for citizens to text in requests for data from the DLT, which is sent to them on their phones (Jones et al., 2019, p. 4).

What makes up the sanitation DLT indicator

The sanitation sector performance indicator used in the DLT is Open Defecation Free (ODF) certification (percentage of communities certified as ODF), as it was a chief concern of both the wider public as well as government. Discussions with CDD-Ghana and the MSWR revealed that the ODF indicator is seen as a multi-sectoral outcome indicator to measure quality of sanitation, with links to health, education and the environment. 'Open defecation free villages' is a composite indicator that is made up of numerous other output indicators relating to systems being in place to keep villages free of visible waste and employing hygiene practices.

For instance, output indicators would monitor latrine construction at the household level, with handwashing facilities with soap or ash close to these facilities, and evidence of handwashing practices being available to ensure hygiene behaviour. These output indicators are tracked by various ministries who carry responsibility for specific elements of the sanitation system. The Ministry of Health engages in the hygiene dimensions of the composite indicator and the illnesses that arise from poor hygiene behaviour; the Ministry of Education engages in the mechanisms around awareness-raising associated with hygiene promotion; while the Ministry of Sanitation engages with latrine construction and overall outcome of the composite indicator.

Promoting the use of the evidence from IAA/DLT

A number of interventions were intentionally used in order to promote use of the evidence emerging from DLT. Many of these interventions built relationships, a sense of ownership and trust in the evidence through enabling interaction between evidence users. For example, the use of workshops and regular meetings to engage government at multiple levels around methodological design resulting in ensuring ownership as well as building of relationships and trust. The interventions also strengthened incentives for evidence use – through, for example, using a ranking system and strengthening awareness and understanding of the value of evidence for improving performance. Table 11.1 provides an overview of the use interventions and change mechanisms activated.

Types of evidence use that emerged

Strengthening capabilities for evidence-based advocacy

According to a formative evaluation conducted on the IAA, its evidence-informed campaigns using DLT data have helped strengthen the confidence and capabilities of citizens to engage through civic groups. This has become a pressure point on government actors to improve service delivery, particularly at the sub-national level, and has also inspired citizens to work with district assemblies to use the DLT evidence to monitor the state of service delivery (Jones et al., 2019). In particular, the role of citizens in interrogating the output indicators and engaging with district assemblies on the accuracy and relevance in how they are used has contributed to improving the quality of district level data in the sanitation sector (Respondent 3 – Civil society).

The work done at the ground level through the IAA has helped create more robust evidence for civil society at a national level to use in their advocacy engagements (Jones et al., 2019; Ntow, 2019).

Supporting evidence-informed advocacy for improved service delivery

The DLT is utilised by CSOs to influence the development of District Medium Term Development Plans and local CSOs use the evidence to convince the district assembly to provide more equitable distribution of national resources to communities living in deprived areas. The Garu Tempane District is a good example of the use of data for advocacy by CSOs. RISE Ghana, a local NGO, and a citizen's group called the IAA Volunteers used district data to put forward a written petition from citizens to the District Assembly. This was successful

Table 11.1 Evidence use interventions around the IAA/DLT and the changes these influenced

Evidence use interventions	Effect – change mechanisms activated that enabled use of evidence
Workshop to review the indicators and to explore new ones for inclusion in the DLT performance assessment	CDD-Ghana and UNICEF organise an annual methodological review consultative workshop, with government data-producing agencies at the central government level responsible for all sectors assessed in the DLT, to review the indicators and to explore new ones for inclusion into the DLT performance assessment. The workshops enable building of relationships, and create a sense of ownership, ultimately strengthening evidence uptake from the findings of the DLT
Training of citizen groups to analyse and utilise data to demand accountability and better services as well as governance and accountability literacy more broadly	Increases awareness of the potential of evidence as well as the ability to analyse and use evidence
Active advocacy by CSOs and citizen groups for government to support the use of evidence	Dialogue and engagement processes enable agreement between and ownership of the evidence by partners as well as district staff
Convening of regular meetings with sectors at district level	Interaction with districts allows for the development of *relationships* between CSOs and District Assemblies, therefore strengthening *trust* in the evidence and building abilities and confidence of district staff to use the evidence
Annual national launch of the DLT hosted by CDD-Ghana and UNICEF and regional- and district-level engagements after the analysis of the report/ production of the scorecard	The regional- and district-level engagements include town hall meetings, meetings with government officials, specific policy planning meetings, e.g. district annual MTDP planning meetings. These forums engage and enable citizens in understanding the data for their own social action together with the media and provide a space for interaction and engagement with politicians and sector-based bureaucrats.
Providing access to data and analysis in user-friendly formats	This allows individuals to understand and relate to the evidence
Presenting the evidence in comparative formats through using a ranking system for districts	Promoting awareness of the evidence and appreciation of the value of evidence, leading to the improved institutionalisation of evidence use by making it a part of professional norms and cultures and thereby creating/ strengthening motivation for use
CDD/UNICEF promoting DLT uptake to have the DLT used as an additional criterion for the DPAT	
Allocation of national budget based on the provision of data and reports	

in convincing the district to construct a toilet and urinal in the Garu market (Jones et al., 2019).

Influencing district performance management systems

Evidence from the evaluation of the IAA confirms that the greatest responsiveness to the DLT data is at the district level. Having sampled staff in four districts across Ghana, the IAA evaluation found that these district assemblies have integrated some citizen priorities into their medium-term development plans and that these have commenced service delivery improvements in three of the four districts noted earlier (Ibid., p. 6). The evaluation found that the publicity and pressure around the DLT has been a significant driver for increased district level responsiveness because it created competition and embarrassment among district officials and the space for citizen dialogue on sector data (Ibid.). DAs that perform poorly on the DLT are flagged at national level as 'problem districts', a status that few district authorities want to be labelled with (Respondent 8 – Government).

The DLT has no reward system beyond peer pressure through benchmarking and so districts are not always motivated to respond to its requirements. This is slowly changing, with greater awareness among districts of the links between the DLT and improved district performance (discussed further around the District Performance Assessment Tool (DPAT) system). This awareness raising is also promoted through nationally led campaigns (Wumbel 2017).

Informing planning and budget allocations

Evidence of civil society use of the DLT can also be found in the IAA evaluation (Jones et al., 2019). The evaluation found evidence that the DLT had been widely disseminated at national level and that most policy and advocacy organisations had used it, and that civil society used the DLT to plan their geographical focus for service delivery interventions, for advocacy at the district level and for policy analysis (Ibid., p. 5). Further evidence through a series of workshops held with national sanitation civil society role players found that the DLT was foundational to the more sophisticated generation of evidence through their service delivery work (Ntow, 2019).

CSOs and citizens use the DLT for advocacy from the district level downwards. The District Performance Assessment Tool (DPAT) is a performance assessment system that relies on the same administrative data that feeds the DLT but is used upwards from the District Assemblies by the MDAs (Government of Ghana, Ministry of Local Government and Rural Development (MLGRD, 2018). The NDPC and MOME noted that the allocation of national budgetary resources by the Ministry of Finance (MoF) is now based on submission of plans, implementation reports and medium-term development plans, certified by NDPC (Respondents 4 and 11 – Government). The growing responsiveness of district assembly officials to how they are ranked through the DPAT system, drawing on the same administrative data that feeds the DLT, has helped motivate improved performance. The carrot is the implication of not being able to access further funds from central government if the assessment in the DPAT for the environment, within which the category of sanitation sits, is low. This behaviour change has influenced the structure and process of the public administration by influencing decision making in budgetary allocation at the district level. This, in turn, has led to greater budgetary support from the national treasury for sanitation at district level because districts are performing better in addressing the systems required to increase the number of villages/settlements that are ODF.

Analysing use and the factors that contributed to use

Interventions undertaken to promote use of evidence

The IAA campaign, drawing on the DLT evidence, has entailed a series of process facilitation activities that are beginning to produce higher-quality data generation at the district level and greater citizen capacity to hold local government to account for sanitation performance. This has been achieved through CSOs and government stakeholders drawing on deliberate and strategic use interventions to ensure use of the district sanitation evidence that is generated at the local level and fed into national administrative systems. Table 11.1 describes these interventions and the effect they had on individuals, which ultimately resulted in use of the evidence at an organisation and systems level.

The interventions used by the IAA campaign (described in Table 11.1) drawing on the DLT evidence was timely, strategic and effective in enabling evidence use.

Process facilitation

Enabling dialogue (through workshops, meetings, etc.), for example, allowed district assemblies and CSOs to work together to co-create the methodologies and approaches used to generate the evidence as well as jointly engage in sense-making of the evidence. The trust, relationships, sense of ownership and understanding that emerged through these interactions were important in building capabilities to use the evidence.

While this has been the general sense, there are still some districts that feel there is room for improvement in how the DLT process is integrated into District Assembly assessments used for the DPAT system. This would enable district officials to gain a better understanding of what the criteria for performance assessments are and how these measurements used are used by national institutions.

Knowledge brokering

As discussed in Chapter 2, linkages between supply and demand of evidence need to be deliberately enabled and supported. Accessing, synthesising and analysing as well as disseminating this data through the use of fact sheets, briefs and forums, and training citizen groups was seen as essential in bridging supply and demand at the local level. These functions also essentially served to translate the evidence into an accessible and useful format thereby strengthening the opportunities to utilise evidence.

Institutionalising evidence use

Formalising the use of evidence through linking it to performance management systems provided incentives and, therefore, motivation for evidence use. CDD and UNICEF, through their efforts to encourage policy uptake and advocacy, are working with MLGRD for the DLT to be used as additional criteria for the DPAT. The use of the DLT as a simple and ready-to-use source of evidence for national performance assessment in sanitation has not yet been institutionalised by MLGRD for use in assessing the performance of district assemblies in relation to sanitation. Nevertheless, two civil society workshops on sanitation indicators held in April and June have indicated that this formalisation is well on its way.[4]

Barriers and enablers of evidence use

There were multiple barriers and enablers that influenced the success of interventions described earlier and overall evidence use.

Enablers

At the outset, Ghana had a developed culture of inclusivity with effective platforms and mechanisms for consultation and participation and the support of development partners to promote social accountability, and well-established collaborative relationships between the different stakeholders. This enabled the flow of information and involvement of civil society, notably in the lead up to decision-making processes (Respondent 2 – Non-government). Of importance to the sanitation sector was the presence of CSOs with capacities to assist in addressing challenges.

This provided a receptive environment for changes to the sector advocated for by external influencers (e.g. the eThekwini Declaration by African water and sanitation ministers)[5] as well as popular pressure from within the country, driven by national coalitions of sanitation NGOs such as CONIWAS (Water Aid Ghana, 2012). However, this may not have been sufficient without the leadership of the newly elected president, who championed the changes necessary to improve the performance of the sector.

The DLT introduced a shift in the types of evidence being generated from input/output levels to outcomes, which better enabled assessment of performance and decision making around service delivery. In addition, the DLT/IAA projects also provided higher levels of brokered knowledge, such as analysing

Barriers

There continue to be insufficient resources allocated to evidence generation, resulting in gaps in the types of evidence generated, and the data does not cover the entire sanitation chain. For example, there is not enough data collected on transport of waste from the household and how it is treated and disposed of. This is further compounded by inadequate coordination of non-state actor-generated evidence, which is needed to understand performance at the district level, particularly in urban areas. The limited scope of the DLT indicators being tracked affects the ability to see the overall bigger picture around sector performance.

One of the most significant barriers to the use of evidence in the sanitation sector is staff capacity. Coordinating directors and engineers in the MMDAs all have first and second degrees. In an environmental unit or department, an environmental health officer who does not hold a degree is often 'found wanting' when they come face-to-face with other staff and directors who are degree holders. Psychologically, there is the feeling that they are not at par or co-equals in the workplace (Respondent 8: Government). This negatively affects their capacity to perform their roles, especially when it comes to regulatory oversight at the district level.

Another barrier around capacity is that, although they appreciate the outputs of the projects, many key state and non-state political and social accountability stakeholders, such as Parliament, CSOs and media, lack the capacity to analyse and use the evidence generated by the IAA and DLT projects to inform policy and demand for responsiveness and accountability in public service provision.

Use of evidence is in itself an enabler to evidence use (or conversely in the case of lack of use as earlier discussed). Although public discussion of engagement with DLT evidence through the IAA is heightened around the release of the annual DLT report, it is not sustained until the next round of the report is released (Respondents 9, 10 – Non-government). This leads to poor use of the evidence or data gathered as people soon forget about the DLT results until the next report is due. Finding social champions to lead advocacy initiatives is needed to sustain the momentum following the national annual launch of the DLT.

Emerging lessons

How context and intervention influenced the use of evidence

Overall, it appears that the environment was appropriate for changes in the use of evidence in the sanitation sector. The political milieu was more conducive to inclusion of all stakeholders in the national development process and Ghana was making strides in political democracy and social cohesion. To address the historically poor performance of sanitation at district level, UNICEF, development partners and a wide spectrum of national CSOs sought to promote greater social accountability between the state, CSOs, and other partners in improving the performance of the sanitation sector.

Moreover, sanitation was on the rise as an area of focus of increased pressure from civil society. This coincided with increasing use of the DLT to help standardise government's own data on district performance, combined with increasing citizen engagement in making sense of district data and using this to lobby for improved district performance in sanitation. The use of information and communication technology for disseminating the DLT data fit well with the wave of interconnectivity and the current, high use of social media in Ghana. This has made the data generated more user-friendly and easily accessible to all citizens.

Overall, the DLT partnership is working well. However, after four years of implementation, partners are now frustrated because broader resource allocation at national level is still not working well through MOFEP, MDAs and the District Assembly Common Fund (DACF). The partners are, therefore, advocating for the District Development Fund (DDF) to become part of a reward system to serve as motivation for the MMDAs to participate in the DLT. The partners are working with Parliament to query budget allocation and push for better resource allocation. Learning from the National Development Planning Commission's 'carrot' reward scheme with the certification of development plans for the receipt of government budget allocations, may be a good way to ensure wider resource allocation at the national level (Respondent 5 – Non-government).

Strengthening and coordinating the data system

Ghana has strong, capable national-level CSOs that have played a significant contribution in moving the sector forward. Their contributions on service delivery, however, are limited to the districts where they are funded to work, and therefore the ability to feed these results into a national picture is non-existent. There has been a long-standing plea from civil society to the Ministry of Sanitation and Water Resources and its institutional predecessors to play this coordinating role so as to be able to better use the various sources of evidence that civil society is generating. The data ecosystem and governance infrastructure in Ghana needs to be strengthened and harmonised to support the production and access to timely, trusted/reliable, relevant data for policy uptake.

Suppliers of evidence need to better understand policy processes

As civil society players are still significant actors in the delivery of sanitation services, they are also the generators of the evidence stemming from this engagement (Ntow, 2019). As noted earlier, this evidence feeds into their monitoring systems, which report to a variety of funders. However, as it is not centralised, it is difficult to gain a broader national understanding of how each project is influencing the progress in systems of delivery.

The systematic practice of evidence use in policy making, analysis and evaluation within and across government and key social actors in Ghana needs to be strengthened. Non-state data producers (CSOs and academia) need to improve their understanding of how, when and which government institutions and other actors use evidence to inform policy design, implementation and monitoring so that they are better equipped to use these opportunities well for improved sanitation services. CONIWAS has been loudest in lobbying the state to address the coordination of data systems highlighted earlier. As a knowledge broker trusted by civil society and the state, CONIWAS could play a valuable role in mentoring civil society in where and when to influence decision making with the evidence they have generated from their service delivery work.

Ownership of the evidence is critical for use

Developing and building an inclusive culture is paramount in promoting evidence use at all levels of society. Evidence tends to be used when government and key stakeholders are involved in the evidence process from the design stage. Uptake of evidence by government is facilitated when government sees the evidence as part of its developmental objectives in ensuring informed decision making. With reference to non-state actors, community and individual ownership of the evidence process is key in creating the environment for policy mechanisms to work for the desired policy outcomes where these require behaviour change by citizens.

Champions are key

The role of champions, such as a president, UNICEF, CONIWAS and CDD, when combined can be catalytic in moving a sector forward. This was illustrated in this case study through the President, declaring his support for a particular policy intervention during his presidential campaign through intense lobbying by CONIWAS. Once in power, he then followed through to create and support the mechanisms for it to happen until the desired policy outcomes are achieved. UNICEF's funding of a Ghanaian adaptation of the IAA and DLT has built the tools to benchmark and expose poor performance in the sector at the district level. Government and other stakeholders act speedily when the evidence shames or embarrasses them.

Collaboration requires trust

Fortunately, the history of an inclusive culture in Ghana has helped build a historically close engagement between civil society as implementors of sanitation, and as such, also valuable knowledge brokers because of their own role in evidence generation. This long-standing state dependency on civil society to carry the sector forward, thanks in large part to development partner funding, has been instrumental in creating the foundations for trust between the state and civil society, an uncommon trait in many other African countries. This also calls for improved and increased access to and use of basic indicators for social development. This makes it easier for all stakeholders and citizens to engage with the data as knowledge and use of data/evidence is empowering for all: citizens, government (at all levels) and CSOs. However there needs to be more trust between policy makers and other data producers, users, evaluators (CSOs/think tanks) to facilitate and amplify learning and innovation around the relevance and use of evidence in policy/decision making.

Conclusion

The IAA campaign and the DLT have begun to effect change in the use of evidence for improving district level performance in sanitation. However, these changes cannot be isolated from broader changes over the last decade with sustained and active engagement by a community of active civil society actors at the national level. These combined efforts have contributed to a series of interventions and investments that demonstrate the state's growing presence in raising awareness through incentive schemes and increasing allocations to this long-neglected sector.[6]

Around the world, many NGOs have demonstrated the ability to undertake high-quality research using results and evidence-based approaches. However, this evidence is not always recognised as credible or legitimate by other actors in accountability processes. The IAA campaign, drawing on DLT evidence, is an illustration of moving beyond this barrier to provide ongoing and sustained evidence that has now become institutionalised within government, at various levels. The need for increased recognition of the potential use of CSO-generated evidence in policy interventions is a key lesson emanating from this study. In terms of relevance for Africa, the findings from this research will be particularly valuable in informing engagements in addressing institutional barriers around greater use of CSO-generated evidence and advocacy tools for promoting greater prioritisation of sanitation in state decisions around budget and human resource allocations.

Notes

1 According to the Mo Ibrahim Index IIAG scorecard on Governance, Ghana ranks fifth in Africa on participation and human rights.
2 Notably UNICEF and World Bank.
3 These include Ghana Education Service (GES); Ghana Health Service (GHS); Community Water and Sanitation Agency (CWSA); Ghana Water Company (GWC); Ghana Police Service (GPS); and Environmental Health and Sanitation and Ministry of Local Government and Rural Development (MLGRD).

4 This progress was confirmed at a meeting between UNICEF, GMEF and the NDPC on 16 December 2019.
5 The eThekwini declaration was part of the second Africasan Conference held in Durban in 2008. Water and Sanitation ministers announced the commitment for a separate budget line for sanitation to enable greater transparency in tracking state resources going towards sanitation as well as an annual budget allocation commitment of 0.5% of GDP.
6 Including substantive budget allocations by the state towards the government contribution of the second phase of the Greater Accra Metropolitan Area (GAMA) sanitation project, funded through a USD 150 million World Bank loan to the Ghanaian government in 2015; increased budgetary allocations to MSWR; a promotion of the development and use of tools such as the Sanitation Index for all MMDAs; and an award scheme launched by MSWR to reward private sector actors supporting MMDAs in a National Sanitation Challenge programme to successfully implement their liquid waste management strategy proposals.

References

Appiah-Effah, E., Duku, G., Azangbego, N., Aggrey, R., Gyapong-Korsah, B. and Nyarko, K. 2019. Ghana's post-MDGs sanitation situation: An overview. *Journal of Water, Sanitation and Hygiene for Development*, 9, 3.

CDD-Ghana. 2017. *Ghana's district league table report 2017*. Retrieved 6 November, 2018, from www.iamawareghana.com; www.cddgh.org/publications

Ghana Statistical Service. 2018. *Snapshots on key findings, Ghana Multiple Indicator Cluster Survey (MICS 2017/18)*. Survey, Findings Report, Accra, Ghana.

Government of Ghana, Ministry of Local Government and Rural Development (MLGRD). 2018. *District performance assembly tool: Operational manual*. Retrieved from www.mlgrd. gov.gh/ctn-media/filer_public/b1/d2/b1d2f2c0-66fb-4f1a-9366-bfc169e49396/2018_ dpat_operational_manual.pdf

Government of Ghana (GoG), Ministry of Water Resources Works and Housing (MWRWH). 2010. *Water and sanitation sector performance report*. Retrieved 20 March 2019, from www. washghana.net/ . . . /Final_2010_Sector_Performance_Report[1].pdf

Jones, E., Amidu, I. and Nyarko, C. 2019. *Formative evaluation of the 'I Am Aware' social accountability project in Ghana*. Oxford, UK: Oxford Policy Management Limited.

Mo Ibrahim Index. 2018. Retrieved from http://s.mo.ibrahim.foundation/u/2018/10/ 26173830/2018-IIAG-scorecard-GH.pdf

Ntow, S. 2019. *Baseline report: Sanitation status in Ghana and the role of CSOs in the policy processes*. Report Commissioned by Twende Mbele.

Progress on Drinking Water, Sanitation and Hygiene. 2017. *Update and SDG baselines*. Geneva: World Health Organization (WHO) and the United Nations Children's Fund (UNICEF). Licence: CC BY-NC-SA 3.0 IGO.

Trend Group. 2003. *Water, sanitation and service delivery in Ghana, Ghana*. Retrieved 20 March 2019, from www.ircwash.org/sites/default/files/WELL-2003-Water.doc

Twende Mbele. 2019. *M&E culture baseline study*. Ghana: Executive Summary.

UNDP. 2019. *Promoting inclusive growth and development*. Retrieved from www.gh.undp.org/ content/ghana/en/home/operations/projects/poverty_reduction/all-projects.html

World Health Organization (WHO) and the United Nations Children's Fund (UNICEF), 2017. Progress on Drinking Water, Sanitation and Hygiene: 2017 Update and SDG Baselines. Geneva. Licence: CC BY-NC-SA 3.0 IGO.

Water Aid Ghana. 2012. *CSOs' assessment of Ghana's eThekwini commitments compiled by Ibrahim Musa, Economic Impacts of Poor Sanitation in Africa, UNDP-Water & Sanitation Program*

Report, March 2012. Retrieved from https://washwatch.org/uploads/filer_public/86/d2/86d2ad38-ae52-4e77-bf3c-36c68cc39d75/cso_ethekwini_assement_-_ghana.pdf

Water and Sanitation Monitoring Platform. 2009. *Status of Ghana's drinking W&S sector.* Country summary sheet. Ghana. Retrieved 18 March 2019, from www.wsmp.org/downloads/country-summary-sheet-09.pdf

WorldoMeters. Retrieved 14 April 2019, from www.worldometers.info/world-population/ghana-population/.

Wumbel, A. *Every day is sanitation day.* Retrieved 28 November 2017, from www.ircwash.org/news/every-day-sanitation-day

12 Using evidence for tobacco control in West Africa

Papa Yona Boubacar Mane, Abdoulaye Diagne and Salifou Tiemtore

Summary

The marketing of tobacco products in poor countries is intensifying. Despite their commitment, in 2010, the 15 countries that make up the Economic Community of West African States (ECOWAS) were still far from a legislative environment conducive to tobacco control. This case study focuses on the application of the World Health Organization Framework Convention on Tobacco Control (FCTC) in West Africa, and how the use of action research to generate evidence and the creation of consensus between the different stakeholders involved in tobacco control can change policy. The process was supported through an action-research process led by the Consortium for Economic and Social Research, based in Senegal, working closely with ECOWAS. Research was conducted in each country, tax rates were modelled, and the situation and possible taxation rates workshopped with stakeholders, including members of the ECOWAS legislature. The evidence produced and the actions undertaken have contributed to the adoption of a new law on tobacco control in Senegal and a new directive on the taxation of tobacco products in the ECOWAS area, which is now better able to comply with the provisions of the FCTC.

Background

Tobacco control is a global public health priority. According to the World Health Organization (WHO), smoking kills more than five million people per year worldwide (WHO, 2015). If nothing is done, by 2030, the number of tobacco-related deaths per year will double. More than 40% of these deaths will occur in developing countries (Goodchild et al., 2018). Strong tobacco control policies are leading to a decline in consumption in developed countries (Chaloupka et al., 2010). This is leading to an intensification of tobacco marketing in poor countries, shifting the future burden of tobacco-related mortality and morbidity to developing countries (IARC, 2011). Under the aegis of the WHO, the international community has decided to take action through the WHO Framework Convention on Tobacco Control (FCTC), which was signed in 2003. All 15 countries that are part of the Economic Community of West African States (ECOWAS) have ratified this framework convention.

Despite their commitment to tobacco control, in 2010, these 15 countries were still far from a legislative environment conducive to tobacco control. National laws for control were either non-existent, incomplete or not enforced. Tax policies were far from sufficient to reverse the trend of increasing tobacco consumption or to control tobacco use. This was due to two main constraints. First, tobacco industry lobbying has been successful in countering or circumventing any laws or regulations made by states. Second, there was a lack of knowledge about the use of tax policy as an effective means of tobacco control and only timid reforms undertaken in this field by tax administrations. In addition, countries ignored the policies of their neighbours, even though they belonged to ECOWAS and some are also part of the West African Economic and Monetary Union (WAEMU).

Other factors were that civil society had not seen the potential of a tobacco tax and researchers were not interested in the issue. Meanwhile, the regional directives that defined the taxation of tobacco products by ECOWAS and WAEMU member states proposed a type of tax, tax rates, and a tax base that did not promote an effective tax policy.

On a global scale, there is renewed interest in protecting health through tobacco control. Since their engagement by the FCTC, ECOWAS countries have increasingly participated in major international meetings on health and tobacco, including the Conference of the Parties to the WHO FCTC and the World Tobacco Conference. This has raised awareness in ECOWAS countries of the challenges of tobacco control and of the need to set up an appropriate framework for the transposition of the WHO Framework Convention. It is in this context that these countries have implemented changes in their tobacco control environment. This chapter presents the process of implementing these changes through a participatory approach based on action research.

This case study focuses on the application of the Framework Convention in West Africa, and the development and passing of a directive with much more punitive tax rates on tobacco. It demonstrates how the use of action research to generate evidence and the creation of consensus between the different stakeholders involved in tobacco control can change policy. The evidence produced and the actions undertaken have contributed to the adoption of a new law on tobacco control in Senegal and a new directive on the taxation of tobacco products in the ECOWAS area, which is now better able to comply with the provisions of the FCTC. The process was supported through an action-research process led by the Consortium for Economic and Social Research (CRES)[1] based in Senegal.

An earlier CRES-led action-research project ran from 2011 to 2017. The research for the case study underlying this chapter used the following methodology. Initially, a literature review was conducted on the taxation of tobacco. The various reports and outputs produced by the previous action-research project were analysed to understand the context and environment of tobacco control, the process of adopting the new directive, the various challenges facing ECOWAS countries and the main results of that action-research project. Following the literature review, nine people were interviewed: the ECOWAS representative and the director of CRES (the two champions in this case study), two representatives of research institutes,

208 *Papa Yona Boubacar Mane et al.*

two representatives of tax administrations, a representative from WAEMU, and representatives from a tobacco control focal point and from a civil society organisation. A questionnaire was submitted to respondents a week in advance. The questions were discussed in a telephonic interview where the respondent lived outside Senegal, and in a face-to-face interview where the respondent lived in Senegal.

The evolution of the tobacco control process

The institutional context

Unlike other cases in this book, this case has a regional dimension. WAEMU and ECOWAS play a growing role in West Africa, particularly in a strategic aspect of tobacco control, namely tobacco taxation. The ECOWAS and WAEMU commissions are the bodies that lead any tax change process in the region. Any draft new directive must be prepared by a technical committee of experts from the member states, which is submitted to the Council of Ministers. The ECOWAS Commission mobilised participants for the regional conferences and provided financial support for the events.

The role of the tax and customs units of national ministries of economy/finance is crucial in any changes to taxation policy. Staff of these ministries analyse the technical aspects of any policy change and make proposals to the ministry for a draft law, decree or directive.

Civil society organisations initiated the fight to protect people's health from the harm of tobacco use, and so also play a key role in tobacco control. A particularity of the taxation of tobacco in West Africa was the lack of country-level studies and data. Research centres and national statistical institutes played an important role in filling these gaps, in collaboration with tax and customs administrations.

Moving from local and national actions to regional

Initial work in Senegal

Figure 12.1 shows a timeline for the evolution of the process that led up to the adoption by ECOWAS and WAEMU of a new tobacco directive in 2017. It started in 2006 with an African tobacco situation analysis (ASTA),[2] funded by the Canadian International Development Research Centre (IDRC) and the Bill and Melinda Gates Foundation. A political mapping approach was used to develop a situation analysis to understand the factors that determine success in tobacco control in 10–14 African countries. This enabled each country to clearly understand the broader context in which their tobacco control priorities are situated. The next step was for each country to work on an immediate action plan to achieve one or two priorities of their choice. The programme required proposing projects that combined research and action.

CRES was a participant in the ASTA research and, in preparing their action plan bid, CRES organised a workshop in 2006 to choose between different

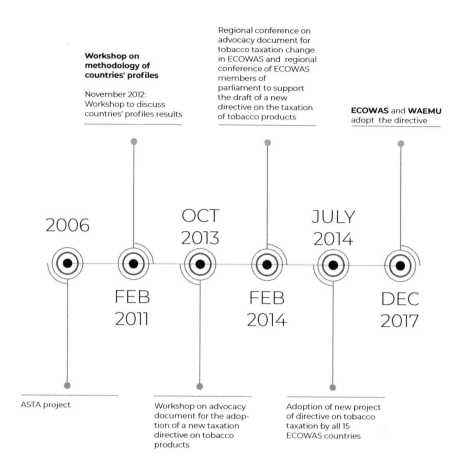

Figure 12.1 Milestones in the ECOWAS new tobacco fiscal directive productsess
Source: Author generated.

priorities. The two priorities selected were Facilitating the Adoption of a Law Responding to the Legislative Need Relating to the Framework Convention on Tobacco Control in Senegal, and Strengthening the Tobacco-Free City of Touba. The first project involved working closely with the Senegalese Ministry of Health and other stakeholders to develop a new draft law on tobacco control. A draft bill was produced in 2011. However, The Bill on the Manufacture, Packaging, Labelling, Sale and Use of Tobacco was only adopted by the National Assembly of Senegal on 14 March 2014 and the implementing decree was signed in July 2016, subsequent to some of the regional work described later.

The second CRES-led ASTA project focused on measures to ban tobacco which have existed for several decades in some religious cities in Senegal such as Touba. As a religious centre of the Mouride Muslim Brotherhood, Touba's influence extends to several other cities and towns spread throughout Senegal, some of which are under the direct authority of the Khalife of Touba. Outside the Mouride religious cities, there are networks of disciples throughout the country and abroad who convey the religious directives and recommendations from Touba. This network would be influenced by a tobacco ban measure in Touba (ASTA Project Technical Report, 2010). Through a mapping of local actors involved in tobacco control, grassroots associations came to support such a measure and a prefectural decree was drafted by the local authorities in 2010 for Touba to move from an unwritten tobacco ban to a formal ban.

Moving to a West African approach

After raising awareness among part of the population and authorities on the need to formalise laws to counter tobacco use in Senegal, CRES decided to widen its scope and look at more effective taxation on tobacco products across the region as a key control measure. As tax policy for the region is governed by ECOWAS, funding was obtained from IDRC for another action-research project in West Africa on tobacco taxation, again with CRES as the project manager. Key stakeholders were identified and brought into the project, notably the chairman of the Customs Commission of ECOWAS. The design and methodology were developed, a steering committee was established in each country and regionally to oversee the project and a scientific committee was set up as the validation body for the documents and procedures.

A first research methodology workshop took place in February 2011 to look at regional decision-making mechanisms, taxation experiments and the levers of the tobacco control strategy. Participants included representatives from each of the 15 ECOWAS member states, the two regional economic communities and technical and financial partners active in the fight against tobacco.

The workshop confirmed the lack of national information on tobacco taxation and the need to take stock of the taxation of tobacco products in the region, including information on the consumption, production, marketing and taxation of tobacco products.

A multidisciplinary research team was set up in each of the 15 countries in 2011. To ensure rigorous data collection and analysis, an academic researcher was appointed as team leader. In addition, there was an official from the tax administration, an official from the customs administration and a statistician, making it easier to collect the required tax and customs data in each country. The methodology for collecting and analysing data was shared with all stakeholders and validated at a sub-regional workshop held in Ouagadougou, Burkina Faso, in November 2012. These teams coordinated the research and ensured the consistent application of methodologies for the collection and drafting of country profile documents, including conducting a survey using the same methodology in all ECOWAS countries to determine the evolution of cigarette prices in the retail trade.

Subsequently, a conference of decision makers was held in Ouagadougou from 26 to 28 November 2012, with the aim of making decision makers aware of the similarities and differences in tobacco taxation policies and practices in the West African region and to determine ways in which they can use the economic unions to harmonise policies and practices. Representatives of each of the 15 ECOWAS member states attended. Each country's ministry of finance and the focal point on tobacco control in the health ministry of each country were represented. The two regional economic communities were also represented by the commission, which is responsible for changing tax directives. Other technical and financial partners active in tobacco control participated in the workshop. One of the major outcomes of this conference was the recommendation to move towards the adoption of new regional directives on the taxation of tobacco products. The ECOWAS and WAEMU commissions provided guidance on the procedure required. This involved draft guidelines being prepared by a technical committee of experts from member countries and submitted to the Council of Ministers. This technical committee is the only body authorised to draw up directives and must be convinced of the need for a change in tax policy, based on solid arguments and evidence. After these directives have been approved by the ECOWAS Council of Ministers, they are submitted to the Council of Presidents.

A position paper was then developed by CRES to support a change in tobacco taxation in the ECOWAS region. This advocacy paper compared the tax situation in ECOWAS countries, drawn from the country profiles, with the tax situation in other countries and economic areas around the world (WHO, 2015). In October 2013, a regional workshop was held to discuss and refine the first draft of the argument. This workshop was attended by several academic researchers and ECOWAS and WAEMU regional organisations.

Once the document was finalised, a regional conference was organised in Abidjan, Côte d'Ivoire, in February 2014 to share the findings. It was attended by representatives of the tax and customs administrations, ministries of health, parliamentarians from WAEMU and ECOWAS, civil society and international organisations including the WHO and the World Bank. At that conference, participants discussed the gap that existed between taxation of tobacco products in West African countries at that time and potential effective taxation. The discussions led to consensus amongst stakeholders on the need to prepare a preliminary proposal for a new directive.

In parallel with the conference of technical staff, an advocacy conference was held with parliamentarians from ECOWAS and WAEMU to present them with the arguments in favour of a change of directive and gain support for adoption. The parliamentarians appreciated the initiative and agreed to support the adoption of the preliminary draft directive, which they embodied in a signed declaration.

> **Box 12.1 Tax categories**
>
> There are taxes that are common to all goods and services, such as VAT and customs duties, and there are so-called excise taxes that are only applied to certain products such as tobacco products. Excise taxes fall into two categories. An *ad valorem* tax is a tax that is applied to a value. The authority sets a rate or range of rates to be applied to a given value called the tax base. For example, in the ECOWAS region, countries apply the rates set on the producer price, that is the amount that the tobacco industry declares as the sum of its production costs and profits.
>
> The second category of tax is called a *specific tax*. It corresponds to a fixed amount that the authority levies on cigarette sales, regardless of the price of the tobacco or cigarettes. In Gambia, for example, for any sale of a packet of 20 cigarettes, the tax authority charged five *dalasi*, regardless of the price. Sometimes the two types of taxes are combined in the same country.

Meanwhile, CRES developed models of combinations of tax types and rates that could lead to higher prices, higher tax revenues and lower consumption (see Box 12.1). A proposal for a combination of two types of taxes was put forward, taking into account the literature, the results of the modelling and, above all, the arguments of the technicians who would have to apply the tax changes. It was recommended that the minimum tax rate of 15% of the sale price be increased to 50%, that the maximum rate be removed and finally that a specific tax of $0.02 per cigarette be introduced into the system.

A final conference was held in Ouagadougou on 10 and 11 July 2014, which was devoted to a review and validation of the draft directive on the harmonisation of excise duties. It brought together representatives of the 15 ECOWAS member countries, of WAEMU, German Cooperation (GIZ), CRES and resource persons. The various articles of the directive were examined and amended. The conference urged the ECOWAS Commission to accelerate the adoption process. Unfortunately, a delay then ensued in the final adoption due to the Ebola epidemic in West Africa, which stopped travel and had a disruptive effect, diverting attention from regional processes. However, the new guidelines were finally adopted in December 2017 by the two sub-regional organisations (ECOWAS and WAEMU).

The research evidence generated

The research undertaken by the country teams produced three main documents – country profiles, a regional synthesis and a position paper, referred to as 'arguments' in French (CRES, 2013a, 2013b, 2013c).

The country profiles covered evidence around key issues such as consumption of tobacco products; the economic importance of tobacco production; the inefficiency of applied taxation; the relationship between tax increases and price increases; and the challenges related to gathering data and measuring the value of smuggling of tobacco products. As well as the 15 country profiles, stakeholders requested a single West African regional profile on tobacco taxation which showed the differences and similarities between countries.

The reports of the national research teams in each of the 15 countries, the resulting regional synthesis and the various workshops showed that reform must focus on the adjustment and harmonisation of tax levels and the tax structure to converge towards common objectives for controlling tobacco consumption. The advocacy document (CRES, 2013c) used the results of these various studies, along with elements from the international literature on tobacco taxation, to provide West African leaders with arguments for tobacco tax reform and the best practices available to them to carry it out. These included, for example, a reallocation of household spending away from tobacco towards health insurance, which would go a long way towards ensuring that basic health care is affordable for a significant proportion of the population. The document also showed that there was a lot of inefficiency in tax uptake. The WHO has set as its main criterion for judging the effectiveness of the tax system on tobacco that tax should be at least 70% of the retail price of cigarettes. Of the 15 ECOWAS countries, only two collected more than 40% of the retail price of cigarettes, while this is at least 60% in some European countries. In addition, the main reasons for the ECOWAS countries' delay in raising taxation were identified and explained. The first is that tax increases are often not regularly adjusted upwards. Increasing the price of tobacco products through taxation is a very effective tool for reducing consumption, but because of the addictive nature of these products and the behaviour of tobacco manufacturers, it is important to increase the value of the price strongly and continuously to reduce consumption.

The second reason was the inefficiency of applying only an ad valorem tax. The regional legislation in force in the sub-region only provided for excise duties in value terms. No West African country had achieved the target of total taxes representing 70% of the selling price of the cigarette packet.

The third reason was the weakness of the tax base. The ex-works price declared by the tobacco industry did not even represent half of the final selling price. Taxation based on the ex-works price can in no way achieve the objective of a tax share in the retail price.

A clear example of use – but the story is not finished

The final version of the tax adopted by ECOWAS was based on the position paper. The process led to specific recommendations based on evidence and was carried out in a manner that built the commitment of the technical staff, who had to develop the proposal and implement it, and the policy makers who had to adopt the directive. According to the representative of the ECOWAS Customs Commission,

> To be able to adopt the directive, it was necessary to make technical reports to convince the states. However, ECOWAS is not a research centre. It is

therefore thanks to the documents produced . . . that we were able to develop them and propose a new range of taxes.

The country profile documents were used in Senegal

> to inform the Minister of Health about the existence of possible tax niches through tobacco that could finance health. . . . Civil society has emerged strengthened by this project. His speeches, which focused on raising awareness among targeted audiences, particularly schoolchildren, have now been expanded to include taxation as the best way to reduce tobacco consumption. These details have greatly helped in political decision making.
> (Tobacco focal point, Senegal Ministry of Health)

A respondent who represented Senegalese civil society indicated that civil society is now invited to participate in technical meetings with the tobacco industry, enabling them to compete with the tobacco industry.

The project also opened opportunities for members of the national teams:

> I was approached as a resource person for a study on smuggling, commissioned by customs, and the research and analysis tools from the Benin country profile were used in the methodology. I also participated in programmes on national television with civil society and the Ministry of Health to inform national opinion on certain aspects, mechanisms to reduce tobacco consumption, updating the law, etc. My contribution was based on the results of the studies carried out as part of the tobacco project. . . . I am often asked to give my opinion on tobacco issues because I led the national research team.
> (The leader of Benin Team)

According to the representative of fiscal administration in the Burkina Faso team, 'The Legislation Directorate worked on amending the code for the increase in tobacco tax based on data collected through the CRES project. Currently we are in the process of increasing taxes to reach the FCTC rate.' (Fiscal administration representative for Benin).

An unintended consequence of the new tobacco fiscal directive process is that greater emphasis has been placed on research into tobacco use in West Africa, with more and more research institutes interested in the topic and doctoral and master's theses supported on these topics. The team researcher in Senegal said:

> My impression has changed considerably. I think that researchers in economics and even sociology can indeed intervene to counter the purchase of cigarettes, which are a heavy expense, and convince public decision makers to fight smoking through tax collection. With regard to the involvement of economists, researchers can have a significant impact and guide public decisions to eradicate the scourge.
> (Team researcher from Senegal)

Tax administrations saw the taxation of tobacco products as an instrument for collecting tax revenue, while civil society actors and ministries of health focused on the health dangers. The bringing together of these stakeholders has shifted the philosophy towards the consideration of taxation as a tool for protecting public health. These stakeholders have thus integrated into their behaviour that tobacco use must be analysed over a long- or medium-term horizon to take into account all relevant aspects in political decision making (CRES, 2014).

After the adoption of the new regional directive, each country's tax administration had to incorporate it into national legislation. However, progress has been slow. Nigeria has introduced a specific tax but keeps the ad valorem tax below the minimum imposed by the new directive. Senegal and Ghana have increased their ad valorem tax rates without introducing a specific tax.

The slow adoption and transposition of the directive into national legislation may be due mainly to two factors. First, as the representative of the ECOWAS Commission pointed out, ECOWAS management teams change every four years. The new management team takes time to understand, carry out and enforce decisions made by their predecessors. Second, the new, more binding directive runs counter to the interests of the tobacco industry, which is trying to influence decision making by arguing that the tobacco industry contributes to the countries' economies through job creation and tax revenue. Its interventions can delay decision making. Lobbying by the tobacco industry delayed the process but the relevance of the evidence and the determination of stakeholders finally won. Thus, stakeholders have changed their vision of tobacco.

Finally, a steering committee must be set up to monitor the process of transcription into national legislation and ensure that the laws are applied. This regional committee is not yet in place and some pressure is needed to ensure it gets established. CRES has initiated a new project to address this.

The purpose of the action-research project was to protect people's health from the negative effects of tobacco. One of the outcomes of this project was to measure the costs of tobacco through non-communicable diseases. The results showed that while tobacco caused some of these diseases, food was a large contributing factor. Thus, CRES has launched a new action-research project in Senegal on the food system and non-communicable diseases.

The factors enabling and hindering evidence use

What types of use do we see?

In this book we have characterised uses of evidence as instrumental, conceptual, process and symbolic (see Chapter 2). We do see *instrumental use*, in that the form of the directive was largely drafted as part of the action-research process. The specific proposal from the simulations of the tax rates to use was also adopted in the directive.

Underlying instrumental use was significant *conceptual use*. As a result of the process, stakeholders had a much better understanding of the challenges arising from tobacco consumption, the limited benefits to the economy compared to the costs to the state, and possible modalities of taxation. This understanding led to the approval of the directive and tax rates. As taxation is a regional issue, each country realised that regional tax harmonisation was the only way to control consumption and reduce illicit trade, and that a regional strategy would have more impact. Another form of conceptual use that emerged is that local evidence on tobacco use is now produced and disseminated widely which makes it possible to talk about real statistics from the region. In terms of research, we can see a flowering of documents that use the statistics produced by CRES. Countries have also used their greater understanding to inform their participation in international meetings such as the Conference of the Parties to the FCTC (Civil society respondent).

The process also greatly raised the profile of the dangers of tobacco consumption in the region, which helped to counteract the lobbying from the tobacco industry. This is an example of *positive symbolic use*.

In terms of *process use*, the establishment of research units in each country led to countries acknowledging the importance of the evidence process.

How evidence use was promoted

A variety of interventions promoted the use of evidence (see Table 12.1), but there were four main levers. An important first lever was the *process facilitation* role played by CRES, along with key *champions* in CRES and ECOWAS. The CRES director used his contacts to bring together all the key players in the fight against tobacco. He understood the multidisciplinary aspects of tobacco control, the need to produce relevant rigorous evidence and the need to master political decision-making mechanisms. He involved his academic colleagues specialising in law and sociology for the draft law in Senegal and the smoking ban in Touba. He used his relationship with the ECOWAS representative to work on tariffs in ECOWAS. The collaboration between CRES and ECOWAS helped them to understand the steps to be taken for a change of directive. The director of CRES also seized on the opportunity of a meeting with the then president of the Republic of Senegal to raise the president's awareness of the need for a new law to control tobacco use.

CRES obtained funding for the action research and immediately started to address the main shortcomings highlighted in the prior situational analysis, namely the lack of synergy in tobacco control between researchers and other stakeholders like civil society, ministries of health, fiscal and customs administrations, and members of Parliament at the national and regional levels. CRES had an understanding of how this synergy could be built that could lead to a new tobacco directive. This process began with the involvement of all stakeholders from the beginning through a methodological workshop to upgrade their knowledge in terms of tobacco use and especially tobacco taxation. This enabled all stakeholders to discuss the subject and to understand actual practice in the region. A key champion in ECOWAS, the chairman of the Customs Commission, indicated,

> I had no knowledge of this issue. I started to get a better idea of the tobacco issue at the first methodological workshop. It was with the country profiles

Table 12.1 Use interventions and their influence

Intervention	Effect
Process facilitation and knowledge brokering	CRES facilitated the overall process over a number of years, managing the IDRC-funded project and using it to conduct the research, liaise with stakeholders, organise effective events and problem-solve to take the process to completion. Many of the following process elements were intended to help *interaction* and building of *trust* between stakeholders, to *agree* and work together on a common cause.
Creation of a civil society coalition in Senegal to support action on tobacco taxation	A key feature with civil society was the need to unite and advocate for tobacco control in-country. A coalition was established which helped to create this.
Scientific committee, steering committee comprising key stakeholders	These structures brought together government and non-government stakeholders and helped to build *agreement*, *commitment* and *trust* in relation to the credibility and importance of the process.
Multidisciplinary research teams were set up in each of the 15 countries	Multidisciplinary teams ensured rigour in producing the evidence and access to tax and customs data. The recommendations gave decision makers *confidence* in their decision making in 2011. These teams increased the *ability* of countries to generate and use evidence, as they undertook much of the research. The composition of the teams made it easier to *access* and collect the required information on each country and strengthened country *ownership* of the data and process.
Database of tobacco control stakeholders in Senegal	CRES initiated a database which they made available to civil society to make civil society actors *aware* of who else is working in the tobacco space. This tool has contributed to the creation of partnerships between the actors.
Targeted events at a technical level and political level	A series of regional events was organised, some with technical staff, some with high-level politicians, some with members of Parliament. The location was rotated between countries to maximise *ownership*. These events developed and agreed content, built *ownership* and *agreement* at different levels, and fostered *trust* between technical staff, politicians and non-state actors. Getting key decisions from decision makers at these events made it easier to *formalise* decisions later.
Collaboration between state and non-state actors to counter the tobacco lobby	CRES received examples of letters sent by the tobacco industry to government and collaborated with civil society in drafting responses. This built government's *ability* to respond as well as *trust* between state and non-state actors.
Reports consolidated arguments for policy makers	The position paper summarised the arguments for policy makers, which helped to build *understanding* and *awareness* of the costs and benefits around tobacco and the options available.

(*Continued*)

Table 12.1 (Continued)

Intervention	Effect
Format of reports	A policy note was produced for each country profile and for key recommendations. The policy notes were in a four-page format, written in both English and French, to make the key results *accessible* and help policy makers be *aware* of them.
Reports public	All reports produced by CRES in this process are publicly *accessible* at www.cres-sn.org, which promoted *access* to evidence.
Knowledge-brokering role of CRES	CRES played a key role in knowing the research world and linking the research world with the public sector and political world. They ensured that effective research teams were set up in each country, that good evidence was *generated* and that it was disseminated in an accessible form, and so easy to *access* and use. They organised events where this evidence was tabled, at technical and political level. They built *trust* with governments and the commission and built the *capability* and *motivation* of the technical staff and politicians who participated.
Use of WHO standards as a reference	Being *aware* of WHO standards provided an external benchmark, for example, in deciding what tax levels could be/should be. This provided some motivation for change as well as *trust* that the proposed recommendations were appropriate.
Use of peer comparison to promote use	The comparison of the 15 countries in reports and in the conferences allowed participants to learn what others were doing and introduced some level of competition to be seen to be doing well.

Note: Change mechanisms are highlighted in italics.

that I learned about the harmful effects of tobacco, especially on young people and vulnerable people.

This process facilitation involved a second lever, the *inclusion of key people in the process* as the intention was that the Council of Ministers would change the tobacco taxation directive on the basis of evidence. In order to achieve this, it was important that the technical staff who had to convince the ministers of the need for this change were involved throughout. Hence, officials from the ministries responsible for the application of taxation had to be involved in the steering committees, be part of the research generation process, participate in key events and so forth.

The integration of the technical experts from the administrative bodies who would analyse the proposals to be made to the ministers was facilitated by their inclusion in multidisciplinary national research teams that were expected to produce most of the evidence.

The third lever to promote use of the evidence was the organisation of workshops and conferences that brought together the 15 ECOWAS member countries led by CRES. All 15 ECOWAS countries were represented by a delegation of at least two people from the tax and customs administrations and the country's ministry of health. The host city for these events was rotated, with workshops and conferences held in Ouagadougou, Dakar and Abidjan. Each of these events was opened by eminent people from the host country in the presence of high-level representatives from community institutions. For example, the two advocacy workshops, the first bringing together tax, customs and health administrations and the second the parliamentarians, held in Abidjan, were attended by the chief of staff of the Minister of African Integration, a vice president of the National Assembly of Côte d'Ivoire, a vice president of the Ivorian Senate, the chairman of the ECOWAS Customs Commission and the representative of the WAEMU Commission.

The fourth lever was the presentation of the results in the form of easy to read policy notes to better disseminate the results. Each country profile was the subject of a policy note in a brief, four-page format focusing on policy recommendations. The policy notes were written in both English and French.

Facilitators and barriers to the use of evidence

The three key facilitators of the use of evidence

RATIFICATION OF THE WHO FRAMEWORK CONVENTION ON TOBACCO CONTROL AT REGIONAL LEVEL

When the action-research project on tobacco taxation in West Africa began, all ECOWAS countries had ratified the WHO FCTC which identified taxation as the most effective way to reduce consumption. Thus, there was a strong commitment by each country to fight the consumption of tobacco products. The need to fulfil this commitment provided an environment conducive to the adoption of a new directive on the taxation of tobacco products and contributed to the active participation of governments.

PARTICIPATION IN INTERNATIONAL MEETINGS

Since ratification of the FCTC, tobacco control stakeholders have participated in international meetings such as the Conference of the Parties to the FCTC and the World Tobacco Conference. These meetings raised awareness of the need for strong commitment against tobacco, and demonstrated that the international community has decided to take action. According to the civil society respondent, the discussions at these conferences provided an opportunity to hear about the strength of taxation as a means of tobacco control.

THE ROLE OF CHAMPIONS

Two main champions were the driving force behind the new tobacco tax directive – the director of CRES and the chairman of the ECOWAS Customs Commission. The director of CRES designed the action-research project to create synergy between research, advocacy and political decision making. CRES's role in process facilitation, led by the director, is described earlier. Second, agreement of a new directive on the taxation of tobacco would not have been possible without the political will of the chairman of the ECOWAS Customs Commission.

At the outset he had no knowledge of the issue, but he was committed to providing ECOWAS countries with an effective tool to control tobacco. He mobilised ECOWAS delegations for the meetings and ensured the preparation of technical notes for the discussions. Once the directive was ready for adoption, despite the considerable delays caused by the Ebola virus crisis in the ECOWAS region, he continued to work towards the final adoption of the process.

The three key barriers to the use of evidence

THE EBOLA CRISIS

After analysis and validation of the draft directive in 2014, the Ebola virus crisis hit West Africa. As some ECOWAS countries had Ebola cases, ECOWAS was forced to suspend all inter-state gatherings to prevent the spread of the disease. This situation slowed down the process of adopting the directive, which delayed the process for about three years. However, as the two key champions were still in their positions in ECOWAS and in CRES, it was relatively easy to pick up the process again.

INTERFERENCE FROM THE TOBACCO INDUSTRY

The tobacco industry took advantage of the Ebola crisis to try to discredit the process. Letters were sent to a few ministers to discourage them from adopting the draft regional directive. The lobbyists denounced the role played by CRES, arguing that it had replaced the administrations as the driver of the process. CRES and civil society shared these letters and helped government to respond to these letters, and the tobacco industry did not manage to derail the process.

THE EXISTENCE OF TWO PARALLEL DIRECTIVES

Both ECOWAS and WAEMU developed directives. The WAEMU directive does not have a specific tax, just an ad valorem figure. Countries belonging to both regional bodies can apply the directives of both. However, this does not make the application of the same directive in the 15 ECOWAS countries any easier. WAEMU, being an economic and monetary union, has more opportunities to meet, because it deals with more economic issues and is more closely integrated. The issues around these multiple tax jurisdictions are discussed in Blecher and Drope (2014).

Conclusions and lessons

How did the context and intervention influence the use of evidence

First, we apply the realist approach to look at what mechanisms are likely to lead to successful outcomes in what contexts. The *mechanisms* applied included the generation of evidence and interventions to maximise the likelihood of use.

Using evidence for tobacco control 221

The hypothesis was that these would lead to the *outcomes* of changes in individual/organisational motivation, in capability and in the opportunity to use evidence, which would lead to behaviour change in individuals/organisations/systems, which would result in policy performance and wider systems change.

The *context* in this case was characterised by fragmented stakeholders with differing worldviews, notably from tax and health perspectives, 15 different countries, and a contentious topic with a strong industry lobby. On a regional dimension, the signing of the FCTC provided some incentive for countries to comply.

Interventions to promote use started with the approval of the action-research project, and an immediate focus on bringing stakeholders together, the start of strong process facilitation by CRES through the project, coupled with an institutional champion in ECOWAS. A series of processes and events was used to build consensus across the 15 countries, helped by the convening power of ECOWAS, and this collective power helped to offset the lobbying from the tobacco industry. *Evidence* was generated through the creation of multidisciplinary virtual research units in each country, which helped to create *ownership* as well as generate rigorous evidence. The research units generated country profiles, a synthesis, models of tax rates and eventually a rationale/argument for a new directive and for the eventual revised tax rates. *Use interventions* after the evidence was produced included producing policy briefs to summarise the argument and recommendations, production of a draft directive, and tabling these at technical and political regional committees.

In terms of *outcomes*, ultimately the directive was adopted, a major achievement, and an example of *instrumental use* of the recommendations. We see increased *capability* of country stakeholders to work together, to produce evidence, and *conceptual use* of the evidence to argue for tobacco control at international fora. The need to address the Framework Convention provided the *opportunity*, which was enhanced by support from high levels in ECOWAS. The process stimulated the *motivation* of stakeholders to produce and approve the directive, even despite the loss of momentum with the interregnum during the Ebola epidemic. Domestication of the directive into country legislation is the next battle.

Emerging lessons

Some of the emerging lessons for evidence use from this case include:

- Undertaking a *situation analysis* at the beginning was important, through which the multidisciplinary aspect of the tobacco issue was identified, as well as key stakeholders.
- The actual evidence generation was probably less than half the effort. *High-quality process facilitation* to support a multi-stakeholder partnership was essential, championing and facilitating processes over time. These skills are

not usually present in government, and such processes can be led by non-state actors, where the key government champion is able to ask for support.
- The *inclusion of all stakeholders*, through a participatory approach, from the beginning of the process created a real synergy between the actors allowing everyone to drive the fight that was needed.
- *Action-research* processes are potentially very powerful, where as much attention is given to the use interventions and process support as to evidence generation itself, and the evidence is located within a wider process.
- The facilitator needs to bridge the understanding of evidence with a *good knowledge of the functioning of government* (and, in this case, regional institutions) and work in an empowering way. According to the director of CRES, 'if we did not know how the two regional organisations work, how the different countries work with these institutions, I do not think we could do this mobilisation work in such a short time'.
- The *lead organisation must be credible*. CRES gained credibility in all the member states through prior work on negotiations for an economic partnership agreement. This made it much easier to mobilise the regional organisations and the 15 member states (CRES director).
- It is important to have *champions* who can carry the momentum effectively over a number of years – in this case, an institutional champion and an evidence/knowledge broker champion.
- *Coalitions of state and non-state actors* can be very powerful, if they can develop a common vision, and the process is well supported. This is particularly important for sectors where industry lobbies are powerful, such as around tobacco, climate change, mining and so forth.
- *Piloting processes* in one country can be helpful prior to applying at the regional level, and this can even work across language and cultural divides.
- An *international/regional agreement* can be used to help large-scale change to happen.

The process of adopting a new directive on tobacco taxation in West Africa has been very rewarding for all stakeholders in tobacco control. The case study provides a number of lessons and demonstrates that it is possible to use evidence to change public policies. However, having good evidence was only one of a number of necessary factors.

The adoption of a new directive on the taxation of tobacco products in ECOWAS is a very significant step forward in tobacco control. ECOWAS countries have the opportunity to use the most effective means to reduce tobacco consumption. This must make it possible to meet the commitments made when ratifying the Framework Convention. Now it remains for ECOWAS countries to transpose the new directive into national legislation in order to implement it, and in Senegal's case to enforce the law. This battle is not yet won.

Notes

1 Consortium pour la Recherche Economique et Sociale.
2 This focused on undertaking a situation analysis to assess current tobacco use, the dynamics of tobacco farming and existing tobacco control policies (including their level of implementation) in 10 to 14 sub-Saharan African countries. At the same time, it endeavoured to build the technical capacity of African researchers to gather, synthesise and analyse data at the country and the regional level.
See www.idrc.ca/en/project/african-tobacco-situation-analyses.

References

ASTA. 2010. *Rapport technique final, Analyse Situationnelle sur le tabac au Sénégal*. Dakar, Senegal: Consortium pour La Recherche Economique et Sociale.

Blecher, E. and Drope, J. 2014. The rewards, risks and challenges of regional tobacco tax harmonisation. *Tobacco Control*, 23, e7–e11. https://doi.org/10.1136/tobaccocontrol-2013-051241

Chaloupka IV, F.J., Peck, R., Tauras, J.A., Xu, X. and Yurekli, A. 2010. *Cigarette excise taxation: The impact of tax structure on prices, revenues, and cigarette smoking*. Cambridge, MA: National Bureau of Economic Research Working Paper No. 16287. https://doi.org/ 10.3386/w16287

CRES. 2013a. *Profils-pays sur la fiscalité du tabac en Afrique de l'Ouest*. Dakar, Senegal: Consortium pour La Recherche Economique et Sociale. Retrieved from www.cres-sn.org.

CRES. 2013b. *Synthèse régionale des profils-pays sur la fiscalité du tabac en Afrique de l'Ouest*. Dakar, Senegal: Consortium pour La Recherche Economique et Sociale. Retrieved from www.cres-sn.org

CRES. 2013c. *Argumentaire pour un changement de la fiscalité sur les produits du tabac*. Dakar, Sénégal: Consortium pour La Recherche Economique et Sociale. Retrieved from www.cres-sn.org

CRES. 2014. *Rapport technique 'Projet régional de recherche-action sur la taxation des produits de tabac en Afrique de l'Ouest'*. Dakar, Sénégal: Consortium pour La Recherche Economique et Sociale. Retrieved from www.cres-sn.org

Economic Community of West African States. June 2009. Directive C/DIR.2/06/09 On Excise Tax harmonization.

Goodchild, M., Nargis, N. and Tursan d'Espaignet, E. 2018. Global economic cost of smoking-attributable diseases. *Tobacco Control*, 27(1), 58–64.

IARC. 2011. *Effectiveness of tax and price policies for tobacco control*. IARC Handbooks of Cancer Prevention: Tobacco Control. WHO International Agency for Research on Cancer.

WHO. 2015. *WHO report on the global tobacco epidemic: Raising taxes on tobacco*. Geneva: World Health Organisation.

13 Lessons for using evidence in policy and practice

Ian Goldman and Mine Pabari

Summary

This final chapter draws together findings and lessons from this study with reference to the analytical framework described in Chapter 3. We reflect on the evidence journeys of the cases in their individual contexts. Diverse sources of evidence were used in across the different cases, and a wide range of evidence use interventions applied. Where an evidence system (such as a national evaluation system) existed, it helped to standardise many of these interventions. Building agreement and trust were key mechanisms leading to change in all the cases, spurring commitment to act. All the case studies resulted in changes in procedures, in some cases extending to changes in policies or budgets. A core message is that evidence use is complex and begins long before an evidence journey starts. Evidence use needs to be planned for and woven into the institutional culture. This needs active facilitation of the process, often in a knowledge brokering role which manages both the supply of and the demand for evidence. Is evidence use the answer to African problems? On its own it is not, but it can make a contribution by helping to lessen the influence of partisan interests and providing some of the answers needed when decisions have to be taken.

Introduction

This book focuses on improving understanding of how using evidence can help inform and strengthen development policy, programmes and practice in Africa. We looked at the evidence journeys in eight cases, learning from the policy process and how this was accompanied by evidence interventions. The journeys included generation of evidence, activities to promote use and eventual changes (or not) in policy or practice informed by the evidence.

We analyse the processes which support or inhibit evidence use rather than focusing on the sources of evidence, of which much has been written. Four of the cases used evaluations and research synthesis as their key source of evidence and four focused on the role of citizen engagement and evidence from NGOs.

In this chapter we first summarise the findings against the analytical framework (Figure 13.1)[1] and then reflect on lessons emerging around evidence use. We start by discussing how the contextual influencers and the demand for evidence influenced the way in which the evidence journeys played out across

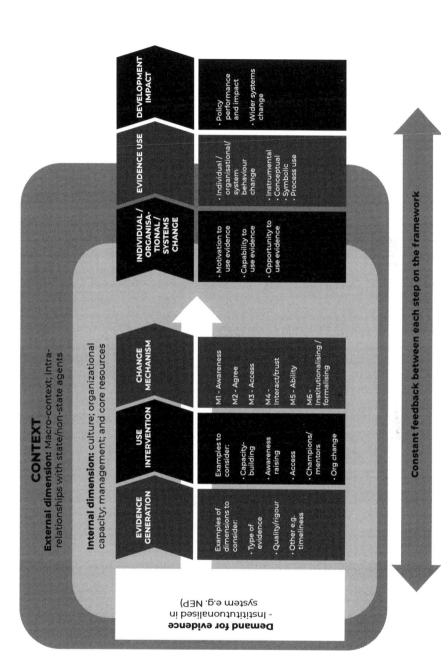

Figure 13.1 The analytical framework showing the Context, Mechanism, Outcome relationships

Source: Langer et al. (2020).

the case studies. We then mention the supply of evidence, evidence use interventions applied in the cases, the change mechanisms these triggered and how these led to immediate outcomes in terms of changes in capabilities, motivation and opportunities and to wider outcomes in terms of changes in policy and practice. Finally we draw out the key messages emerging for promoting evidence-informed policy and practice (EIPP).

Emerging findings

Contextual factors influencing use

As succinctly expressed by Weyrauch et al. (2016), 'context matters'. Across all of the case studies, the context within which the evidence journey took place had a significant bearing on how evidence was used. Table 13.1 summarises the contextual influencers identified from across the eight case studies, relating these to the original framework for context. These are discussed in more detail following the table.

Table 13.1 Contextual influencers of evidence use emerging in the case studies

Category	Dimension of context	Contextual influencers identified in the cases	Examples from case studies
External	Macro-context	Significance of the policy challenge/question	Commitments made to international or regional agreements
			High levels of financial investments
			Legal requirement for legislative review
		Broader political and socio-cultural environment	Timing, for example, proximity to election period
			Space for public participation and civil society engagement
			Level of interest and engagement of stakeholders
		Catalysts of change	Crises
	Intra and inter institutional linkages		Pressure from development partners
			Pressure from civil society
Internal	Culture Organisational capacity Management & processes Other resources	Institutional environment	Systems and processes
			Evidence champions
			Leadership
			Mandates and capacities
			Culture – learning and accountability
			Linkages and relationships

Perceived significance of the policy challenge/question

The perceived level of significance of a policy challenge is an important consideration in whether an investment in evidence is seen as worthwhile, and if so, the types of use interventions that may be necessary to use to raise the profile of the policy issue. In all of the case studies in this book, countries already had high levels of commitment to the policy issue. For example, a number of the countries had signed international or regional agreements and there was pressure to meet their commitments.[2] The evidence itself can also help to inform judgements on the significance, such as the magnitude, distribution of effects and causality.

Political and socio-cultural environment

The broader political and socio-cultural environment influenced whether or not it was worth investing in sourcing and using evidence to support a change process.[3] For example, how power is distributed and decisions are made had a bearing on evidence use. In some of the cases, presidential proclamations were important in driving policy changes. In other cases, the macro-context enabled public participation and citizen engagement, which allows the decision-making space to be more inclusive. For example, in the agriculture case in Benin, the opening up of spaces to include non-state actors changed the power relationships and resulted in a significant shift in the extent to which evidence was used in the sector to inform decision making and planning.

Perhaps of equal importance was the level of stakeholder engagement and interest as well as the nature of relationships between stakeholders. Where stakeholders were highly fragmented and/or had polarised values and positions, this significantly influenced the level of effort and skill required to manage the evidence process (also discussed later in this section). In the Sanitation, Wildlife and Agriculture cases, citizens felt strongly about the issue, were well organised, had strong capabilities as well as relationships and there was an enabling environment for participation. In these cases, civil society organisations (CSOs) and citizens were an important resource and citizen engagement helped to ensure evidence use.

Catalysers and influencers

In some cases particular events or actors triggered the need for change, thereby creating an environment conducive to ensuring that the evidence generated was taken seriously and, in these cases, used. For example, a poaching crisis in Kenya and a crisis of education in South Africa provided the impetus and created a sense of urgency which, in these instances, triggered the demand for evidence. In other cases, it was pressure from development partners to generate evidence that was the main trigger for lobbying and advocacy by civil society. We must also recognise that crises may lead to rapid decisions being taken without using the best available evidence, but rather based on beliefs and opinions.

Institutional environment

Across all the cases, the capabilities of the organisations involved in the evidence journey and the extent to which they were fit for purpose was an important influencer of evidence use. Aspects of institutional capability included the following.

Competent leadership emerged as important for ensuring that the opportunities for evidence use within the wider context were utilised and barriers navigated. Examples of leadership characteristics identified as being significant included broad-based respect and trust across different stakeholder groups; recognised experience and knowledge of the sector; and having well-established networks and alliances and being seen as politically wise. Another factor was the stability of leadership.

Evidence champions were important in all cases, driving both the generation and use of evidence. Evidence champions were not always in senior leadership positions, although it was helpful when they were; in some cases, they were in civil society. An important lesson was the need for champions to remain in place and to be able to sustain their efforts, as the process of changing policy tends to be lengthy. Champions at the centre of government were important in the evaluations, particularly where the policy issue cuts across sectors, as in the violence case. Knowledge brokers also emerged as playing an important role.[4]

Other important capabilities included *skills and knowledge*, for example, the ability to access and utilise evidence for decision making and action. Chapter 4 showed that in Benin, Uganda and South Africa, 25%–33% of managers do not have the skills to understand and use evaluation recommendations. The limited skills and ability of decision makers and other evidence stakeholders to access, absorb, analyse and synthesise information emerged as a barrier in several of the cases.

Appropriate structures and processes were also important. Organisational silos, competition and overlapping mandates were identified as barriers to evidence use, particularly as coordination and positive relationships are important to enable the dialogue, debate and consensus building necessary for effective use of evidence.

Chapter 4 outlines issues in *organisational culture* around evidence use in Uganda, Benin and South Africa, indicating that around 50% of managers support evidence use, but report challenges around hierarchy and fear of punishment for perceived failure. This was confirmed in the case studies where those more open to new ideas and encouraging of change were more likely to enable evidence use. Similarly organisations that are more deliberate in *enabling learning and accountability* were more likely to utilise evidence than those that do not, for example the Department of Social Development in the violence case study. This was linked to *organisational incentives*, which emerged as an issue either as a burden (as in the Rapid Response case) or as a motivator (the reward system in budgetary allocations for districts in Ghana).

Demand for evidence

The next element of the framework in Figure 13.1 is *demand for evidence*. This may come from government or from other stakeholders. The source of the demand had a bearing on the design of the evidence journey. In some cases demand was institutionalised, for example in a country's national evaluation plans. Where donors were the key demanders, the significance of investing in national and local ownership emerged as being critical to evidence use. In the sanitation case study, civil society was the primary driver behind the demand for evidence which led to lessons around the need to put time and energy into ensuring government trust, buy-in and ownership. In all these cases we see a demand for evidence from the evidence users rather than a research push.

Supply of evidence

Evidence generation is also a part of the framework but not a focus of this book. The different cases show examples of generation through evaluations, research, research synthesis and citizen engagement, and we draw lessons on evidence use across these different methods of generating evidence.

The evidence use interventions

Table 13.2 shows the range of *evidence use interventions* that we could see across the cases. In three of the countries there was an NES (national evaluation system) which specified certain interventions and these have been distinguished

Table 13.2 The range of evidence use interventions, as part of, or external to, national evaluation systems

Associated with a NES	*Elements seen outside the NES*
• Demand from government • Evaluation Steering Committee, managing collaboratively the evaluation process • Process facilitation/knowledge brokering by central government unit • Capacity-building of key stakeholders around evaluation • Developing theory of change with stakeholders • Independent evaluators to ensure credibility • Validation workshop with stakeholders • Simple evaluation report • Management response/ improvement plan • Quality assessment of the evaluation • Report public on website • Approval by Cabinet	• Demand from outside government, e.g. from donors/other stakeholders • Use of international standards and conventions as a reference • Creation of coalition to support, e.g. civil society coalition in Senegal to support action on tobacco taxation • Process facilitation/knowledge brokering role of internal unit, either in government (eg Procurement), Parliament (Wildlife) or CSO (Sanitation) • Scoping study/situation analysis • Frequent briefings of key stakeholders during the process • Capacity-building of stakeholders e.g. CSOs • Sharing drafts amongst stakeholders • Sharing evidence in accessible formats e.g. short evidence briefs • Presenting and showcasing evaluation findings at different forums • Ongoing dialogue in the sector • Variety of dialogue methods including debates and 1:1 meetings • Templates and processes for stakeholder inputs • Proactive outreach and engagement with communities • Use of peer comparison to promote use

from other interventions which varied by case. This table provides a useful (but not exhaustive) list to consider in promoting evidence use.

The evidence use interventions that we saw could be applied *throughout* the process (e.g. maintaining stakeholder involvement), *prior* to evidence generation (e.g ensuring demand), *during* the generation (e.g. checking quality and credibility of processes) or *after* the evidence generation (e.g. dissemination processes).

A key finding that emerges is the importance of *facilitation* of the evidence journey, often in a *knowledge brokering role* which manages both supply and demand sides (discussed in Chapter 2). In all cases this brokering role was played by some organisation, sometimes internally, such as an internal monitoring and evaluation (M&E) unit, and sometimes externally, such as the Centre de la Recherche Economique et Social (CRES), the lead think tank in the tobacco case. Facilitation of the process to promote *agreement, ownership, commitment* and *trust* was critical in all the cases. Even where an external entity plays this role, it needs an internal counterpart to work with the evidence. This happens before, during and after the evidence generation process.

Examples from the case studies of these roles include the following:

- Deliberately *convening forums and platforms* to enable dialogue and debate between the different stakeholder groups.
- Ensuring *skilled facilitation*, allowing all parties to have an equal voice and creating safe and trusted spaces for meaningful dialogue. In the case studies where this took place this included facilitating negotiation and consensus building, and managing conflict and power dynamics.
- Creating spaces for *jointly making sense* of the evidence and providing the opportunity for difficult conversations around beliefs and value systems.
- *Awareness raising* through informal and formal interactions, trainings, meetings and so forth. Dialogue and interaction is also essential to build trust, for example by knowledge brokers with their policy clients – something that ideally needs to happen well before evidence is requested.
- *Collaboration in planning and managing* the process, so co-creation of the evidence journey. Steps that could be seen were stakeholders working together to frame the problem, develop ToRs, finalise and approve of the methodological framework and timeline, and jointly manage contracts.
- *Convening of regular meetings* and working hand in hand with programme managers to ensure regular interaction and contact with decision makers, as well as validation workshops with stakeholders.

The change mechanisms triggered by the evidence use interventions

In order for capabilities/opportunities/motivation to use evidence to be activated, there has to be a change mechanism which inspires people and organisations to do things differently. The list of change mechanisms from Chapter 3 is adapted in Table 13.3, based on what we have seen in this research. Drawing on the experiences of the case studies, we suggest a few changes to the original change mechanisms which are added to the table in italics.

Table 13.3 The change mechanisms

Mechanism	Example of interventions to promote use arising in the cases
Awareness of the potential of evidence (M1)	Training senior managers in the public service in South Africa, Benin and Uganda on evidence (Goldman et al., 2019) Training and awareness raising on the potential and value of evidence (e.g. Rapid Response Services) Training of citizen groups in Ghana to analyse and utilise data to demand accountability and better sanitation services as well as in governance and accountability literacy more broadly
Agreement/*understanding*/commitment (M2)	Establishing dialogue processes to build agreement and commitment Use of evaluation steering committees to formalise partnerships
Access to evidence (M3)	Producing accessible short reports and policy briefs Workshops Knowledge repositories
Interaction *and trust* (M4)	Dialogue processes Knowledge brokering Workshops/breakfast meetings Networks and communities of practice
Ability *and confidence* (M5)	Capacity-building (e.g. learning by doing, workshops and formal training courses) Coaching/mentoring Experiential learning Online learning
Institutionalising/formalising (M6)	Use of management responses and improvement plans to formalise action needed Embedded support e.g. knowledge brokering Institutionalisation of NES Making public the analysis

Across the cases, building *agreement* and *trust* amongst the different players in the evidence journey was key and led to the *commitment* to act. In some cases, it was necessary to strengthen ability. For example, in the tobacco case, it was necessary to strengthen the ability of technical staff to generate and use evidence, and of politicians to understand the evidence and make decisions. *Understanding* could also be seen as important in many cases, which links to the importance of conceptual, and not just instrumental, use of evidence.

Outcomes of evidence use in the cases

Immediate outcomes – changes in capabilities, opportunities and motivation to use evidence

Our analytical framework is based on a behaviour change model where a combination of *capability, opportunity* and enhanced *motivation* to use evidence at both individual and organisation level leads to behaviour change. In our analytical framework, this corresponds to the immediate outcomes of an evidence process, that is changes in behaviour at the individual, organisational and systems levels which manifest as changes in policy or practice.

In most of the cases strengthening the capability to use evidence emerged as a key component of change. Sometimes the *capability* was to generate and use evidence, but also we see examples of *capacity* to advocate for the programme or policy, or for *funding* and even for the evidence itself.

Motivation to use evidence is an antithesis of the compliance mindset that is common in all these countries. In Chapter 4 we found that around 50% of managers were motivated to learn and improve policy making, while around 50% were not. In terms of motivation, Michie's definitions suggest the difference between a reflective motivation based on knowledge and understanding, and an instinctive one, triggered by the topic (Michie et al., 2011). We clearly see examples of increase in motivation of the producer association (PNOPPA) to take forward the agricultural policy in Benin, or the impact of the dialogue in strengthening motivation in the violence case.

In some of the cases with a NES, the *institutionalisation* of the system created *opportunities* to use evidence. For example, part of the institutionalisation in South Africa was that national evaluations would go to Cabinet, providing an opportunity for Cabinet to endorse the findings, and this stimulated motivation for the custodian department to use the findings. Some of the mechanisms such as 'trust, agreement, commitment' are also important in opening up opportunities.

And in combination

In most cases it was the combination of increased capability, motivation and opportunity which made the evidence journey significant and sustained. For example, in the wildlife case, the opportunity to provide inputs into drafting the new Wildlife Act was taken up by a skilled civil society sector and thereafter matched by increased capability of the Kenyan Parliament to manage a participatory process, and to supply and use evidence. The motivation is often driven by key champions, but also by the collective energy from stakeholders. In the Wildlife case, if the motivation of key champions or stakeholders had not been sustained, the Act might have passed, but the drive to take forward the key elements of the Act might have been compromised.

Wider outcomes – changes in policy and practice

The eight cases selected were purposely selected for being in some way influential, as we sought to understand how and why that influence occurred. The wider outcomes from the different processes resulted mainly from instrumental use of evidence and included policy change, changes in procedures and processes, in budgets and other resources as well as changes in capacity.

Four of the cases showed changes in *policies or legislation*. In all cases there were changes at *process or procedure* level, such as guidelines, criteria, thresholds for procurement and so forth. Direct evidence of changes in *budget allocations* was rarer, seen in only two to three of the cases, at least partly because resources to fund the recommendations were not available. In none of the cases were there recommendations to close whole programmes or elements, nor were there findings or recommendations that were significantly controversial/in contradiction to policy makers' beliefs and values.

There were also *unintended uses*, sometimes arising where there has been conceptual or process use. Unintended uses can have significant long-term impact. For example, the 2009 evaluation of agricultural policy in Benin was not used instrumentally – but the improved understanding from the stakeholders who participated led them to use the evidence in later evaluation and policy processes.

Other unintended uses included:

- The evidence being used to inform other work;
- The lessons being used to widen the work, for example in the wildlife case from community participation in one sector to development of guidelines for public participation with Parliament more generally;
- Strengthening the capacity of particular stakeholders;
- Rebuilding trust between government and stakeholders;
- The evaluation being used for teaching;
- Promoting further research in the area.

What have we learned about promoting the use of evidence?

In a nutshell, our core message is this:

> Evidence use is complex. It begins long before an evidence journey and needs to be planned for and woven into the individual and institutional culture. It is a worthwhile investment.

This research explored interventions to promote evidence use – actions not to generate the evidence but to enable and ensure use. These have to be thought through in an intentional way – what change do you wish to bring about, what change mechanisms need to be triggered and so what evidence use interventions will be needed? Some of the key lessons that emerged in this regard are described below.

The analytical framework is valuable for strengthening evidence use

For evidence to be utilised, it is important to recognise that evidence use is a journey and not a set of activities focused solely around generation of evidence. The journey involves a series of interconnected processes that can be influenced by the wider environment at all stages. Using the analytical framework, we were able to identify and understand the different stages of the journey and develop insights into the relationships between them. In doing so, we recognised the potential of the framework to support evidence generators and users to be more purposive in designing an evidence journey towards ensuring use. Key is understanding the change mechanisms you wish to activate (e.g. agreement/ownership), how this will build the capability/motivation of managers or the opportunity to use evidence, and the evidence use interventions you need to undertake to generate this change.

Evidence use takes place in multiple ways

We learned the importance of recognising the multiple uses of evidence that can take place (instrumental, conceptual, symbolic, process use, etc.) and the value of designing an evidence journey to be cognisant of these different uses. In focusing simply on evidence and instrumental use, valuable opportunities may be lost. In a number of cases, for example, process and conceptual use were key to bringing about transformational changes that ultimately created the space for positive and sustained impact. Later we discuss the importance of knowledge brokering and facilitation, particularly with regards to process and conceptual use.

Context matters – make sure you understand it

The evidence journey does not take place in a vacuum and there are multiple factors that influence this journey. We earlier quoted Carol Weiss stating that 'evaluation is a rational enterprise that takes place in a political context' (Weiss, 1993, p. 94). The case studies amplified the importance of understanding this wider context, in line with a core message expressed by Weyrauch et al. (2016). As described earlier, there are contexts where the prevailing political situation is unlikely to allow for evidence use and therefore the investment of an evidence journey may simply not be worthwhile. In other cases, understanding the context can ensure that there is a clearer understanding of relevant entry points and opportunities in the policy process, the change mechanisms necessary to ensure evidence use and the interventions that are most likely to be effective in triggering these mechanisms.

Ensure there is demand

Much of the writing on EIPP has been by researchers seeking to push their research or evaluation. In this book we take a policy-maker perspective, where policy makers or other stakeholders have requested evidence. In the cases studies we saw a number of ways of ensuring demand:

- Through national evaluation systems requiring evaluations to be done;
- Through policy makers requesting research or research synthesis;

- Through parliaments requiring citizen inputs into development of legislation;
- Through civil society analysing government data, and the analysed data then being used by government.

The experiences in the cases demonstrate the importance of demand for evidence originating from the evidence users, particularly policy makers. This ensured ownership, strengthened the alignment of the evidence to the policy needs and therefore, ultimately, evidence use.

Ensure credibility, quality and legitimacy in the evidence journey – often it is the messenger as well as the message

The cases provide examples of different ways in which the credibility of the evidence journey was enhanced. The reputation and track record of the actors generating the evidence as well as those delivering it was extremely important. In a number of cases, consultants were contracted to carry out an evaluation as part of ensuring the independence of the evaluators. Peer reviewers or content experts were also used in several cases to comment on the evidence. The violence case showed the importance of legitimacy in terms of the cultural and racial makeup of the research team. Another important lesson was that transparency and effective communication were important in perceptions of legitimacy of process. A key role for internal and external knowledge brokers was ensuring the quality and credibility of the evidence process, as did stakeholder structures such as steering committees.

Apply evidence use interventions to build capability and motivation

Passive provision of evidence does not work

Langer et al. (2016) reviewed the facilitators of research uptake and came to the conclusion that research use requires active steps to facilitate access to evidence, to enhance skills in understanding evidence, increase motivation to use evidence, and the formalising of these steps in structures and processes. A passive approach alone, such as seminars or policy briefs will be insufficient.

What we see in the case studies supports these findings. We see where the impact of formalising systems has made a significant contribution, for example through an NES or a formalised citizen engagement process. We see how working to improve decision makers' capability, understanding, motivation and commitment are essential ingredients. In no cases did isolated communication functions play a major role.

The process needs active facilitation and knowledge brokering

The experience from these cases would suggest that knowledge brokering (also described earlier) is important in the overall evidence journey. These roles include keeping policy makers and other stakeholders involved and informed in planning and implementation of the evidence generation process, so keeping them committed and motivated. A key part of the facilitation role was building positive and trusting relationships between stakeholders and with the evidence generation teams. While structures such as steering committees were important, it was essential that they were facilitated effectively. Similarly, where the relationship with the researcher/evaluator was good, there was flexibility in delivery of the evidence, improving recommendations and so forth.

Overall, what emerges is that the process of knowledge brokering is complex, sensitive, and requires strong facilitation skills, and linkages between governmental and non-government stakeholders. These roles currently tend to be under-appreciated and the functions of knowledge brokers in government need to be reviewed to ensure they have the skills and mandates to be successful.

Establishing formal structures to manage the process and maintain ownership of stakeholders

In all but one of the case studies, committees were established to enable different types of engagement across the different stakeholders and sectors, which became a formal expression of the *coalitions of stakeholders*. These were meant to ensure *ownership by key stakeholders* in the evidence process. The committees included steering committees to provide overall guidance and decision making and scientific or technical committees involving subject matter specialists from key evidence stakeholder groups (often including development partners). Other forums were sector-driven platforms, such as the Violence Prevention Forum facilitating ongoing dialogue on EIDM in violence prevention in South Africa.

These committees/forums were instrumental to the use of the evidence in a number of different ways. They enabled interaction and the building of relationships between the evidence generators and evidence users, strengthened the abilities of the evidence stakeholders to understand and make sense of the evidence, and helped to ensure the quality, relevance and responsiveness of the evidence, so ensuring a greater sense of ownership of the process as well as the evidence produced.

Build capacity of managers, decision makers and stakeholders

In a number of cases, investments were made in strengthening the abilities of stakeholders to use evidence. This helped them to play effective roles in the evidence journey. For example, in the sanitation case, citizen groups were trained to analyse and utilise data to demand accountability and better services as well as governance and accountability literacy more broadly.

Package and communicate the evidence simply and effectively

Evidence was packaged and communicated in a number of ways to ensure it was appropriate, relevant and accessible to decision makers. Examples included:

- Ensuring the evidence was *relevant* to the policy concerns, the evidence stakeholders and the wider context;
- The evidence going beyond simply describing a problem to providing *practical and realistic solutions*;
- Evidence and recommendations being as *specific* as possible – the more generic, the less likely they are to be used;
- The evidence recognising *the values of its recipients*. In the case of violence, for example, there was a disconnect in the underlying values of researchers and public servants. Recognising this, the researchers focused the findings on systems and processes rather than engaging with beliefs and values, which, in turn, mitigated risks of rejection and enabled use;
- *Formats* of reports being *readable and accessible*, for example using a format for evaluation reports including a 1-page policy summary, 5-page executive summary and 25-page main report format, to ensure reports were readable.

There emerged a number of examples of sensitivity to the dynamics and the need for responsive communication throughout the process. Examples could be seen where findings and recommendations were discussed with higher-level decision makers prior to wider engagement, strengthening their ownership of the evidence and their comfort with the recommendations, so that they would be more likely to implement them.

The experiences of a few of the case studies demonstrate that wider *dissemination of the evidence* can be as important as the evidence itself, both in terms of how it is shared as well as with whom. In some of these cases, significant effort was made to share the evidence widely using multiple communication media and platforms targeting specific audiences. This included the use of repositories/websites, policy briefs, national dialogues, workshops and seminars. This in turn enabled transparency, ownership and uptake for implementation across multiple stakeholders. In a few of the cases, the evidence was given to trusted and respected individuals to present to stakeholders, as it was recognised that the messenger is often as important as the message itself.

Having an evidence system makes some of the elements automatic

Five of the eight cases[5] are from Benin, Uganda and South Africa. These three countries had established a NES which formalise the use of evidence. This includes formalised requirements for evaluations, competencies and standards (benchmarks of evaluation quality, guidelines, peer review mechanisms, etc.).

In addition, in South Africa formal *management responses* and *improvement plans* are required whereby different departments and stakeholders respond to findings and outline how recommendations will be taken up and institutionalised. Developing of the improvement plan again involves stakeholders to ensure quality and ownership of the plans going forward.

Established systems and processes better enable evidence use to be anticipated which, in turn, can improve timely responses to demands.

Lessons on the analytical framework

The analytical framework we used in Chapter 3 was developed by Langer, deriving from his earlier work (Langer et al., 2016), and that of Vanessa Weyrauch (Weyrauch et al., 2016b). The framework proved very useful in structuring the research and analysing the findings. It evolved slightly in the use. It proved very helpful to be explicit about the behaviour change required for evidence to be used, and to understand what leads to that change. The framework should be valuable for policy makers and practitioners seeking to expand the use of evidence in their work. The context matters framework proved complex to use, and we have simplified it somewhat in our analysis of the contextual influencers. We added additional words in the descriptors, such as commitment and understanding. The version at the beginning of this chapter includes these minor changes.

Conclusions

Is evidence use the answer to African problems? On its own it is not, but it can make a contribution by helping to lessen the influence of partisan interests in decision making and strengthen its empirical grounding. Evidence can link the implications of decisions to their likely impact on society and ensure that decisions relating to the complex and emergent realities we face are supported or challenged by independent analysis and evaluation. By bringing evidence to the table in a systematic way, anticipating the evidence needs of policy makers, and developing and answering evidence agendas for organisations and the country, it can help to provide some of the answers needed when decisions have to be taken.

The cases we draw from in this book are all examples where evidence has contributed to decision making. They demonstrate that it is possible to use evidence to get improved policies and improved practice, though it is not yet possible to conclude that this results in improved longer-term societal and developmental impact.

The main aim of this research was to find out how can we best facilitate the use of evidence to improve policy and practice and facilitate social outcomes in an African context, and second to test out an analytical framework for understanding evidence use. We conclude that the key factors in the successful use of evidence to improve policy making include understanding context, involving stakeholders continuously, ensuring demand for evidence and an appropriate supply, using change mechanisms, building capability and motivation, establishing buy-in at higher levels, and exploiting opportunities within the policy process.

To make evidence more influential requires strengthening the role of knowledge brokers internal and external to government, enabling trusted relationships and creating stronger dialogue between government and stakeholders so that wider influences can inform policy and practice. This requires stronger process skills in government, as well as partnerships with external bodies such as think tanks which have the skills to facilitate and sustain processes.

To do this effectively the key roles of process facilitation and knowledge brokering have to be given more weight, in centre of government and internal evidence/M&E units, and in the skill sets and job descriptions of the people employed there. This is also true for researchers who seek to influence policy and practice.

Postscript

Where next?

The book is part of a process to reflect on African experience and to apply this in policy processes and practice across the continent. The book accompanies other materials, notably videos and policy briefs, intended as resources to help these processes. We hope these resources will inform training and the practice of policy makers, practitioners, parliaments and knowledge brokers. We look forward to continuing the journey with these partners. *A luta continua!*

Limitations of the research

The research is built on eight case studies with between 8 and 20 interviews per case. In some cases the researcher of the case study had been involved in the case as a participant observer and so brought considerable richness to the analysis. Clearly, these numbers of interviews are limited. The case studies were undertaken by different researchers so there were some differences in interpretation and how the research was conducted, and how the cases were written up, despite a common template. This has been minimised in that the co-editors then took the cases and turned them into chapters, with the content validated by the authors.

There are several cases of evidence from evaluation and citizen engagement, with only one example of the use of research and one which used research synthesis. However, what we sought to unpack was the process by which evidence use happened, and deliberately take a diversity of evidence generation modalities.

There are some limits in how critical each chapter is, as policy makers involved were co-authors. It was a deliberate strategy to involve the policy makers to acknowledge their role and to bring in the richness of their direct experience, but also because the intention was not just to write a book, but to use the content to influence processes in the five countries and the region more widely. Hence the book itself is a change intervention meant to promote interaction and trust between researchers and policy makers, build awareness and commitment to take evidence more seriously in policy and practice, and to strengthen the institutionalisation of evidence. We hope in the process to have built the *capability* of these policy makers and of the researchers to understand the process by which change happens, increased the *motivation* of the policy makers to use evidence more actively, and in the remaining part of the project (to June 2020) to support them where *opportunities* occur to apply the learnings.

Notes

1 The analytical framework is described in Chapter 1 and discussed in detail in Chapter 3.
2 Such as the ECOWAS countries which had ratified the Framework Convention on Tobacco Control (Chapter 12); and Uganda's commitment to the global guidelines as well as the East, Central and Southern Africa food fortification guidelines and regulatory manual (Chapter 8).
3 In the wildlife case, for example, previous experiences had demonstrated that proximity to an election period meant that there were higher risks of influences and interests other than evidence dominating the decision-making spaces.
4 In the education case, for example, the Chief Directorate Strategic Planning, Research and Coordination had a good reputation as an entity that facilitated the use of evaluations within the Department of Basic Education. In the case of Kenya, on the other hand, there had been a loss of trust in the government during previous policy review processes which meant that there was scepticism around the sincerity of government in its invitation to the wider public to participate in the Wildlife Conservation and Management Act review process. In Benin there was a loss of trust as, while new policies had been developed in response to political changes and these were informed by evidence, these policies did not result in concrete changes in the sector.
5 DBE, VAWC, Procurement, Rapid Response, and Benin.

References

Goldman, I., Deliwe, C.N., Taylor, S., Ishmail, Z., Smith, L., Masangu, T., Adams, C., Wilson, G., Fraser, D., Griessel, A., Waller, C., Dumisa, S., Wyatt, A. and Robertsen, J. 2019. Evaluation2 – Evaluating the national evaluation system in South Africa: What has been achieved in the first 5 years? *African Evaluation Journal*, 7(1). https://doi.org/10.4102/aej.v7i1.400

Langer, L., Goldman, I. and Pabari, M. 2020. Analytical framework used to guide case study research. In *Using evidence for policy and practice – Lessons from Africa*. London: Routledge, Taylor & Francis Group.

Langer, L., Tripney, J. and Gough, D. 2016. *The science of using science: Researching the use of research evidence in decision-making*. EPPI-Centre, Social Science Research Unit, UCL Institute of Education, University College London EPPI Centre.

Michie, S., van Stralen, M.M. and West, R. 2011. The behaviour change wheel: A new method for characterising and designing behaviour change interventions. *Implementation Science*, 6(1), 42. https://doi.org/10.1186/1748-5908-6-42

Weiss, C.H. 1993. Where politics and evaluation research meet. *Evaluation Practice*, 14(1), 93–106.

Weyrauch, V., Echt, L. and Suliman, S. 2016. *Knowledge into policy: Going beyond 'Context matters'*. Politics & Ideas and the International Network for the Availability of Scientific Publications.

Index

Note: Page numbers in *italic* indicate a figure and page numbers in **bold** indicate a table on the corresponding page.

3ie *see* International Initiative for Impact Evaluation
2010 Kenya Constitution 172–173
2016 Community Survey reports 94

accountability 2–3, 20–21, 55–56, 58–61, 77, 116–118, 156, 192–194, 200, 228
ACE *see* African Centre for Evidence
action-research project 207, 210, 215, 219, 221
active facilitation and knowledge brokering 235–236
activity-based learning 35
administrative data 2, 15, 69, 77–79, 82, 89, 160, 194, 197–198
administrative red tape 163
AEN *see* African Evidence Network
AfDB *see* African Development Bank
AfrEA *see* African Evaluation Association
AFRED *see* African Evaluation Database
Africa, combined GDP of 2
Africa Centre for Rapid Evidence Synthesis 35
Africa Evidence Network 3, 22, 35
African Centre for Evidence 22–25
African Centre for Health & Social Transformation 6
African Development Bank 1–2, 119, 134
Africa Network for Animal Welfare 174
African Evaluation Association 21
African Evaluation Database 73n6
African Evidence Network 21, 25, 36–37
African National Congress 75
African Parliamentarians' Network on Development Evaluation 6, 21, 24
African tobacco situation analysis 208–210

agreement 40, 107, 109, 123–124, 162, 165, 196, 217, 219, 230–232
agriculture 22, 24, 62, 125, 153–155, 157–159, 161, 163–164; policy 153, 155, 164, 232–233; *see also* Benin agricultural sector development policy
ANA *see* Annual National Assessments
analytical framework 1, 4, 34–36, 39, 45–46, 49–50, 54, 56, 160, 224–225, 231–233, 238; combined 44, *45*, 46–47, **47**, 48; simplified version of *9*, 9–10, 224, *225*; strengthening evidence use 233–234; *see also* combined analytical framework
ANAW *see* Africa Network for Animal Welfare
Annual National Assessments 78–79
anti-retroviral (ARV) therapy 1
apartheid policies 75, 93
APNODE *see* African Parliamentarians' Network on Development Evaluation
ASTA *see* African tobacco situation analysis
authority 66, 70, 117, 120–122, 127, 143, 190, 210
autonomy 7, 145

barazas, community 118
BCURE *see* Building Capacity to Use Research Evidence Programme
behaviour change 107, 198, 202, 221, 232, 238; interventions 41; in terms of evidence use 42
'behaviour system' 41
Benin 3; accountability of government 59–60; agriculture sector 1990–2009, landmarks in **166**; levels of governance

Index 243

7; M&E policy 7; Mo Ibrahim index 59; national-level evaluations 8; national M&E systems 21; ownership of M&E function 61; *see also* M&E culture in Benin, Uganda and South Africa
Benin agricultural sector development policy 8, 152, *154*; CNOS role in 159; conceptual use of evaluation for 160; context and intervention influencing 164–165; Declaration of Rural Development Policy 153; donor conditionalities for 163; 2009 evaluation report 155–157, **158–159**, 159–160, 165; evidence generation 163; evidence use arising from 164–165; factors enabling evidence use 161, 163; factors inhibiting evidence use 163–164; Farmer Memorandum 160–161; instrumental use of evaluation for 160; interventions influencing use of 161, **162**; Letter of Declaration of Rural Development Policy (LDPDR) of May 1991 153; for maize sector 160; non-state actors' commitment 161, 163; PNOPPA role in 153, 155, 159–160; process use of evaluation for 161; PSDSA 2017 156–157; PSRSA 153–154, 157, 160; stakeholders in 153, 157; symbolic use of evaluation for 161; unintended consequence of 160
Benin Chambers of Agriculture 159
BEPP (Bureau for Evaluation of Public Policies) 161
BEPPAG *see* Bureau of Public Policies, Evaluation and Government Action Analysis
biased production 28
Bill on the Manufacture, Packaging, Labelling, Sale and Use of Tobacco 209
bounded rationality model 18
budget allocations 65–66, 72n2, 92, 201, 204n6, 228, 233; for evidence generation 200; and planning using DLT 197–198; for violence prevention 100–101
budgetary resources 181, 197
Building Capacity to Use Research Evidence Programme 35
bureaucratic hierarchies 60–61
Bureau of Public Policies, Evaluation and Government Action Analysis 7, 155

cabinet 5, 6, 78, 81, 82, 83, 86, 96, 98, 99, 112, 115, 118, 124, 129, 134, 161, 229, 232

Campbell Collaboration 21, 22
Canadian International Development Research Centre 208
capabilities 10, 21, 41, 42, 45, 47, 62, 130, 146, 165, 180, 195, 218, 221, 225, 226, 227, 231, 232, 235
capacity builders 27
capacity-building programmes 35
capacity development 27, 67, 165
'carrot' reward scheme 201
CBOs *see* community-based organisations
CDD-Ghana *see* Ghana Centre for Democratic Development
Centre for Learning and Evaluation for Results for Anglophone Africa 7, 21, 62; NES diagnostic study 5, 6, 8
Centre for Research on Evaluation, Science and Technology 21
Centres for Learning on Evaluation and Results 3
champions 45, 75, 87, 127, 128, 141, 147, 162, 185, 202, 207, 222, 225, 228; evidence champions 48, 87–89, 147, 226, 228
change, theory of 9–10
change intervention 4
change mechanisms 9–10, 44–45, 48, 84–86, 124, 128, 179, 183, 195–196, 225–226, 230–231, 233–234, 239
CITES *see* Convention on International Trade in Endangered Species
citizen engagement 6, 178, 201; in policy-making processes 177; process 173, 235
citizen participation in sanitation sector: CDD-Ghana 192–194; CONIWAS 192, 202; constraints to 192; CSOs and INGOs 191–192, 199; needs of 192
Citizens' Social Action Groups 193
civil society 26–27, 29, 58–59, 134–135, 177, 179, 190–193, 195, 197, 199, 201–203, 214, 216–217, 226–228; with established relationships 180; and government, rebuilding of trust between 177; involvement in evaluation 24, 29; involvement in M&E systems 59
civil society actors 43, 158, 192, 215, 217
civil society organisations 92, 94, 98, 104, 106–107, 118, 153, 193, 195–205, 227, 229; and government, connections between 101; role in sanitation sector 191; role in tobacco control 208
CLEAR *see* Centres for Learning on Evaluation and Results

CLEAR-AA *see* Centre for Learning and Evaluation for Results for Anglophone Africa
CNOS *see* Conseil National d'Orientation et de Suivi
coalition 78, 165, 190, 199, 217, 229, 236; Coalition of NGOs in Water and Sanitation 190, 192–193, 199, 202
Cochrane Centre, South African 7
Cochrane Collaboration 22
coherent theory of research use 36
collaboration 202–203
COM-B system 41–42, 49
COM evidence 49
communication: mechanisms 59, 62; with stakeholders 58–59, 82, 107, 112, 118, 128, 129, 147, 157, 163, 173, 183, 216, 227, 236, 239
community-based organisations 170, 175
competencies 126, 237
compliance reporting 59
comprehensive rationality 18
conceptual use 16, 82, 99–102, 122–123, 140–141, 160, 215–216, 221, 234
CONIWAS *see* Coalition of NGOs in Water and Sanitation
Conseil National d'Orientation et de Suivi 159
conservancies 171, 186n1, 186n3
Consortium for Economic and Social Research 9, 210–213, 220–223, 230; ASTA projects 208–210; and ECOWAS, collaboration between 216, 218; process facilitation role of 216, 218–219, 221; *see also* West Africa, tobacco taxation action-research project in
context 1, 4, 9–10, 35–39, 42, 44–45, 47–49, 54, 70, 79, 88, 93, 102, 104, 108–111, 116, 122, 126, 128, 130, 134, 141, 148, 154, 161, 164, 170, 182–183, 189, 200, 207–208, 220–221, 225–226, 234
Context Matters framework 34, 38, 226; aim of 42, 44; dimensions of context according to 42, **43**, **44**, 48; and Science of Using Science, synergies between 44, *45*, 46–48; sub-dimensions of 42
Context-Mechanism-Outcome configuration 109, 128
contextual influencers 224, 226, 238
Convention on International Trade in Endangered Species 173
coordination 43, 58–59, 70, 87, 109, 127, 134, 190–192, 202
corruption in government 117

Country Procurement Assessment Review 2001 119–120
County Wildlife Conservation and Compensation Committees 186n4
CPAR *see* country procurement assessment report; Country Procurement Assessment Review 2001
credibility 16, 85–86, 124–126, 129–130, 144, 148, 217, 229–230, 235; and ownership 125, 148; and trust 86, 129–130
CRES *see* Consortium for Economic and Social Research
CREST *see* Centre for Research on Evaluation, Science and Technology
criminal justice departments 96
crises 43, 70, 78, 79, 86, 89, 178, 226, 227
cross-organisational silos: and competition between departments 107; interventions with 109
CSOs *see* civil society organisations
culture 42–43, 45, 48, 54–56, 55, 60–61, 66, 70–72, 125, 127, 225–226

DACF *see* District Assembly Common Fund
DAs *see* district assemblies
data: access and usability of 19; collection in Africa, obstacles to 19; curation and interpretation of 27
DBE *see* Department of Basic Education
DCENR *see* Departmental Committee on Environment and Natural Resources
DDF *see* District Development Fund
decentralisation 145, 153, 191
decision making 63–65
Declaration of Rural Development Policy 2, 5, 152–154, 159, 193, 224
demand for evidence 9, 23–25, 44, 46, 48
demand-side frameworks and models 37–38
Departmental Committee on Environment and Natural Resources 173–174, 177–181, 180, 185
Department for International Development 25, 118–120
Department of Basic Education 7, 90; Annual National Assessments 78; barriers to use of evidence 87–88; Basic Education Sector plan 78; context and intervention influencing 88–89; educational planning system 77; Education Management Information System 77; evidence work of 7; experts as co-authors 78; factors enabling use of

evidence 86–87; Funza Lushaka Bursary Programme 80–82; M&E unit 79, 84; 'monitoring and evaluation' activities in 79; National Development Plan 78; National Evaluation Policy Framework 78; National School Nutrition Programme 82–84; officials in 86–87; research and evaluations 79, **80**; Schools Register of Needs 77; structures to use evidence in 77–79; textbook availability crisis and 78, 86; use interventions 84, **85**

Department of Basic Education, national evaluation system of 89; designing 78–79; elements of **85–86**, 89; ESCs and 79; evaluations under 79–80

Department of Basic Education, Policy Support Unit 77

Department of Education 75

Department of Higher Education and Training 75

Department of Planning, Monitoring and Evaluation 7, 23–25, 30n16, 57–59, 62, 66, 68–69, 76, 78–80, 83–88, 93, 98–99, 103–104; and DSD 94, 96, 98, 106; and JET Educational Services 81; National Evaluation Plan 96; Quality Assessment Report 82

Department of Social Development 92–94, 96–101, 103, 106–107, 109, 228

Descriptive and experiential evidence 15

development partners 96–101, 104, 116–120, 129–130, 135–138, 142, 153–158, 162–163, 165, 199, 201, 226–227

DFID *see* Department for International Development

DHET *see* Department of Higher Education and Training

DHO *see* District Health Officer

Diagnostic Review 8, 78, 92, 96–97, 99, 109; conceptual uses of 101–102; instrumental uses of 100–101; interventions and decisions 102, **103–104**; knowledge broker role 106; macro-contexts 102, 105

dialogue forums, evidence 24

Directorate of the Environmental Health and Sanitation Division 190

district assemblies 190

District Assembly Common Fund 201

District Development Fund 201

District Health Officer 139, 145

District League Table 188, 192; data collection 194; design and launch of 194; district performance management systems 197; evidence use interventions around 195–200, **196**; information and communication technology for 201; MLGRD for 199; objectives of 194; outcome indicators 194–195; partnership 201; planning and budget allocations using 197–198; supporting improved service delivery 195, 197

District Performance Assessment Tool 197–198

DLT *see* District League Table

DoE *see* Department of Education

donor-driven initiatives 19

donor funding for government programmes 24–25

donors, roles of 24–25

DPAT *see* District Performance Assessment Tool

DPDR *see* Declaration of Rural Development Policy

DPME *see* Department of Planning, Monitoring and Evaluation

DPs *see* development partners

DSD *see* Department of Social Development

Early Childhood Development 79

East Africa Wildlife Society 172

EAWLS *see* East Africa Wildlife Society

Ebola virus crisis 220

EBPM *see* evidence-based policy making

ECD *see* Early Childhood Development

E-CIMES *see* electronic county integrated M&E system

Economic and econometric evidence 15

Economic Community of West African States 5, 9, 155, 206, 216; and CRES, collaboration between 216, 218, 220–221; delay in raising tobacco taxation 213; Ebola virus crisis 220; promotion of workshops and conferences 218–219; ratification of FCTC 206; tax policy for tobacco control 207, 208–209, *209*; and WAEMU developed directives 220; WHO FCTC ratification by 206, 219; *see also* West Africa, tobacco taxation action-research project in

economic growth 2

Economic Policy Research Centre 6

ECOWAS *see* Economic Community of West African States

education 6, 35, 40, 75–77, 80, 88, 194–195

Educational Endowment Foundation 27

Education Management Information System 77

education system, South Africa 75
EHSD *see* Directorate of the Environmental Health and Sanitation Division
EIDM *see* evidence-informed decision making, analytical framework for
EIPP *see* evidence-informed policy and practice (EIPP)
electronic county integrated M&E system 5
electronic national integrated M&E system 5
engagement, important ingredients for 184
E-NIMES *see* electronic national integrated M&E system
Environmental Protection Agency 8
ESC *see* evaluation steering committee; Evaluation Sub-Committee
eThekwini declaration 204n5
ethical evidence 15
evaluation evidence 13; stage at which countries use **65**
evaluation process 16, 27, 64, 83–84, 89, 97, 110, 124, 129–130, 229; being undertaken 63; emergence of 21–22; involving civil society in 24; recommendations 59, 62, 64–65, **65**, 69, 71, 84, 86, 160–161, 228; senior managers requesting 24; values and culture barriers to **61**; *vs.* monitoring 20
evaluation reports 59, 70, 76, 81, 83, 85, 103, 122–123, 155, 157, 160–161
evaluation steering committee 79, 85, 92, 97–98, 103, 106, 108, 115, 118, 124, 231
Evaluation Sub-Committee 118
evaluation systems 8, 21, 24, 27, 78, 87, 89
evidence: credibility, quality and legitimacy in 235; definitions 11n3, 15–16; demand for 23–27, 29, 44–46, 48, 96–97, 141–142, 145–149, 156, 163, 224–225, 227–229, 235; forms 15; historical development of forms of 18–19; packaging and communicating 237; passive provision of 235; policy dynamics 26, *26*; for policy and practice 13; supply, demand and knowledge brokering for *25*, 25–26; supporting enabling environment for 27–29; use of 14, 16–18, 20, 25, 29, 36–38, 41, 58, 62, 86–89, 106, 238; value of 127, 195–196, 231; ways of ensuring demand of 234–235
evidence-based advocacy 195, 197–198
evidence-based policy 1, 3, 13–14, 17

evidence-based policy making 7, 14, 24; movement for 3, 5; policy/programme cycle for *17*, 17–18
evidence culture 5
evidence demand-constrained countries 26, *26*
evidence ecosystem 27–29, 37, 48, 58–59
evidence generation 3, 4–5, 8–10, 9, 29, 46, 48, 64, 87, 88, 89, 92, 109, 127, 128, 156–157, 159, 193, 200, 229, 230, 236
evidence-informed decision making 3, 14, 34–38, 40, 42, 49–50, 100, 144, 236; challenges to 148–149; leadership of 44; mentoring 47
evidence-informed decision making, analytical framework for 34; demand-side frameworks and models 37–38; developing 39–48; need for 35–36; organisational context and 56; potential application and limitations of 49–50; supply-side frameworks and models 36–37; theories of change and practice-informed 38–39
evidence-informed policy and practice (EIPP) 3, 14, 25, 226, 234
evidence maps 22–24, 30n16
evidence models 38
evidence revolution, waves of 21, 22, 27
evidence stakeholders 228, 236–237
evidence-supply-constrained countries 26, *26*
evidence synthesis *see* research synthesis
evidence systems 27, 29, 37, 47, 224, 237
evidence use 29, 37, 238; capabilities needed for 62; context and intervention influencing 88–89; contextual factors supporting or hindering 86–88; contextual variables of 38; demand side of 37–38; development of 20; factors influencing 58; as form of behaviour change 41; as link between supply and demand 25; meaning of 16–18; by policy makers 18; in policy making 14; in public policy, facilitators and barriers to 93; shift in conceptualisation of 37; spaces for dialogue in 106; supply side of 36–37; *see also* Context Matters framework
evidence use, barriers and enablers to: in procurement sector 125–128; in RRS 144–148; in sanitation sectors 199–200; in VAWC sector 102–108
evidence use, contextual factors influencing: catalysers and influencers 227;

institutional environment 227–228; perceived significance of policy challenge 226–227; political and socio-cultural environment 227
evidence use, outcomes of: changes in capabilities and opportunities 231–232; changes in policy and practice 232–233; motivation to use evidence 231–232
evidence use interventions 10, 46, 48, 49, 88, **229**, 229–230, 233; analytical framework for 36; to build capability and motivation 235–238; change mechanisms triggered by 230–231, **231**; context 234; design of 38; evaluations of effectiveness of 38–39; fragmented state of conceptualisation of 35; frameworks and typologies of 39; mechanisms for structuring 41–42; micro-level theories of change relating to 38; multiple ways 234; outcomes of 46–47; potential for synergies 36; range of 35–36; *see also* analytical framework
evidence use mechanisms **40**, 40–41
evidence use strategies: analytical lens for 39–42; evaluation of 35

facilitation 87, 112, 153, 184, 191, 224, 230, 234, 235, 236
farmer-based organisations 193
FBOs *see* farmer-based organisations
FCTC *see* Framework Convention on Tobacco Control
FLBP *see* Funza Lushaka Bursary Programme
Food and Drugs Act (Food Fortification) Regulations 136
food fortification programme 136–137, 140–141
Framework Convention on Tobacco Control 206–207, 216, 219, 221; ratification by ECOWAS 206, 219, 221
funding 79, 81, 101, 119–120, 129, 135, 137–138, 142, 155, 158–159, 210, 216
Funza Lushaka Bursary Programme 75, 76, 80, 81, 82, 86

GAIN *see* Global Alliance for Improved Nutrition
Garu Tempane District 195
GEF *see* Government Evaluation Facility
gender-based violence 97
Gene Xpert results for TB 139, 140, 141

Ghana 5, 8–9, 201; *see also* sanitation sector in Ghana
Ghana Centre for Democratic Development 188–189, 192–194, 196
Ghanaian Environmental Protection Agency 48
Ghana M&E Forum 8
Ghana Statistical Service 8
Global Alliance for Improved Nutrition 136
Global EIDM index 39
government: agencies 8, 43, 58, 105, 122, 193; assessment reports 65; institutions 42, 58, 105, 110, 116, 170–171, 181, 202; internal evaluation and research capacity 111; relationships within and between 3, 29, 40, 42, 43–46, 58, 82, 104, 105–107, 130, 143, 145, 148, 177, 179, 180, 183, 184, 185, 195, 196, 198, 212, 216, 225, 226, 227, 228, 234, 236
Government Evaluation Facility 6
Government of Uganda 116
Government Results and Performance Act of 1993 20
guidelines 23, 55, 81, 83, 118, 119, 120, 123, 126, 130, 136, 177, 184, 211, 212, 232–233

health sector 3, 6–7, 22–23, 134–135, 148; *see also* Rapid Response Service
Health Sub-district (HSD) management team 134
HIV/AIDS incidence, decline in 2
human development outcomes 93
Human Sciences Research Council 7

IAA Volunteers 195
I Am Aware (IAA) initiative 188, 192; CSO partners 193–194; data facility centre 193; district performance management systems 197; DLT evidence dissemination 194; evidence use interventions around 195–200, **196**; goals of 193; process facilitation activities 198
IDRC *see* Canadian International Development Research Centre
IEs *see* impact evaluations
IMC *see* inter-ministerial committee
impact 21, 22, 79–82
implementation evaluation 81
improvement plans 81, 87
incentives 19, 43, 71, 88, 146, 173, 174, 177, 195, 199, 221

INGOs *see* international non-government organisations
initial teacher education (ITE) programmes 80
Institute for Public Policy Research 6
institutional culture 184
institutional environment 227–228
institutional framework 8, 155–156, 160, 164–166, 174
institutionalising 10, 40, 45, 85, 103, 199, 225, 231
instrumental use 16, 122, 123, 140; definition of 99; of Diagnostic Review 100–101
interdepartmental cluster system 58
inter-ministerial committee (IMC) on VAWC: establishment of 96; improvement plan 98; root cause analysis study 96–97; *see also* Diagnostic Review
internal government policy-making processes 112
International Initiative for Impact Evaluation 22
international meetings, participation in 219
international non-government organisations 191–192
intra- and inter-institutional linkages 58–60, 105–108
investments 19, 47, 59, 101, 226, 234, 236
ITE Directorate 81

JBSF *see* Joint Budget Support Framework
JET Educational Services 81
JMP *see* Joint Monitoring Programme
Joint Budget Support Framework 118, 124, 129, 131
Joint Monitoring Programme 189
J-PAL 30n13

Kenya 5–6
Kenyan Parliament 170
Kenyans United Against Poaching 174, 180
Kenya Wildlife Conservancies Association 171, 173, 180
Kenya Wildlife Service 171–172, 175, 180, 186
knowledge brokering 25–28, *28*, 84, 85, 89, 99, 110–111, 179, 198–199, 217, 224, 230, 234–236
knowledge-brokering entities 30n17, 31n17
knowledge brokers *26*, 26–27, 29, 34, 40, 103, 109, 111, 145, 148–149, 180, 202, 228, 230, 236, 239
knowledge management and learning culture 182
knowledge managers 27
knowledge transfer 35
knowledge translation 6, 27, 133
knowledge utilisation, two-communities theory of 36–37
KUAPO *see* Kenyans United Against Poaching
KWCA *see* Kenya Wildlife Conservancies Association
KWS *see* Kenya Wildlife Service

land-use management 177
leadership 43–44, 57–58, 62, 66, 68, 70, 86, 89, 180, 185, 190, 226, 228
learning outcomes, assessments of 77–78
legislative/legislation 9, 14, 57, 104, 160, 169, 170, 171, 173, 174, 175, 178, 179, 183, 184, 215, 222, 232, 235
legitimacy 65, 85, 163, 177, 191, 235
Letter of Declaration of Rural Development Policy (LDPDR) of May 1991 153
linkage agents 27

macro-contexts 42–43, 45, 48, 56–58, 70, 102, 144, 225, 227
Makerere Rapid Response Service in Health *see* Rapid Response Service
Makerere University 6
management and processes 48
M&E 3–5, 7–8, 18, 20, 76, 93, 106, 110, 115; central coordinating bodies for 62; culture 54, 55–56, 61, 67; development of 19–25; legislation for overarching 57; limitation of 21; organisational capacity for 62; organisations with roles related to 59; ownership of 61; political recognition 55; sector 37; systems, championing 56; units 57–58, 61–62, 66, 69–70, 79, 115, 126
mechanisms of change 40, 46
M&E culture in Benin, Uganda and South Africa **70**, 70–72; culture 60–61; enabling factors to 66; evaluation process 63; evaluation recommendations 64, **65**; evidence for decision making 64–65; evidence for planning and budget 65–66; hindering factors to 66, 69; information for decision making 63–64; intra- and inter-institutional linkages 58–60; linking plans to individual performance 63; macro-context of 56–58; monitoring implementation 63; organisational capacity 62; organisational context of 56; strategic planning 63; strengths and

weaknesses of 61, **67–69**; systems in place 62
M&E Directorate 5
Medium-Term Strategic Framework 101
M&E systems 3, 4, 21, 55–57, 56, 59, 62, 65, 71, 118, 159; civil society involvement in 59; factors influencing development of 56; government-wide 57; influence of 57–58; leadership changes and 56–57; situation with regard to 56, 57
Metropolitan, Municipal and District Assemblies 189–190, 193, 200–201
Ministry of Finance, Planning and Economic Development 116–119, 117, 127, 134
Ministry of Local Government and Rural Development 190–191, 193, 197, 199
Ministry of Sanitation and Water 190–191, 193–194
misoprostol, community distribution of 137–139
MLGRD *see* Ministry of Local Government and Rural Development
MMDAs *see* Metropolitan, Municipal and District Assemblies
MoFPED *see* Ministry of Finance, Planning and Economic Development
Mo Ibrahim index 59
monetary compensation 175, 177
monitoring and evaluation *see* M&E
motivation 1, 9, 10, 41, 42, 43, 44, 45, 47, 67, 89, 128, 129, 144, 162, 165, 183, 196, 199, 201, 218, 221, 225, 226, 231, 232, 235, 239
MSWR *see* Ministry of Sanitation and Water
MTSF *see* Medium-Term Strategic Framework
Mukono DHT, Gene Xpert results for TB 139, 140, 141
Mukono district, community distribution of misoprostol in 138–139

National Bureau of Statistics 5
national development plan 8, 63, 70, 78, 95, 116, 144, 190, 201
National Development Planning Commission 8, 190–191, 197
National Evaluation Plan 24, 45, 80, 96, 225, 228
National Evaluation Policy Framework 68, 78, 96, 97, 98
national evaluation system 3, 5–7, 37, 54, 59, 70–71, 75–76, 78–79, 92–93, 128–129, 152, 161, 165, 229

National Guidance and Monitoring Council *see Conseil National d'Orientation et de Suivi* (CNOS)
national integrated M&E strategy (NIMES), Kenya 5
National Platform of Agricultural Farmer and Producer Organisations 153, 155, 159–160
national public procurement system, evaluation of 6
National School Effectiveness Survey 77
National School Nutrition Programme 7, 75–76, 80, 82–84, 86, 88–91
national statistics offices 18, 19
National Strategic Plan 92, 99–100, 104
National Student Financial Aid Scheme 81
national task force 119
National Working Group (NWG) on Food Fortification 136
NDP *see* national development plan
NDPC *see* National Development Planning Commission
NEP *see* National Evaluation Plan
NEPF *see* National Evaluation Policy Framework
NES *see* national evaluation system
networking event 40
New Public Management 20
NGOs 24, 94, 100, 104–106, 110, 118, 163, 170–175, 177, 180–181, 188–190, 192
non-governmental organisations *see* NGOs
non-state actors 5–6, 70, 155, 157, 161–165, 171, 191–192, 202, 217, 227
NPM *see* New Public Management
NSFAS *see* National Student Financial Aid Scheme
NSNP *see* National School Nutrition Programme
NSOs *see* national statistics offices
nutrition interventions, evaluation of 30n3

Office for Evaluation of Public Policies (BEPP) 152
Open Defecation Free (ODF) certification 194
organisational capacity 42–43, 48, 56, 62, 70, 104, 226
organisational cultures 44, 48, 55, 60, 228
organisational incentives 228
organisational performance 60–61
organisational silos 107–108, 228
ownership 125

parent/teacher associations 193
parliamentary committees, demand for evidence from 23–24

Index

Parliamentary Research Services 23, 173, 174, 180, 183
parliamentary research units 27, 30n17
participant observation 11n5
partnerships 4, 80, 104, 192–193, 217, 231, 239
PASCiB *see* Platform of Civil Society Organisations in Benin
patriarchy 94
PDE *see* procuring and disposing entity
PDU *see* procuring and disposal unit
PEDs *see* provincial education departments
perceived cultural imposition 106
performance agreements 63
performance control 20
PFM *see* public financial management
Platform of Civil Society Organisations in Benin 153
PNOPPA *see* National Platform of Agricultural Farmer and Producer Organisations
poaching 169
PoA:VAWC *see* Programme of Action on Violence against Women and Children
policy-based evidence 14
policy: challenge, perceived significance of 226–227; decisions 3, 14, 46, 110, 119, 127–128, 133, 146, 170; makers 17, 18
policy making 14, 134–135; definition 125; evaluations in 115, 117, 119, 123, 125, 127, 129; politically sensitive sectors 125–126
policy/programme cycle *17*, 17–18
political and socio-cultural environment 227
politically sensitive sectors, policies for 125–126
political sabotage 178
political will 86
Population Service Initiative 138
postpartum haemorrhage 137
Poverty Eradication Action Plan and Poverty Action Fund 119
PPDA *see* Public Procurement and Disposal of Public Assets Authority
PPH *see* postpartum haemorrhage
PPMS 127 *see* public procurement management system
practice-informed frameworks and theories of change 38–39
practice, policy and 2, 10, 13, 14, 34, 88, 183, 211, 224, 226, 232, 238
Primary School Nutrition Programme 82
process use 13, 16, 30n4, 45, 64, 81, 99, 161, 177, 216, 233

procurement sector 128, 129; *see also* public procurement reforms
procuring and disposing entity 117
Programme for Accessible Health Communication and Education (PACE), Uganda 138–139
Programme of Action on Violence against Women and Children 95–96, 99–100, 107–108
provincial education departments 81, 82
PRS *see* Parliamentary Research Services
PSI *see* Population Service Initiative
PSNP *see* Primary School Nutrition Programme
PTAs *see* parent/teacher associations
public (procurement) finance regulation of 2001 119
public finance (Tender Board) regulations of 1977 119
public financial management 117
public participation 169–187, **179**, 226, 233
public policies 7, 43, 57, 62, 93, 152, 156, 161, 192
public procurement 116–122, 127
Public Procurement and Disposal (PPD) Act of 2003 116, 117, 120; amendment of 120
Public Procurement and Disposal of Public Assets Authority 117–118, 129; bottlenecks and issues identified by 131n2; capability of 130–131; context 128–129; credibility and trust 130; cultures, systems and capacities of 127; decision-making structures within 127; demand for 123–124; establishment of 120; evaluation of 120, 122–125, **124**, 126–127, 128–129, 130, 131n2; familiarity with context 126; final report 122; findings of 122–123; influence of DPs 126–127; management system supporting 120, 122; objectives 120, 122; ownership of evaluation process 129–130; reliability of data 128; research unit 127; sense of ownership 125; timing of 126; use interventions influencing 124, 124–125
public procurement management system 130–131
public procurement reforms: Country Procurement Assessment Review 2001 (CPAR) 117–120, 125–126; evaluation of 116, 118, 127–128; policy timeline of 119–123, *121*
public sector evaluations 118
public sector M&E policy 118

public service 7, 23, 54, 57, 69, 71, 107, 189, 192

qualitative evidence 15–16
quality assessment 86, 229

Rapid Response Service 23, 24; accessibility to evidence 143; challenges to 148–149; community distribution of misoprostol 137–139; context and intervention for 148; credible processes of 143–144, 148; decision-making cultures and 142–143; demand-driven approaches 143; demand for evidence from 141–142; Gene Xpert results for TB 139–141; interaction between decision makers 143, 148; knowledge translation innovation 133; piloting of 135; positive attitudes towards 142; scope of services 135; service model design 135; at sub-national level 135; support to DHT decisions 134; training to decision makers 144; 'urgent' definition of 133; use at national level 133–134
Rapid Response Service, barriers and enablers to use of: autonomy to make decisions 144, 145, 146–148
rapid results initiative 5
RCME *see* Research Coordination, Monitoring and Evaluation
REACH-PI *see* Regional East African Community Health Policy Initiative
realist approach 1, 88, 108, 220
Regional East African Community Health Policy Initiative 133, 135
regional initiatives 21
regional tax harmonisation 216
relationships 3, 29, 40, 42, 43–46, 58, 82, 104, 105–107, 130, 143, 145, 148, 177, 179, 180, 183, 184, 185, 195, 196, 198, 212, 216, 225, 226, 227, 228, 234, 236
representivity 111
Research Coordination, Monitoring and Evaluation 77
research: councils 7; evidence 9, 39, 41–42, 93, 107–108, 112, 135, 183; research processes 110–111; teams, representivity in 111; tools 4; use 40–41, **40**; utilisation 16
research synthesis 1, 4–7, 13, 15, 22–23, 29, 35, 224, 229, 234, 239
resource allocation for liquid waste 191
resource limitations and consequences 181–182
Rural Initiatives for Self-Employment Ghana (RISE Ghana) 195

RRI *see* rapid results initiative
RRS *see* Rapid Response Service

SAMEA *see* South African Monitoring and Evaluation Association
sanitation policy-based oversight 190
sanitation provision in Ghana 188, 189, 190
sanitation sector in Ghana: 190–192, 193, 201; *see also* citizen participation in sanitation sector
sanitation sector in Ghana, evidence use in: barriers to 200; collaboration 202–203; context and intervention influencing 200–201; enablers of 199–200; for policy processes 201–202; for process ownership 202; state and non-state agencies for 193
school education: challenges 76, 77–79
Schools Register of Needs 77
Science of Using Science project 39–42, **40**, *41*
scientific research methods 16
Senegal 206–210, 214–217, 229; country profile documents 214
Senegal, tobacco control measures of 209–210, 214
service delivery 78–79, 188, 191, 194–195, 199, 201
social sector departments 96
social welfare services 94
societal values 94
South Africa 1, 3, 6–7; democracy 93; evaluation demand of parliamentary committee 23–24; Mo Ibrahim index 59; national M&E systems 21; as pathfinding country for VAC 101; policy makers' use of evidence 14; population 93–94; *see also* M&E culture in Benin, Uganda and South Africa; violence against women and children (VAWC), South Africa's response to
South African Monitoring and Evaluation Association 7
South African National Evaluation System, evaluation of 59, 62, 93
South Africa's education 76–77; *see also* Department of Basic Education; Department of Education; school education
SRs *see* systematic reviews
staff capacity 200
stakeholders 58–60, 67, 85, 107, 109–110, 112, 117–118, 127–130, 137, 143–148, 155, 159–165, 173–181, 183–184, 209–211, 215–217, 221–222, 226–230, 232–234, 236–239

252 Index

standards 15, 29, 115, 116, 118, 120, 121, 123, 130, 136, 237
Statistical Capacity Development Outlook 2019 19
statistical evidence 15
Statistics South Africa 77
strategic planning 63
structural adjustment programmes 20
supply-side frameworks and models 36–37
sustainability 120, 137, 142, 144, 165
symbolic use 16, 65, 71, 122–123, 128, 141, 148, 160, 161, 216
systematic reviews 15, 22, 24, 27–28, 35, 38–39
systems in place 62

Tanzania Essential Health Interventions project 135
TASU *see* Technical Administration Support Unit
taxation/taxes 9, 213–216, 218–219; administrations 207–208, 210, 215; categories 212; policy, tobacco 207, 210–211
teacher education models 82
Technical Administration Support Unit 120
technical working group (TWG) 97
TEHIP *see* Tanzania Essential Health Interventions project
textbook availability crisis 78, 86
theories of change and practice-informed frameworks 38–39
Think Tank Initiative 24
tobacco: ban measure in Touba 209–210; consumption 213–214, 216; control 206, 207, 216, 219–220; deaths related to 206; industry lobbying 207, 215, 220; tobacco taxation 9, 207–211, 213, 216–219, 229; *see also* West Africa, tobacco taxation action-research project in
Total Shutdown movement 102
training 7, 17, 35, 63, 76, 80, 143, 144, 148, 177, 194, 199
trust 59, 85, 86, 89, 103, 104, 109, 112, 124, 127–130, 143, 145, 148, 177, 183–184, 195–196, 198, 202, 217–218, 224, 228, 230–232
Twende Mbele initiative 4, 10, 11n4, 35, 54, 64

UBOS *see* Uganda Bureau of Statistics
UEA *see* Uganda Evaluation Association
Uganda 3, 5, 72n2, 115; accountability of government 59–60; budget support to 116; corruption in 117; food consumption survey 136; government-led study tour to 107; health care funding 134; health care system 134–135; health sector 6; health sector in 148–149; levels of government 6; maternal mortality rate in 137–138; M&E policy 6; Mo Ibrahim index 59; national M&E systems 21; NIMES 6; OPM 65; population 134; public procurement 116; university sector 6; *see also* M&E culture in Benin, Uganda and South Africa
Uganda Bureau of Statistics 118, 137
Uganda Evaluation Association 6
Ugandan MOH Health Sector Strategic Plan 136
unintended use 16, 82, 233
United States Agency for International Development (USAID), funding from 171, 172
use intervention 9, 10, 34–36, 38–42, 44–46, 48–49, 51, 75, 84–85, 88–89, 93, 99, 102, 109–110, 124–125, 128, 142, 144, 162, 164, 179, 195–196, 198, 217, 221, 225–226, 229–230, 233–235

VAC *see* violence against children
VAWC, national policies related to 94–96, *95*, 97, 98
VAWC sector 107–108
VAWC sector, evidence use in: enablers and inhibitors of 102, **104**; evaluation process 97–99; identifying need for 96–97; interventions and mechanisms facilitating 108–110; lessons around 110–112; types of 99–102
VEP *see* Victim Empowerment Programme
vicious circle countries 26, *26*
Victim Empowerment Bill (2017) 100
Victim Empowerment Programme 107
violence against children 92, 97, 101
violence against women 92
violence against women and children (VAWC), South Africa's response to 92–93; approval by Cabinet 98; balancing knowledge 108; cabinet memorandum 98; commitment to resolution 99; competition between departments 107–108; coordinating structure 100; DSD's evaluation unit 96; evaluation process 97; government-led study tour to Uganda 107; government's configuration and capacity 94; improvement plan 98–99; organisational silos 107; problem identification 97; Programme of Action (PoA) 99; researchers and government

105–107; submission process 98; *see also* inter-ministerial committee (IMC) on VAWC
violence prevention, budget allocation for 100–101
Violence Prevention Forum 106
virtuous circle countries 26, *26*
Vision 2040 116
Voluntary Organizations for Professional Evaluation 30n7
VOPEs *see* Voluntary Organizations for Professional Evaluation

WAEMU *see* West African Economic and Monetary Union
WAMU *see* West African Monetary Union
water, sanitation and hygiene (WASH) activities 190–191
Water Director and Environmental Health and Sanitation Directorate 190
WCMA 2013 *see* Wildlife Conservation and Management Act 2013
Weiss, Carol 16, 36, 39, 234
West Africa, tobacco taxation action-research project in 221–222; conceptual use of evidence 215–216; conference of decision makers 211; context and intervention influencing use of evidence 220–221; country profiles 212–214; data collection and analysis 210–211; delay in raising taxation 213; draft guidelines 211; emphasis on research 214; final version of tax 213; funding for 210; inclusion of key people 218; increase in tobacco tax 214; instrumental use of evidence 215; national legislation 215; Nigeria 215; opportunities for members 214; organisation of workshops and conferences 218–219; position paper 213; process facilitation role of CRES 216, 218; process use of evidence 216; proposal for tax types 212; regional committee 215; regional synthesis 213; research evidence generated 212–213; research methodology 210; slow adoption of regional directive 215; stakeholders of 210, 215; symbolic use of evidence 216; tax administration 215; use interventions 216, **217–218**
West African Economic and Monetary Union 207–209, 211–212, 220
West African Monetary Union 9
White, Howard 21–22, 27
WHO *see* World Health Organization
Wildlife (Management and Conservation) Amendment Bill (1989) 170–171
wildlife: conservation 177; crime, offences and penalties for 177; management in Kenya 169, 170–173, 181; poaching 173; sector 5, 169, 171, 177, 181, 183, 185
Wildlife Conservation and Management Act 2013 6, 169, 173–177, *176*, 177, 178, **179**, 182–183
Wildlife Conservation and Management Act (1976) 170
Wildlife Policy and Act, draft 171–172
World Bank 93, 116, 123, 127–128, 134, 211
World Health Organization 134, 138, 144, 189, 204, 206, 211, 213; *see also* Framework Convention on Tobacco Control
World Wildlife Fund 171
WWF *see* World Wildlife Fund

Taylor & Francis eBooks

www.taylorfrancis.com

A single destination for eBooks from Taylor & Francis with increased functionality and an improved user experience to meet the needs of our customers.

90,000+ eBooks of award-winning academic content in Humanities, Social Science, Science, Technology, Engineering, and Medical written by a global network of editors and authors.

TAYLOR & FRANCIS EBOOKS OFFERS:

A streamlined experience for our library customers

A single point of discovery for all of our eBook content

Improved search and discovery of content at both book and chapter level

REQUEST A FREE TRIAL
support@taylorfrancis.com